Sustainable Site Design

Sustainable Site Design

*Criteria, Process, and Case Studies
for Integrating Site and Region
in Landscape Design*

Claudia Dinep
Kristin Schwab

John Wiley & Sons, Inc.

Library of Congress Cataloging-in-Publication Data:

Dinep, Claudia, 1968-

 Sustainable Site Design: Criteria, Process, and Case Studies for Integrating Site and Region in Landscape Design / Claudia Dinep, Kristin Schwab.

  p. cm.

 Includes bibliographical references and index.

 ISBN 978-0-470-18783-8 (cloth)

 1. Ecological landscape design. 2. Sustainable design. 3. Building sites. I. Schwab, Kristin, 1961- II. Title.

 SB472.45.D45 2010

 712—dc22

                                    2009018430

Printed in the United States of America

10 9 8 7 6 5 4 3 2 1

Contents

Preface

INTRODUCTION

This book was written to assist landscape architecture practitioners, students, and clients in developing dynamic sustainable landscape design resolutions. As sustainable landscapes are increasingly requested and required, landscape architects are expected to respond to ever more complex sustainable programs. All too often conventional—and even sustainable—design approaches fall flat in responding to critical challenges by failing to comprehend them within a broader context—a consideration that provides potential two-way benefits for both site and context. Our examination of sustainable design approaches employed in the United States within the last ten years revealed that the primary characteristics distinguishing the most successful outcomes were those that incorporated the qualities of the context within the site design. Multi-dimensional integration of contextual elements, whether in the immediate adjacency or regional scale, has shown itself to be an essential ingredient in achieving sustainable goals such as ensuring environmental quality, connecting to significant open space, cultivating community, and improving regional aesthetics. This book provides criteria, a process, and case studies for looking beyond site-only solutions to integrate regional and site concerns and maximize sustainable landscape design potentials.

The built projects examined for this book, all designed by leading firms in the profession, successfully integrate regional phenomena with site sustainability resulting in efficient, purposeful, and meaningful places that cultivate connections between people and the landscape. Study of these projects revealed the following conclusions:

1. Site sustainability encompasses cultural as well as ecological concerns.

2. A design process inclusive of stakeholders is the basis for a landscape's long-term success.

3. Regional factors interrelate with and are inseparable from factors critical to site design.

4. Strong design form actualizes sustainable concepts in the landscape.

5. Constructions designed to achieve multiple purposes are efficient and cost effective.

6. Places that hold meaning for people encourage stewardship.

This book addresses a variety of needs within the environmental design industry. Practitioners such as landscape architects, architects, and developers can use this book to tailor their own design processes toward sustainability, students can use it as a framework for envisioning new directions, and clients can utilize it as a resource to direct and substantiate their visions.

THE SUSTAINABILITY CRITERIA AND DESIGN PROCESS

Over the last fifty years, many have contributed to the development of contextual sustainable design. Perhaps most influential has been Ian McHarg's *Design with Nature* with its focus on assigning value to regional processes. Others, such as Frederick Steiner's *The Living Landscape*; Joan Woodward's *Waterstained Landscapes*; Wenche Dramstad, James Olson, and Richard Forman's *Landscape Ecology Principles*; William Marsh's *Landscape Planning: Environmental Applications*; and Carol Franklin's *Fostering Living Landscapes,* offer useful guides to landscape sustainability. Still others such as Kevin Lynch's *Site Planning* and James LaGro's *Site Analysis: Linking Program and Concept in Land Planning and Design* have provided general site planning guides that encourage the consideration of context.

As these sources testify, while a process is a useful guide, the design of landscapes can never be formulaic and attempts at confining the process produce uninspired results. Landscape architect Steven Krog writes, "We delude ourselves in believing that by energetically invoking the process we will definitely arrive at a creative design solution. We can only dissolve this obeisance by facing the great risk-by recognizing that creation/invention is an emotion, intuition, intellect, and energy-intensive task" (Krog 1983). Yet armed with the requisite energy and skills, a process does provide critical direction for the complex task of defining and developing sustainable site goals and outcomes.

At the heart of this book's examination are two ingredients essential to achieving successful sustainable site design— the defining of *sustainability criteria* and a *process* to fulfill them. The rationale for the sustainability criteria and process is rooted in a review of existing literature that explores sustainability within the context of landscape architecture, site design, and planning. This framework values environmental health and function, site access and spatial organization, as well as aesthetics to reconcile people with nature, to balance development practices with natural resources, and to foster healthy communities. As such, it differs from conventional design approaches as its emphasis is broader in scope and its sustainability potentials extend outside traditional project limits.

In Chapter 1, the notion and significance of context integration is examined and the set of five criteria, gleaned from the case study research, is developed. Each of the criteria contributes to and expands on the relationship between a site and its context:

Connectivity

Purpose

Meaning

Efficiency

Stewardship

In Chapters 2 through 7 of the book, the design process is developed, led by six essential questions that fulfill the criteria. These questions focus on areas where the sustainable design process differs from that of conventional design in generating sustainable outcomes—*Program Development, Stakeholder Influence, Regional and Site Assessment, Form-Making, Design Efficiency,* and *User Experience.* Finally, strategies and methods for addressing the question are paired with a sustainable design case study that strongly exhibits that particular aspect of the design process.

Program Development

What people, resources, and strategies guide sustainable site programming?

Stakeholder Influence

How are the philosophies and needs of neighbors, community members, and other project stakeholders purposefully incorporated into project scoping and direction?

Regional and Site Assessment

What sustainable site design potentials are revealed by the consideration of context?

Form-Making

How is sustainable design articulated through cohesive, imageable, and artful form and space?

Design Efficiency

How does design efficiency serve multiple goals in sustainable landscape design?

User Experience

How can design incorporate "meaning" to connect user and place?

THE CASE STUDIES

A report summarizing research commissioned by the Landscape Architecture Foundation in 1997 concluded that the case study method is a highly appropriate and valuable approach to advancing the knowledge of the landscape architecture profession.

> The primary body of knowledge in landscape architecture is contained in the written and visual documentation—that is, stories—of projects...

> ...these cases provide the primary form of education, innovation, and testing for the profession. They also serve as the collective record of the advancement and development of knowledge in landscape architecture . . .

> From the range of knowledge that can make up a case study, at least three levels of information are possible in a case study analysis. The first, and simplest, is a project abstract. The second is a full project case study. The third is a more in-depth case study with contextual or specialized material. While each may have a different audience, the greatest need, especially in teaching, is for the more detailed case studies of the second and third nature. (Francis 1997)

This study and report spurred an increase in case study publications, begun by those published by *Process Architecture*, and *Spacemaker Press* in the United States. The Landscape Architecture Foundation has been instrumental in continuing this progress with the publication of case studies that center both on more general landscape types (*Urban Open Space: Designing for User Needs*), and on specific seminal landscapes (*Village Homes: A Community by Design* and *Paris-Lexington Road: Community-Based Planning and Context Sensitive Highway Design*).

At the same time, while a variety of sustainable tools and checklists are available, most are specialized to focus on theory or techniques but do little to offer case study analyses of built work. In addition, at the time of this writing, we found most case study books analyze finished designs but do not deconstruct the design-journeys that led to project completion. In seeking successful design strategies, we interviewed top firms, took note of projects highlighted in industry journals, and visited award-winning projects. The six projects selected represent a breadth of design styles, scales, locations, designers, and processes.

To develop the mapping diagrams and background information for the case study projects, we traveled across the United States from Connecticut to the Pacific Northwest to the Virginias and the Desert Southwest. The projects are found within diverse biomes and settings from a densely settled industrial park to a suburban residence to a pristine rural park. Each area with its unique cultural qualities, regional character, natural limitations, and cultural practices, revealed forms, functions, and philosophies that shaped the sustainable approaches taken. The map diagrams in the case studies, created specifically for the book, are based on the design process information provided by the landscape architecture firms. While the mapping shown does not necessarily reflect the mapping produced by the firms, it illustrates issues inventoried, assessed, or considered that are evident in the design resolutions.

Each case study is used to illustrate a particular dimension of the design process but also to more generally exemplify the contextual landscape basis of the landscape sustainability framework and criteria. Toward this end, the case studies first lay out the regional conditions that form the landscape context and later the sustainable site design outcomes of six widely varied projects. They are formatted for ease of comparison to one another. The projects are:

Menomonee Valley Industrial Center,
Milwaukee, Wisconsin

Sandstone Visitor Center, Sandstone, West Virginia

Whitney Water Purification Facility,
Hamden, Connecticut

Paradise Valley Residence, Paradise Valley, Arizona

Gannett/USA Today Headquarters, McLean, Virginia

Tanner Springs Park, Portland, Oregon

The format for the case studies, which unfolds through the mapping and analysis of the projects' site/context relationships, forms the basis for the sustainable design process guidelines. The presentation of the case studies is not meant to interpret each designer's own design process, but rather to reveal to the reader the sustainable outcomes in relation to both site conditions and context conditions. The format includes:

Overview

The project's inception is explained and the design concept is briefly introduced.

The client and designer philosophies are outlined through an examination of their project goals and previous experiences. General sustainability trends in land use and program types comparable to the case study subject are also explored.

Context

The project's context is explored at a variety of scales from the entire United States, down through its multi-state region, watershed, metropolitan, or local area and neighborhood, to the immediately adjacent conditions of the site. This context is described through three dimensions: form, (the physical features of the context), function (the ecological and human systems and processes at work in the region), and philosophy, (the attitudes toward development and conservation in place in the region). The overall sustainability of the regional context is evaluated as a basis for examining the site and its design solution as either a *sustainable integrator* or a *sustainable pioneer*.

Site

Design considerations are first presented in the form of an examination of the predesign site, an analysis of the most influential scales of context, and an explanation of the ecological and cultural dimensions of the program development. An example of a conventional (versus sustainable) approach to the same type of project that exists in proximity to the case study site is also presented.

The design solution is analyzed at a variety of scales with regard to two sustainability dimensions that were also used in the regional context analysis: landscape form (the site's organization, spatial framework, and materials), and site design function (the site's stormwater management, planting, human use systems, and site management strategies), as well as site design integration (the creation of meaning through elements that engage the user with dimensions of sustainability).

Outcomes

The project's predesign and postdesign conditions are compared with regard to the program/site/context relationship. The use of design techniques that contribute to site-level sustainability are identified and distinguished from techniques that contribute to sustainability of the larger landscape beyond the site. The case study's specific fulfillment of the five landscape sustainability criteria developed in Chapter 1 is outlined to establish its exemplification of the framework. Finally, other examples of similar sustainable projects are identified.

Acknowledgments

We are indebted to the following landscape architects for providing us insight into their design processes: Tavis Dockwiller of Viridian Landscape Studio, Matthew Urbanski and Chris Gates of Michael Van Valkenburgh Associates, Herbert Dreiseitl and Gerhard Hauber from Atelier Dreiseitl, Mike Abbaté of Greenworks PC, William Wenk and Greg Dorolek of Wenk Associates Inc., Steve Martino and Andrea Cooper of Conservation Design Forum, and Michael Vergason and Doug Hays of Michael Vergason Landscape Architects.

Special thanks to Joe Bivona for his dedication and skill in mapping research, obtaining image permissions, and generating graphics. We would also like to acknowledge University of Connecticut landscape architecture students Katherine Liss, Jameson Secco, and Mary-Kate Casey. We are grateful to the anonymous reviewers of this book and give thanks to colleague Mark Westa for his review, Dan Buttrey for graphic assistance, and Dr. Mary Musgrave for her guidance and encouragement. This research was supported by a faculty grant from the University of Connecticut. The editorial staff at Wiley, especially Margaret Cummins and Lauren Poplawski, were helpful with the evolution and development of the manuscript.

Additional thanks to the Oriental Café in Storrs, Connecticut, where we had the good fortune of spending many working lunches. We owe this work to the patience and support of our families, especially Rich, Emily, Garrett, Ted, and Katia.

1 LANDSCAPE SUSTAINABILITY FRAMEWORK AND CRITERIA

Achieving sustainable environmental design encompasses myriad efforts on the part of both professionals and the public. These efforts—grassroots awareness campaigns that challenge individual citizens to come together to champion good planning for their communities, the realignment of our regulatory structures to facilitate and encourage healthy patterns, the retooling and retraining of our construction and materials industry, and the development of planning and design methods that inform and guide professionals' design processes and ultimately the built environment—are all essential to reversing the destructive patterns of sprawl and the subsequent loss of nature and community that permeate contemporary development of our environment. The complexities and interrelationships of these needed efforts are daunting, yet nearly every person, organization, and profession has a role to play and perspective to contribute.

LANDSCAPE + DESIGN + SUSTAINABILITY

The relationship between and intersection of these three concepts—*landscape, design,* and *sustainability*—form the basis for this book and define the role of the profession of landscape architecture. *Landscape*, referred to by Frederick Steiner as the connective "tissue" of our world, is the medium that hosts, links, and conveys the vast complex of ecological and cultural systems in an intricate fabric of landform and habitats. Though it can be divided into many types of units, it does not and cannot exist independent of its larger whole. Through *design*, humans plan their technological interventions and express creative urges to satisfy individual and societal needs. When deployed in the landscape, design takes on the dynamism of a living, fluid, and changing medium, where decisions made at a site scale have direct impact on and connection to larger scales and vice-versa. Finally, the urgent call for *sustainability* of human development of the environment requires that we begin to recognize the critical role landscape and its design—landscape architecture—must play in uniting fragmented places, healing degraded systems, and engaging people in healthy relationships with nature. From this perspective, land is a continuum of cultural and ecological influences and responses, where a site boundary acts as a filter rather than a wall, and design holds the potential to draw and propel positive influences to and from the site.

EVOLUTION

Sustainability in landscape architecture until recently was viewed as a specialized branch of the field, heavily associated with ecological design. However, the synthesis of the cultural and ecological qualities of landscape architectural design reflected in contemporary built work blurs the once sharp line between ecological design and culturally resonant "high design."

Several critical benchmarks in landscape architectural theory and practice have contributed to current views about sustainability within the profession (Ndubisi 1997). These benchmarks can be considered within three significant "generations": the first generation occurring roughly between 1960 and 1975 and sparking a general awakening and shift in design approach toward ecological awareness; the second generation occurring between 1975 and 1995 and developing more scientific and specialized areas of interest; and the third/current generation from 1995 to present, which can be characterized as moving toward integration of sustainability within the more generalized practice of landscape architecture.

First Generation: 1960–1975

Systems-Based Model for Landscape Planning. Alongside public outcries critical of the status quo such as Rachel Carson's *Silent Spring* and the founding of environmental movements such as Greenpeace, Ian McHarg's landscape planning techniques in his book *Design with Nature* in 1969 represents the first explicit and systematic consideration of natural and cultural resources in landscape architecture (McHarg 1995). His "layer-cake" approach to determining land use suitability remains the gold standard for design methodology across all disciplines dealing with land use analysis and planning and set the stage for later technological development of Geographic Information Systems. McHarg's work and that of his contemporaries and colleagues, most notably Philip Lewis, focused on large-scale planning projects such as The Woodlands residential community in Texas. These concepts and methods were also applied to site-scale design in determining both the suitable uses for a site, as well as how it might be designed to fit within its surroundings.

Second Generation: 1975–1995

This period is benchmarked by several divergent outgrowths of land planning models developed in the earlier generation.

Regenerative Design. The work of John Lyle, practitioner and professor at California Polytechnic State University at Pomona, developed the concept of regenerative design focused on site-scale subjects. Regenerative design is the idea that development does not just consume resources, but also can regenerate or produce them. Examples of regeneration are recharging groundwater, reusing graywater, producing edible crops in the landscape, or harvesting solar energy (Lyle 1992). The Center for Regenerative Studies at California Polytechnic State University is a living laboratory for these concepts.

Ecological Design Firms. Meanwhile, ecological design firms such as Andropogon Associates in Philadelphia and Jones & Jones in Seattle, both early proponents of landscape sustainability, developed systems-based and context sensitive ecological approaches evident in landmark designs such as the Crosby Arboretum and Paris Pike.

Reclaiming Landscapes. Also during this period, a bold social approach to reclaiming abandoned human landscapes can be identified through projects such as Lawrence Halprin's Freeway Park, which reconnected the divided pieces of Seattle; Richard Haag's Gasworks Park, which reclaimed the waterfront site of a former gas utility for recreation; and later Hargreaves Associates' Byxbee Park, a former industrial site along the San Francisco Bay.

Regional Identity. A focus on regional identity, both cultural and ecological, is part of this generation's contribution. The insight of Michael Hough in his book *Out of Place* (1992) and regionally inspired built work by practitioners such as Phoenix-based Steve Martino embody the value of distinctive regional context in creating landscapes that are "of the place."

Schism between "High Design" and Ecological Design. Along with the more specialized identity of ecological design within the larger profession of landscape architecture, a growing dialogue and debate about the role of creative form-making in sustainable design was forming. There was a strong impression that the profession was still rewarding design work that did not give adequate consideration to ecological function or health, while there was also a common observation that many of the ecologically conceived projects lacked inspiring or memorable form. This debate was crystallized in a 1992 forum featured as a cover story by *Landscape Architecture Magazine* entitled "Is it Sustainable? Is it Art?"

Third Generation: 1995–Present

The Metrics Approach. The current generation of sustainability in landscape architecture is characterized first by a growing interest in the metrics for ecological function and economics in the built environment. The Leadership in Energy and Environmental Design (LEED) Green Building Rating System, developed by the United States Green Building Council, provides a detailed checklist for incorporating a range of ecologically based sustainable design principles into architectural development projects. Site-related components are not a central focus of the system.

Construction-Based Sustainability. The *Sustainable Landscape Construction* book produced by William Thompson and Kim Sorvig in 2000 provides important site-based technical focus for sustainable design implementation. Advances in native plant production and construction technologies have bolstered the ability to implement site elements that were once not possible within conventional construction practices. In a similar vein, the concept of *low-impact design* calls for recharge, filtration, and other on-site treatment methods for stormwater engineering in a time when water resource conservation has become a focus.

Applied Ecological Principles. Articulation of applied ecological principles at the landscape scale has been a critical contribution of Dramstad, Olson, and Forman as developed in their 1996 book, *Landscape Ecology Principles in Landscape Architecture and Land-Use Planning.* The ecological structure and functioning of land in corridors, patches, mosaics, and matrices provide a new language for land-use planning that protect ecological integrity and connectivity.

Ecorevelatory Design. Eco-revelatory design is intended to reveal and interpret ecological phenomena, processes, and relationships (Brown, Harkness, Johnston 1998). This concept has brought exciting synergy of visual drama/appeal and ecological process of such phenomena as stormwater conveyance and reuse that has fueled a new brand of innovative form-making.

Mainstreaming of Sustainability. A particularly prominent aspect of the current generation is that sustainability is moving away from being viewed as a specialized type of landscape architectural practice, focused exclusively on ecological concerns, toward a more mainstream concern for all landscape architecture projects. The concerns of "high design" that emphasize rigorous attention to form-making are being merged with the concerns for ecological integrity.

The Next Generation

As nearly all of the influences just outlined begin to converge, built work is exhibiting a critical synthesis of ecological, social, and cultural landscape considerations. As the "green revolution" takes hold in the global environment, a chief concern for the future of sustainable site development is the need to integrate larger planning efforts to combat sprawl, conserve ecologically intact open space, and create more livable communities with the more specific and detailed design of sustainable sites. The projects reviewed for this exemplify the benefits of such integration. Future approaches must utilize context-informed site design to address the broader range of criteria included in planning-scale projects.

CONTEXT

The information age has brought a dizzying and seductive amount of unfiltered data to our fingertips. Often it is tempting to simply tune out context, as it provides too much information and can derail the process of defining a problem and taking action. Yet, the tremendous efforts we mount to make objects and technologies sustainable and "green" must all be viewed within the appropriate context. The energy efficiency of using corn as a biofuel, for instance, has been rejected, viewed within the context of how much energy it takes to produce the corn. Similarly, a central problem with sustainable site design is one of contextual scale and integration, where piecemeal solutions negate possibilities for larger cohesive ecological and social function and identity. Simply put, individual green buildings or sites do not necessarily add up to green neighborhoods, communities, or regions:

> Not that all our earnest recycling, our water-scrimping showers, our labors to cool the planet are futile, but our larger lapses raise the fundamental question of where and how—and whether—we should be building anew. …The vision of a sustainable planet begins with the individual but requires planning on a large scale—not just locally, but regionally, nationally and internationally—to endure. It becomes increasingly clear that only if we encourage and participate in land planning on a larger and political scale can we consider ourselves builders of a truly sustainable world and not just hammer-wielders building little green islands in a sea of subdivided land.
>
> —Jane Holtz Kaye 2002

The U.S. Green Building Council has recognized this need for larger-scale planning through its LEED ND (Neighborhood Development) program, which is aimed at neighborhood-level planning to provide better control and coordination of larger systems of transportation, building massing, and other elements. This is on the heels of its widely followed and highly influential program for sustainable building construction, in recognition of the growing concern for the larger community context.

Yet this is not a book about land use or community planning per se. While professional planning activities address important analysis, strategy, and policy direction, they rarely result in direct built work. Rather, this effort is aimed at approaching the basic building block of development: the site, that singular piece of the larger land complex, whether it contains a building or exists primarily as a landscape—with an eye toward regional context, applying planning principles to site design. Sites that are conceived with an overview of the larger, hierarchical systems of the environment, both ecological and cultural, stand a much better chance at protecting and enriching—sustaining—the site environment and its inhabitants. Further, sites that design experiences, elements, and visual character that help site users "read the texts of their surroundings" go beyond physical resource conservation achievement to create meaning based on understanding of our relationships and interactions with our environments (Steiner 2002). Designing with context in mind holds potential not only for the sustainability of the site itself, but also for the greater sustainability of the neighborhood, area, or region.

Now more than ever, information without clear and appropriate frameworks for selection and application can be counterproductive and even damaging. The framework presented here retains focus on site design, but aims to strengthen or repair connections to context that are lost or unrealized through piecemeal site planning. Further, it aims to utilize sensitive and artful site design to reveal and express regional values and identity.

This framework offers a way to consider and integrate information about context—in the form of physical constructs such as watersheds and neighborhoods, and in the form of nonphysical constructs such as local history and community attitudes—in the process of site design. It identifies two basic contextual situations for a sustainable site design problem: pioneer and integrator.

Sustainable Pioneer

Where the project's region is generally more challenged in ecological and/or cultural terms, the site can be considered a *sustainable pioneer*. Three of the case studies presented later in the text, a corporate headquarters in McLean, Virginia, a private residence in Phoenix, Arizona, and an industrial development in Milwaukee, Wisconsin, fit this description. The design for a sustainable pioneer site can introduce sustainable form, function, and philosophy to a larger area that lacks integrated cultural and ecological health. The term *pioneer* connotes the idea that these projects are trailblazers, leading a trend that will grow and transform the larger environment. The sustainable pioneer site can impart its trailblazing effect in a variety of ways. It can revitalize lost or broken networks of cultural or ecological function between the site and its surroundings, or reintroduce forgotten heritage or invisible bioregional character of the area. Nevertheless, it can also create self-reliance and wholeness for the site independent of its surroundings. In other words, it may have an important catalyzing effect on the surrounding lands or it may simply be one small island of sustainability unto itself, which when repeated across the region will create the transformation.

Sustainable Integrator

A *sustainable integrator* is a site whose design can reflect the health and stability of its sustainable context. Three of the case studies presented later in the text, an urban park in Portland, Oregon, a water purification facility in Hamden, Connecticut, and a park visitor center in Sandstone, West Virginia, fit this description. The success of each can be said to be linked to the intact political, cultural, and ecological character of its region. These projects answer the question: How do we build upon the success of the surroundings? Integration or connectivity of ecological and human systems is recognized as one of the key criteria for sustainability in this framework. There are two kinds of contextual connectivity addressed here: *physical* and *symbolic*. Physical connectivity, such as improvement of a portion of a stream buffer along a larger system, improves regional ecological health. Symbolic connections, such as use of repurposed local materials, provide a vehicle for human engagement critical to sustainable site making. The sustainable integrator project can knit together discontinuous intact systems and typically improves upon the site's predesign value and health.

CRITERIA

Existing frameworks for creating and evaluating sustainable design fall primarily into two categories: those that offer qualitative, theoretical, or values-based criteria; and those that prescribe specific quantitative or standards-based criteria (Edwards 2005). While many of the former tend to be highly influential and formative, the most actively utilized and applied systems tend to be the latter, where focused, tangible, and measureable directives and benefits are identified. The widely followed LEED program, mentioned earlier, for instance, is a point system for design and certification of high-performance green buildings. This program considers the embodied energy of materials and systems used in the building process and the operation of a building and its site. The benefits of certification, in addition to the energy savings and other environmental resource gains, include long-term economic benefit and the cachet of social consciousness that accompanies the attainment of silver, gold, or platinum certification levels. It rates sustainability in the areas of sustainable sites, water efficiency, energy and atmosphere, materials and resources, indoor air quality, innovation and design process. A similar program for the measured evaluation and recognition of designed landscapes has been introduced with the Sustainable Sites Initiative, a joint effort of the American Society of Landscape Architects, the Ladybird Johnson Wildflower Center, and the United States Botanic Garden. The areas of focus for this program are hydrology, soils, vegetation, materials, and human health and well-being.

An essential characteristic of these types of frameworks—and what makes them so eminently attractive and useful—is that they can be applied to nearly any project, regardless of site or its place within the urban to rural transect of the developable environment. Another key characteristic is that they retain clear focus on measureable technical and scientific criteria, leaving artistic, cultural, and social criteria cleanly out of the mix for the most part.

Alternatively, the framework presented here is centered on crafting sustainable landscapes based largely on a site's relationship to its unique natural and cultural context. This context may be rural or urban, Northeastern or Southwestern, environmentally or economically stable or distressed—all these and many other contextual conditions create distinct opportunities and challenges for sustainable design. Context relevant to site design occurs at a range of strategic scales that begins at the regional level—the Central Plains/Midwest region for instance—and proceeds through state, watershed, local, and neighborhood levels, right down to the site-adjacency context where a site's physical relationship to its neighbors is direct and tangible. In some contexts, native plant communities may be a particularly relevant factor; in other contexts, patterns of historic development and land use may be a more relevant factor. While these aspects cannot be easily measured, they do offer specific opportunities and needs for sustainability.

The aesthetics of sustainability in the landscape have long been a point for debate, some arguing that attention to visual quality has been sacrificed by the concern for sustainability, others pushing for new conceptions of beauty and imageability to embrace the "messiness" of nature. To this end, the framework also develops qualitative criteria that address questions of form-making and meaning related to sustainability and context.

With the ultimate goal to derive sustainable site *design process* guidelines, what follows here is a baseline establishment of *criteria* for sustainable landscapes. These criteria serve both to further define a sustainable landscape framework in which site and regional concerns are integrated and to provide the basic parameters used for the selection of the case studies, which illustrate the qualitative outcomes. The criteria draw from many wide-ranging and foundational developments in thinking about land, landscape, planning, design and case study research, and place these within five major themes for implementing and evaluating landscape sustainability. The five landscape sustainability criteria: connectivity, meaning, purpose, efficiency, and stewardship, each in their own way forge a relationship between a site and its context.

Comparative Criteria for Sustainable Landscape Design

The following provides brief comparative outlines for several frameworks that exist for sustainable design.

Qualitative Frameworks:

Andropogon Associates' Ecological Site Design Guidelines

- Create a participatory design process
- Preserve and re-establish landscape patterns
- Reinforce the natural infrastructure
- Conserve resources
- Make a habit of restoration
- Evaluate solutions in terms of their larger context

- Create model solutions based on natural processes
- Foster biodiversity
- Retrofit derelict lands
- Integrate historic preservation and ecological management
- Develop a monitored landscape management program
- Promote an ecological aesthetic

Sanborn Principles—Urban Design Foundations for Sustainable Communities

- Healthy indoor environment for occupants
- Ecologically healthy
- Socially just
- Culturally creative
- Beautiful
- Physically and economically accessible
- Evolutionary

Values of Place—Essence of Timeless Design, Human-Centered Building, and Personal Responsibility

- Diversity
- Beauty and aesthetics
- Accidental meeting places
- Surprise and discovery
- Resource efficiency
- Leaving your mark
- Human form emerging naturally from its place

Principles of Smart Growth—www.smartgrowth.org

- Range of housing opportunities
- Walkable neighborhoods
- Community and stakeholder collaboration
- Distinctive attractive communities with sense of place
- Development decisions are predictable, fair, and cost-effective
- Mix land uses
- Preserve open space in critical areas
- Variety of transportation
- Place new development where existing infrastructure/development occurs
- Compact building design

Sustainable Landscape Construction Principles—Thompson and Sorvig

- Keep healthy sites healthy
- Heal injured sites
- Favor living, flexible materials

- Respect the waters of life
- Consider the fate and origin of materials
- Know the costs of energy over time
- Celebrate light, respect darkness
- Quietly defend silence
- Maintain to sustain

Quantitative Frameworks:

LEED—New Construction v2.2

- Sustainable Sites
- Water Efficiency
- Energy and Atmosphere
- Materials and Resources
- Indoor Air Quality
- Innovation and Design Process

LEED-Neighborhood Development—Pilot Program

- Smart Location and Linkage
- Neighborhood Pattern and Design
- Green Construction and Technology
- Innovation and Design Process

Sustainable Sites Initiative

- Water Waste
- Water Pollution
- Biodiversity and Invasive Species
- Resource Waste
- Energy
- Soil
- Air

Connectivity

Sustainable landscape solutions must evidence:

- site to context connections

- cultural systems and natural systems connections

- temporal connections that recognize the life of landscapes over time

We live in an era and culture where phenomena like fractal geometry and Google Earth have begun to give us new views of how things are interconnected and in many cases, how these connections have become compromised or destroyed. Fractals, a term coined in the 1980s by mathematician Benoit Mandelbrot, are objects with geometric structure that display self-similarity at various scales. Magnifying a fractal structure reveals small-scale details similar to the large-scale characteristics. Although fractals have similar patterns at a variety of magnified scales, the smaller-scale details are not *identical* to the whole. In fact, its structure is infinitely complex, though the process of generating it is based on an extremely simple equation. The phenomenon of similarity at various scales provides a window on the order, structure, and organization of complexity. With a visual appeal that comes from its balance of complexity and unity, the concept of fractals has been applied and examined in the creation of fine art and other fields in which geometry is relevant.

Fractal patterns are found across vast scales everywhere in nature in small objects such as snowflakes and ferns, as well as large landscapes such as coastlines and mountain ranges. Ian McHarg, in *Design with Nature,* first directed environmental designers to notice these patterns and build with environmental fitness in mind, so that these patterns could be preserved and woven throughout the built environment. The book *A Pattern Language,* written by architect Christopher Alexander in the 1970s, applies the idea of observing and linking successful or proven human patterns at different scales to the built environment. From regions, communities, neighborhoods, and sites, down to buildings, rooms, and windows, *A Pattern Language* proposes a hierarchical, structured way of designing. Whereas McHarg developed a systems-based methodology that responds to each design subject's unique qualities and circumstances, Alexander's methodology uses more of a "recipe" approach with a list of somewhat idiosyncratic patterns that can be applied to any problem and location.

Technological advances in digital geographic information systems and satellite imagery allow us to instantaneously zoom from viewing the entire earth from outer space to our own backyard or latest project site. A vast array of geographic systems information floats out in cyber space, and though there are widely varying scales of accuracy and precision, designing with spatial context in mind has never been more possible.

Site to Context Connections

The most tangible work of landscape architecture—the creation of places of meaning, visual delight, and spatial identity—occurs at the site scale at which human perception operates. But we can look to critical contributions of landscape architecture that occur at larger scales of planning like the neighborhood or community, which, though less tangible and visually iconic than site-scale design outcomes, are equally compelling and arguably more valuable. Much of the most important 19th-century work of landscape architect Frederick Law Olmsted—the "Emerald Necklace" of the Boston Parks system, the Stanford campus, Chicago's Columbian Exposition—occurred at the larger planning level, where study and understanding of the neighborhood, the community, and the region allowed for sensitive siting and land use relationships. These same planning examples, with their far-reaching impacts on whole communities, however, also come with familiar sites that have imageable, physical qualities. The Backbay Fens, Commonwealth Avenue Parkway, and the Public Garden are memorable landscapes precisely because they fit within and enhance their urban context and larger open space framework. The linking of larger community planning concepts and knowledge of site context with more immediate site planning and design concepts provides powerful results on many levels.

The *new urbanism* movement is an example of society's growing recognition of the need to think outside the building and think outside the site, to address the needs of sustainable smart growth. With its combination of principles that emphasize pedestrian connectivity, mixed land uses, compact development that allows for open space preservation, well-defined districts, and the importance of the civic realm, new urbanism calls for a return to the patterns of traditional town planning and a rejection of the patterns of unplanned sprawl that dominated the second half of the 20th century. More importantly, it places the design of sites and architecture within a very contextual realm—each piece of the community is dependent on its neighborhood, district, and community structure. Many of the concepts of new urbanism can be traced back to the ideas of Kevin Lynch and his theory of good city form. In *Image of the City*, Lynch defines the memorable elements of the city as related to him by everyday citizens—landmark, district, node, path, edge. These are connective elements and structures that organize urban environments and make them legible, interesting, diverse, and whole.

In creating site-to-context connections, we can think about *functional* physical connections such as circulation corridors, vegetation patches, or hydrological features, which encourage the larger flow and health of the landscape. We can also think about *spatial* connections such as how a site may be configured as an open or a wooded site to either link with or contrast against its surroundings. Another way to think about site-to-context connections is in *program development*, where the type of park you might wish to develop is highly dependent on the surrounding land uses and the variety of other parks that are available in the local area. Finally, we can use *formal* connections to context to create unity and meaning related to regional vernacular materials and architecture and natural forms.

Natural and Cultural Systems Connections

An end to thinking of natural and cultural landscapes as occurring in two separate realms was suggested by McHarg and elaborated on by Anne Whiston Spirn in *The Granite Garden*. The growing trend toward renewal of natural process in urban environments through stream daylighting and dechannelization, urban forestry, green roofs, and permeable paving is proof that integration of natural process in human development is not only possible, but needed and desired.

The scientific concept of ecology has, until very recently, been studied primarily within the realm of the natural world and has not been applied to the physical development, or design, of the human world. While the notion of "human ecology" was explored as a branch of sociology and geography in the early 20th century, it became disconnected from the physical world to focus on more economic, demographic, and political approaches. Frederick Steiner proposes a new interpretation of human ecology, which denies this historic disconnection and encourages more integration of physical and social science. Ecologist Richard Forman and his colleagues broke this barrier in their development of landscape ecology principles that were specifically developed for use in landscape architecture and land use planning. Steiner, a landscape architect, proposes that the critical issues of sustainability and sustainable development require that we more actively and aggressively engage these principles in applying the concepts of ecology to the planning and design of built human environments (Steiner 2002). The integration of human and natural forms and functions—as in regenerative human ecosystems such as wetlands stormwater treatment systems—is a critical expression of connectivity.

Temporal Connections

The concept of historic preservation originated through the effort to preserve historic buildings and other antiquities. Buildings are nearly completely human constructs; they can be enormously imposing and influential, but can easily and instantaneously be demolished. They represent very particular eras of human culture, evoking powerful form associated with history and a society's collective memory. Alternatively landscapes endure and evolve over millennia, but are in many ways ephemeral and transformable. The image of cultural history reflected in landscape can be subtle and vulnerable, especially when intermixed with that landscape's natural history. The landscape acts as a canvas over which cultures and ecological forces play out; seasonally, yearly, in eras and epochs. The concept of historic preservation has evolved to encourage a less static, more layered notion of history, in which ruins and artifacts of older ideas can comfortably and functionally coexist with new uses, forms, and ideas. Scholars of the cultural landscape, including most notably May Watts, J. B. Jackson, Kevin Lynch, Roderick Nash, and William Cronon, have examined the American landscape for its imprint of our history and changing cultural constructs. Designers such as Richard Haag, in his 1970s Gasworks Park, were among the first to apply a new, more layered and living historic sensibility to the design of open space sites.

Meaning

Sustainable site design solutions must evidence:

- a well-defined sense of place
- engagement of site users with landscape process and phenomena

In the study of the social scientific concept of hermeneutics, which is "the art of understanding," philosopher Wilhelm Dilthey proposed the notion of the *hermeneutic circle*: "In order to understand the determinate meanings of the parts of any whole, we must approach the parts with a prior sense of the meaning of the whole; yet we can know the meaning of the whole only by knowing the meanings of its constituent parts. This is not a vicious circle, in that we can achieve a valid interpretation by a mutually qualifying interplay between our evolving sense of the whole and our retrospective understanding of its component parts." (Abrams 2005)

The hermeneutic circle of emotional, intellectual, and conceptual meaning and identity in the landscape is an important component of sustainable design within the In Site/Out framework, and a concern that is relatively absent in most other frameworks. While many indigenous landscapes hold specific meaning for people in their natural form, created landscapes can utilize creative expression that interprets and reveals human ecological and cultural interactions with the landscape, and conveys an attitude for protection of and integration with intact indigenous landscapes. The conveyance and understanding of site meaning associated with sustainable processes and phenomena can create affinity for landscapes that inspire stewardship for the site itself and greater understanding of its place in the larger environment. Yi Fu Tuan's study of environmental perception of the landscape created the term *topophilia*: "the affective bond between people and place or setting," to describe this force of environmental experience.

The creation of meaning in the landscape can take the form of the gestalt—through the creation of a holistic sense of place. It can also take the form of smaller elements within the site that provide momentary engagements of the site user with specific processes or phenomena, such as a boardwalk that brings the user through a restored wetlands, or a bench placed at a point that focuses the user on a distant view of landform.

Sense of Place

Genius loci, latin for the "spirit of place," is a concept that has been linked to landscape and place-making ever since 18th century poet Alexander Pope wrote his *Epistle IV*:

> Consult the genius of the place in all;
> That tells the waters to rise, or fall;
> Or helps th' ambitious hill the heav'ns to scale,
> Or scoops in circling theatres the vale;
> Calls in the country, catches opening glades,
> Joins willing woods, and varies shades from shades,
> Now breaks, or now directs, th' intending lines;
> Paints as you plant, and, as you work, designs.

Since that time it has developed as one of the most widely agreed principles of landscape architecture: that landscape design should be inspired by and seek to preserve and enhance the unique character, function, and history of a site within its context. The creation of meaningful and memorable landscapes—landscapes that sustain us physically and mentally—is nearly always derived from a careful analysis and expression of the spirit of the place.

Reflection of and respect for regional culture and ecology is one of the most powerful forms of deriving meaning and sense of place. Michael Hough in *Out of Place* advocated for a regional sensibility in the development of landscapes at a time when the homogenization of our built environment was beginning to be recognized. The unique built patterns and forms of an area which have evolved in answer to its particular geographic and historic context comprise the communal identity that sets one region apart from another—such as the southwestern United States with its arid climate and mid-20th century era of development as compared with the northeastern United States with its temperate climate and mid-18th century base of development.

Recognizing a site's place within the urban/rural transect is a critical aspect of creating appropriate patterns of density and character in the built environment. The concept of transecting was first developed as a methodology for documenting and understanding the physical world, where a line was drawn across a landscape and sampling of biological or geophysical phenomenon performed to draw conclusions about the larger landscape's pattern and character. Applied to human development and environmental planning, the concept has been used to combat the indiscriminant application of the sprawling pattern and character of suburban development to nearly all new development, regardless of context. This has begun to bolster both compact and dense development in more urban areas, as well as clustered and open space conservation-minded development in more rural areas.

Process and Phenomena Engagement

Joan Woodward, in *Waterstained Landscapes,* offers a compelling and poetic call to integrate bioregional character, form, and function in the design of sites. The concept of "waterstain" is explained as the regional patterns of contrasting conditions—wet spots in a dry landscape for instance—that create the figure (or matrix) as perceived against the ground (or patches) in a landscape. While suggesting an ecological imperative, she emphasizes the spiritual and aesthetic urge for identity and meaning that can be satisfied with landscapes that reflect the combined imprint of natural systems and cultural systems. In answer to our vast and growing collection of generic and overly standardized places which James Kunstler skewers in *The Geography of Nowhere,* Woodward chronicles her ficticious character's quest to know and understand the "waterstain" of her arid Colorado Front Range region and apply this knowledge to the design of her home landscape. This requires looking beyond the heavily irrigated urbanized regions into the larger regional scales of the landscape.

The concept of eco-revelatory design was articulated and explored in the 1998 traveling exhibition of work mounted by three colleagues from the University of Illinois at Urbana-Champaign. The concept centers on the design of landscapes to reveal and interpret ecological phenomena, processes, and relationships (Brown, Harkness, Johnston 1998). The exhibit included both real and visionary projects from a variety of academic and private practitioners that innovatively expose, juxtapose, or narrate ecological processes from regenerative fire, to stormwater conveyance and reuse, to urban soils regeneration. This concept is in part a reaction to a conventional treatment of landscape to hide or disguise "unsightly" processes such as piped stormwater, and in part a reaction to the standard practice of costly and artificial suppression and control of ecological landscape process, as with monocultural landscapes of lawn and heavily pruned shrubs.

These themes were sounded earlier through the work of Robert Thayer, professor of landscape architecture at the University of California at Davis, who explored the challenges of sustainable landscape design in his 1994 book *Gray World, Green Heart.* Thayer posits that in contrast to mainstream landscape architecture of the time, which remained driven by cosmetic notions of aesthetic quality, design that fosters active and engaging user experience of regenerative processes, such as open stormwater conveyance, is a powerful tool for creating understanding, acceptance, and diffusion of sustainable practices. "One of the problems today is that the average citizen no longer realizes he or she is a part of nature. Landscape architects, more than almost any other profession, have the potential of reconnecting that citizen with nature by immersing him or her in an experience; by promoting, for example, urban forestry and allowing the land to breathe instead of imposing extensive paving . . ." This was the salient conclusion of architect Bob Berkebile on the proper role and greatest potential contributions of landscape architecture to sustainable development in a 1992 forum sponsored by *Landscape Architecture* magazine.

Purpose

Sustainable site design solutions:

- treat landscape as spatial and living medium
- fulfill land-based cultural and ecological program goals

The landscape is omnipresent and everywhere—often thought of as the ground upon which figure is set, or the blank canvas—and as such there is the tendency for it to be thought of and treated as background or negative space in development. Most environmental designers recognize the positive spatial, living, and dynamic qualities of landscape and the need to create hierarchy by assigning relative importance to some landscapes as primary spaces and allowing others to be treated as the connective tissue or interstitial spaces. Due to unawareness, this distinction often gets lost in translation to the built environment.

Landscape as Spatial and Living Medium

The treatment of landscape as background has a number of distinct unsustainable effects. First, it generally diminishes the care and attention given to land and its critical ecological and cultural systems which collectively form the basis for regional sustainability. The spatial qualities of landscape—the creation of enclosure, canopy, and a sense of scale and proportion, to name a few, through the configuration of landform and vegetation—can provide strong physical identity that generates focus on and value for the landscape, independent of understanding and meaning discussed above. This was the original impetus for the recognition of the value of the types of landscapes that now comprise our National Park system. While it is difficult for most people to relate the landscape of Yosemite to that of their own backyard or neighborhood park, the living and life-giving physical systems and their need for care are the same. In developed landscapes, the creation of positive, highly valued form and function is not dependent on its size or on the funds invested, but rather, the spatial treatment and organization of the elements used in the landscape.

A second unsustainable consequence of allowing the landscape to be treated as background is that it diminishes the understanding of the landscape as a living, dynamic, integrated organism. Segmenting the land into individually owned parcels, unrelated to landform patterns, creates a framework by which this understanding is thwarted and the site landscape is treated as independent of its neighbors, its larger functional identity and physical lifelines.

Land-Based Program Goals

Common land use designations assign purpose to land primarily through architectural identity: commercial, residential, or industrial, for instance. In this schema, the purpose and potential function of the landscape is reduced to supportive roles such as entry, parking, visual framing, etc. The sole category in which the landscape itself is the primary subject is typically "open space," which conveys a sort of blank quality and little sense of value or function. Within the realm of open space, landscapes are defined as park, preserve, greenway, green, etc.—also not very useful for directing program development. Sustainable landscape design is aided by the development of landscape-based programmatic function for all landscapes, whether open space sites or sites that accommodate development. People live in houses, shop in stores, and get medical treatment in hospitals. These are architectural program types that are based on how people use different types of buildings. In the landscape, we don't typically accommodate these specific types of cultural uses, but instead are concerned with satisfying a combination of cultural and ecological purposes. Cultural functions such as civic or social gathering and quiet contemplation are integrated with ecological functions such as stormwater management and landscape restoration. The notion of integrating concerns of context in sustainable site design supports the need for land-based programming as it expands the potential function of a site by connecting to its larger neighborhood or regional opportunities and goals.

Efficiency

Sustainable site design solutions:

- require relatively low resource inputs for implementation and maintenance

- create economic, human health, and social benefits

- satisfy multiple land uses

The relationship between conservation and efficiency was first explored during the progressive conservation movement of the early 20th century, at a time when the perception of unlimited resource abundance was beginning to fade, but rapid scientific progress instilled a sense of power to extend the resource base, using good economic and political planning and technology. The reclamation ideal whereby marginal lands were improved to become more useful, such as draining swamps and irrigating desserts, exemplified this interpretation of conservation as efficiency (Nash 1990). By the 1990s, the flaws in this exploitative approach had become evident to all but the most entrenched. Vice-president Al Gore, with his book *Earth in the Balance* and later film *An Inconvenient Truth*, brought unprecedented awareness of the natural resource and global warming crisis to a listening and sobered public.

Conservation of natural resources through the "reduce, reuse, and recycle" mantra was the original plea that led to our current green revolution. Most widely accepted contemporary criteria for sustainability are still centered on the concept of efficiency, primarily as pertains to use of energy, water, and other materials so as to maintain a dependable, renewable supply of these resources. But increasingly a more comprehensive view of conservation connects such efficiency to healthy systems—physical systems such as atmospheric and hydrological systems, agriculture and public health; as well as social systems such communities, economics, and education.

Low Inputs

The xeriscape movement, where drought-tolerant plantings are suggested as a replacement for irrigated landscapes in arid zones, is a landscape-based example of efficiency required as a result of expanding need for a limited resource. The *Sustainable Landscape Construction* handbook developed by William Thompson and Kim Sorvig was the first comprehensive landscape-focused set of guidelines that addressed efficiency in the developed landscape. With principles that encourage low-input landscapes through water, soil, and indigenous vegetation conservation; site protection and repair; impermeable surface reduction; light and noise pollution control; and recycled, renewable, and low-embodied-energy materials use, the strategies are primarily geared to design implementation- and construction-stage decisions rather than site planning and visual design decisions.

The treatment of water in the landscape is perhaps one of the most crucial and evolving forms of resource efficiency. While elaborate and costly stormwater systems aggressively remove water from conventionally designed and engineered sites, conversely, substantial energy is expended on introducing off-site water to sites to irrigate plant material. So a basic means of reducing water and energy inputs is through the creative harvesting of water from where it is not desired—on structures, pavements, and high-traffic areas—and applying it where it is desired—in vegetated areas and subsurface aquifers.

Self-Maintaining

Another important aspect of the efficiency criteria related to low inputs is the need for landscapes to be more self-maintaining. The postconstruction life of built landscapes, whether planned as such or not, typically ends up involving intensive and "one-size-fits-all" maintenance regimes. Endless mowing, irrigating, fertilizing, and replanting cycles are aimed at maintaining a cultural landscape ideal that is not in tune with natural cycles or patterns. While small, or even larger, areas of the landscape may be desired as lawn or more controlled or culturally expressive vegetation, these areas should be more targeted while larger areas of the landscape could be allowed to exist as naturalized areas that are established to eventually require little to no maintenance. Natural plant communities and landscape forms such as meadows, woodlands, and wetlands provide readily adaptable forms that can be meshed with larger landscape context or exist as isolated patches. While no managed landscape can truly be "maintenance free," these naturalized types of spaces offer reduced labor and cost, visual drama inspired by nature, and ecological biodiversity. In undeveloped nature, landscapes evolve and change completely in response to natural forces; it is important to distinguish between these and human naturalized landscapes that do involve some degree of control and management.

Economic, Health Benefits: Value-Added Landscapes

In *The Ecology of Commerce*, economist Paul Hawken likens the evolution of economic systems to that of ecological systems. In immature ecosystems, such as an early successional grassland, there is lots of biomass production, little biodiversity, lots of energy expended, and rapid change. As the ecological system goes through successional change toward a more mature stage, it gains biodiversity and makes use of its biomass to become elegantly free of waste. Hawken likens this contrast to our economic system, which in its early stages did not assign the true costs of waste, inefficiency, and environmental degradation to the market, to encourage mass-production, mass-consumption, and massive waste and destruction. In what he hopes will be our more mature and wiser next stages, Hawken sees economics and development becoming much more aligned with environmental systems to make the reduction and elimination of waste, inefficiency, and environmental degradation profitable (Hawken 1994).

Many of the most basic sustainable landscape elements such as native plants and permeable paving were previously often deemed by project clients as too expensive to implement. This was largely a function of the major markets for plant materials, design and engineering expertise, and skilled construction labor being geared to provide exotic plant palettes and impermeable paving systems. As the extreme inefficiency and cost of building exotic landscapes that require constant infusions of water, fertilizer, and energy becomes increasingly economically unsustainable, and ideologically undesirable, new types of landscape treatments are fueling the rapid retooling and reeducation of our markets and workforce to provide relevant and responsive solutions.

As the economic, social, and health value of landscape becomes more highly documented and quantified—increased values for property located next to protected open space; energy savings, oxygen production, air pollution control, and water purification attributed to urban forests—it is increasingly viewed not as simply an amenity, but as critical infrastructure.

The United States is slowly beginning to connect modern childhood health epidemics such as obesity, allergies, depression, and attention deficit disorder with lifestyles that emphasize sedentary "virtual" activities such as computer use and television viewing, and living environments that offer little access to nature and unstructured play. The "No Child Left Inside" campaign of the Connecticut Department of Environmental Protection is an example of programs that are aimed at addressing what journalist and child advocate Richard Louv has termed "nature-deficit disorder":

> As open space shrinks across America, overuse increases. Meanwhile, the regulatory message is clear: islands of nature that are left by the graders are to be seen, not touched. . . . . The cumulative impact of overdevelopment, multiplying park rules, well-meaning (and usually necessary) environmental regulations, building regulations, community covenants, and fear of litigation sends a chilling message to our children that their free-range play is unwelcome, that organized sports on manicured playing fields is the only officially sanctioned form of outdoor recreation. . . . Countless communities have virtually outlawed unstructured outdoor play, often because of the threat of lawsuits, but also because of a growing obsession with order. . . . These dense donuts of [modern suburban] development offer fewer places for natural play than the earlier suburbs. In some cases, they offer even fewer natural play spaces than the centers of old industrial cities.

In nature-deficit disorder, Louv is talking about "nature" as ecologically functional and biodiverse landscapes in which there are few prescribed uses. He uses examples of both designed and naturally occurring landscapes that offer experiences to children that are open-ended, dynamic, and self-directed, thus stimulating creativity and curiosity, as well as physical challenge and activity—benefits that provide real answers to declining childhood health trends. This phenomenon can easily be extended to the adult population, also plagued by similar health problems. This is both a cultural and an environmental issue in which the landscape offers efficient alternatives to costly and controversial medical treatment.

The concept of "low-impact design" is aimed specifically at the design of stormwater management systems that encourage on-site treatment, thereby creating fewer potentials for negatively impacting downstream sites. Another less pejorative way of thinking about design is to think of the net positive effects that a "high impact" project might have—as in remediating a brownfield, creating improved air quality, or restoring a degraded habitat area.

Multi-Use Landscapes

Another aspect of efficiency is the maximization of landscapes by allowing them to serve multiple functions. Just as we are beginning to realize the efficiencies of mixed-use architecture to reduce travel needs, increase pedestrian-friendly environments, and create new synergies for communities and commerce, we can see the benefits of encouraging landscapes to satisfy more than one focused need. Infrastructure such as water treatment can be satisfied simultaneously with the needs of public open space and of environmental repair. The contemplative landscape of a residential site or a park can also provide biodiverse habitat for wildlife and new understanding of the function and beauty of the natural world. The prescriptive use and identity of landscapes for very specific functions—a detention pond, for instance—limits the possibilities for multiple functions that energy expended on such an element might produce. Detention ponds are typically formed and managed for one single purpose: to temporarily hold stormwater at the low point of the developed site and release it at a controlled rate to prevent flooding downstream. When such ponds are also formed and managed to provide visual beauty, wildlife habitat, or recreational functions this increases the efficiency of the resources being expended on the pond.

The green infrastructure movement is in part a reaction to growing awareness of the negative effects of creating single-purpose, highly technological utilities and infrastructure that are viewed as undesirable neighboring land uses, as described by the NIMBY ("not in my backyard") syndrome. Decreased property values and visual quality, and often dangerous or unhealthful conditions have been associated with highway systems, water treatment facilities, energy and communication grids, and other infrastructure facilities and systems. This is causing us to reconsider both the function and the form of these utilitarian land uses on which we all depend and which are omnipresent in the landscape. Rob Thayer's examination of the perceptual, functional, and symbolic dimensions of technology in the landscape suggests that technologies that are generally perceived to be sustainable (highly productive, renewable, environmentally benign, and safe), such as wind farms, have higher acceptance from the public. He posits that conventional infrastructure utilizes technologies and forms that are typically perceived of with fear or distaste and therefore is approached with disguising strategies in its site design (fencing, screening, hiding). Sustainable technologies, especially when integrated with open space, can be a wonderful neighboring land use to a variety of developed areas, including residential neighborhoods.

This approach extends to nearly all other land use relationships; directing program development and improving landscape character to benefit both the site client and neighboring sites makes for not only "good neighbors," but increased property values through improved neighborhood cohesiveness and identity.

Stewardship

Sustainable site design solutions:

- involve collaborative and participatory design processes
- evoke a sense of long-term responsibility of site users, constituents

One of the standard tag lines of the landscape architecture profession has been "stewardship of the land." Bob Scarfo chronicled the notion of land stewardship through the ages with his seminal article *Stewardship: The Profession's Grand Illusion,* and argued that the profession's claim on this title is generally unsupported by its body of work. As stewards in the more historical sense, subsistence farmers intimately knew their land and understood its limits and capabilities, facing severe and immediate consequences when they did not manage their land sustainably. As stewards who are many steps removed from direct contact with the land, landscape architects have not typically been trained nor do they have the incentive to create designs that are truly sustainable in this sense. In the global era in which we live, the polar forces of interconnectedness and specialization have created an environment for which no one takes specific responsibility and in which narrow dimensions of environmental problems are studied to the exclusion of integrated, holistic thinking.

At the root of the modern stewardship dilemma is the concept of environmental ethics. Aldo Leopold was among the first to articulate a new branch of ethics that would address the relationship of humans to the environment. At this time, prior to the later revelations of Rachel Carson on the environmental and human health effects of industrial development, Leopold, a forestry scientist with the Soil Conservation Service, was alarmed by recreational exploitation of the natural environment. His concept of the "land ethic" would suggest the later movement of deep ecology in which nature holds intrinsic value of its own, apart from its value to humans. Scarfo and others have argued that ethical training for landscape architects has been focused on professional business ethics and not on the land ethic. Ecological thinking is being addressed in some cases, but less by way of ethics than through technical and scientific training. Of course, this issue only underscores the lack of a land ethic that is espoused by our general population. In an age where ethical lapses on the part of corporate and government leaders is at the fore, sustainability is less linked with a land ethic than it is with economic survival and national security.

In *Grey World, Green Heart* Thayer examines the "cognitive dissonance" that results when we are aware that something—such as landscapes that are dominated by the car culture—is bad for our health and the environment, yet that same something is permeating our world in a seemingly intractable cycle of continuation. The *ideal landscape* of our personal, controllable environments (which subtly accommodate our cars) is out of sync with the *real landscape* of the uncontrollable and chaotic wide world. Making sense of this dissonance and bringing the two landscapes into better balance requires a willingness to work toward and recognize the nature and value of incremental improvements in the larger landscape, as well as coming to terms with the real impacts of our personal ideals and lifestyles (Thayer 1994). Promoting public and professional adherence to a land ethic can be aided by the creation of places that reveal the connections between ideal and real landscapes.

Participatory Design

The need to effectively, appropriately, and meaningfully involve clients, users, and constituents in both developing the design goals and crafting a design solution for a site is a well-recognized component of sustainable design outcomes. Users who have been involved in the process can offer valuable first-hand knowledge of the design site and its history, as well as commitment to manage and care for the site into its future. Randy Hester in his book *Community Design Primer* distinguishes between community design—designing *with* people, and professional placemaking—designing *for* people. Originally associated with aiding underprivileged populations in overcoming environmental injustice and anomie through the empowerment of design decision-making, the community design movement has been widely applied to sustainable design efforts to create better ecological outcomes and public stewardship. The art of involving stakeholders in the design process is a delicate one, requiring a balance of the need for professional expertise with the sensibility and insight of the user. But it yields outcomes in which stakeholders are invested and which reflect the values and spirit of cooperation that make for sustainable sites.

Long-Term Care and Responsibility

In addition to stakeholder involvement during the design process, stewardship is derived from the involvement of stakeholders in the long-term management of the landscape site. This means both the physical maintenance of the site, as well as the general sense of ownership and responsibility for the site, that stems from the combined impact of clients, site neighbors, and maintenance providers. For many public landscapes the client may be the technical owner, but the neighbors who surround the site are the eyes and ears who watch over the site and inhabit it most directly, while the maintenance provider controls the actual care given to the landscape.

The care of sustainable sites typically involves unconventional and relatively new maintenance regimes that revolve around more naturalized types of landscape process. While this is greatly aided by the explicit specification of site management guidelines provided by the designer, adjustment and monitoring of the management regime as the landscape establishes, changes, and matures is critical.

2 PROGRAM DEVELOPMENT

What people, resources, and strategies help guide sustainable site programming?

Menomonee Valley Industrial Center

> Sustainable design is not a reworking of conventional approaches and technologies, but a fundamental change in thinking and in ways of operating.
>
> —Carol Franklin

(Credit: Nancy M. Aten of Menomonee Valley Partners)

BACKGROUND

"Programming" is visioning and determining key features to include in a site design. Any kind of programming, whether for conventional or sustainable projects, follows a circuitous path from initial project inception to final project installation. The sequence from program definition to program resolution is at turns exhilarating and frustrating because of the ever-changing variables that encompass working with the live mediums of landscape and people. There is no silver bullet to simplify the task as it unfolds in relation to myriad factors unique to the particular project type, the client and designer philosophies, the project stakeholders, the site location, regulatory requirements, and so on. Perhaps Kevin Lynch offers the most comprehensive yet simple guide to programming in his book *Site Planning*, where he describes it in terms of four key dimensions: package, population, performance, and pattern. The "package" is the set of elements or activities the design needs to satisfy, the "population" considers the needs of prospective users of the site, the "performance" signifies the function of site elements, and finally "pattern" suggests the use of relevant examples or precedents for certain types of individual program elements or project types. These four elements synthesize the basic building blocks of all design programming.

Chapters 3 through 7 in this book each contain aspects of site design that specifically facilitate sustainable site programming—stakeholder involvement, landscape analysis, the creation of form, construction techniques, and consideration of the site visitor. As each of these chapters will illustrate, the first and most significant aspect of sustainable programming is the *integration* of sustainability into every consideration both large and small; from site planning that acknowledges neighboring functions to the smallest detail that references local industry, sustainable goals must be at the forefront of decision-making. Often sustainability is applied as an "add-on" to a conventional approach to programming, where performance is the main dimension affected while the other dimensions are largely unaffected. For example, a parking lot element of a design could specify permeable paving rather than impermeable paving to encourage on-site stormwater management. This decision makes a slight, albeit valuable, change in its function but does not alter the use or perception of the site design. These types of projects can reduce the negative environ-

mental impact of the design, but not necessarily represent a net gain for the site. The Paradise Valley Residence project illustrates a clear departure from this type of approach, where the parking element of the program is developed as an outdoor entry courtyard space that happens to accommodate cars and use permeable desert paving that gives a sense of regional identity. In this example, an approach to sustainability is integrated throughout all four of Lynch's dimensions of program, not as an end-point decision about the type of paving or drainage to use. This chapter on sustainable program development offers a specific look at consensus building, visioning for sustainability, and the potentials of the program/site/context relationship.

STRATEGIES FOR PROGRAMMING DEVELOPMENT

- *Assess the client's attitude toward the landscape, knowledge of sustainability, their needs and desires.* While many clients who pursue sustainable design are very well informed, to some, sustainability is a goal they have little knowledge of. They may not fully understand what a sustainable landscape might look like, how it functions, what it offers the user, its costs, or what it requires to maintain. In either case, misconceptions are common such as assuming sustainability means a no-maintenance landscape or that a meadow is as low-growing as a lawn. On the other hand, a client may have one overarching concern, for example a deer problem that will drive their interest in sustainability to the exclusion of other issues of equal or greater importance such as stormwater quality. During the programming process assess the client's understanding of your expertise and the end product they are seeking. Invest the time to discuss both your own and the client's conceptions of sustainability. Visit sustainable sites with the client. As much as possible, work toward aligning your and the client's expectations to avoid potential misunderstandings later in the design process.

- *Find precedents to emulate.* Successful, time-tested programmatic elements in previously built designs are sources of inspiration and offer proof to you and to the client that the techniques are valid. Precedent projects demonstrate what has worked and what has not and reveal areas of potential for what has yet to be tried. Because the practice of sustainable landscape design is still relatively new, nearly all built work has experimental aspects. Even tried and true elements must be adapted to fit the particular requirements of a different project. Speak to the clients and designers of built projects for feedback on its failures and successes.

- *Assess regulatory opportunities and constraints toward sustainable direction.* Many towns and states are requiring single-purpose regulations on issues specific to their region, such as strict water usage controls in Arizona. Others overregulate, rendering any development near to impossible. Still other towns, despite the need and interest, do not have the resources or expertise to develop sustainable regulations. Assess regulations and determine how to go beyond merely complying to improve upon them. Demonstrate to a town, for example, how pervious reinforced grass rather than impervious pavement can comply with fire truck access requirements. Landscape architects can be key partners in helping towns develop sustainable regulations which frequently occurs on a project-to-project basis as towns scramble to acquire stricter environmental protections and restrict rapid growth. Use the regulatory process of submissions and meetings to set program benchmarks and to clarify sustainable measures to implement.

- *Write a "manifesto" to guide the program development over the course of the design process.* Clearly stated goals and principles of a project in a mission statement help focus all participants (Franklin 1997). It can be as simple as one sentence, such as "The site design will tell the regional watershed story" or as complex as a detailed itemized report. Using clearly outlined principles help the designer, the client, and project team define a course for the project philosophy; whether these goals are to connect natural and social systems, balance material resources, focus on adaptability, and so on. Design team consensus, while important on all jobs, is critical to the success of sustainable projects because the concept requires customization of long standardized cookie-cutter methods. An understanding between team members can be especially strong if the client drives the sustainable program or a unified sustainable program focus can be facilitated by a specialized consultant.

- *Employ a collaborative approach to problem definition and programming.* Whether the landscape architect is the prime consultant on the project or not, involve experts critical to project success early in the process. For example, retain a soil scientist on a project requiring constructed soils to ensure proper drainage, the longevity of plantings, and the client's investment. Tapping local experts knowledgeable of natural processes and cultural resources also lends credibility and ensures professional advice on techniques to be employed. Make use of the design team's unique backgrounds, philosophies, skills, and strengths. Whether they are LEED-accredited professionals or nursery workers, sustainable projects require copious dedication from the unique perspectives offered by a broad spectrum of professionals. Strong team support brings about richer projects with more resources.

METHODS FOR PROGRAMMING DEVELOPMENT

We know that the final product, the goal of the installed design, is sustainability, but how does one go about devising a clear sustainable program that endures from project inception to project outcome without being diluted as other factors take priority? In other words, what specific activities of program development build sustainability into the program and into the built product? The following tools catalyze the development of sustainable programming.

- *Sustainability Criteria Application:* Employ the 5 sustainable landscape criteria to develop goals with the client and to inform a landscape analysis.

- *Program/Site/Context Relationship*: What are the primary influences that will drive the project scope?

Sustainability Criteria Application

The lion's share of programming occurs during the first half of the design process alongside the site and context evaluation when opportunities for connection, revitalization, site function, and meaning reveal themselves. The five criteria outlined in Chapter 1, offer a starting point for sustainable programming in two important ways. First, they are points of discussion for the client and designer that help shape solutions to specific design problems. While important on any project, clarifying client expectations is especially valuable for sustainable design because its ideas and techniques are still relatively new. Second, the criteria identify critical issues in the site and context to inventory and assess. The criteria are:

* *Connectivity:* connections between site and context, ecological and cultural systems, and temporal elements

* *Meaning:* a sense of place with active connections between people and environmental processes

* *Purpose:* landscape as places, not merely settings

* *Efficiency:* efficient resource use of land, materials, and energy to satisfy multiple uses with each construction

* *Stewardship:* ensuring an inclusive design process carried through to the long term care of the changing landscape

The example below uses these criteria to illustrate programmatic considerations developed by the design team for the Menomonee Valley Industrial Center, the case study presented later in this chapter. This former industrial site along an urban riverfront involved copious and energetic dedication to cultural, ecological, and economic sustainability by multiple team and client entities, from the client, to the client representative, and the community nonprofit who spearheaded the project. Employing the broad-based goals, such as these criteria, moves the program beyond the application of performance-only solutions.

Connectivity

How can the site design…

* reconnect the disturbed and disconnected site ecologically to the river system and physically to the surrounding neighborhoods along either side of the valley?

* if not truly connected because of soil contaminations, still model a healthy stormwater system, by improving site runoff and rejoining the site to the greater Menomonee River watershed?

* connect adjacent neighborhoods to one another through trailway and bikeway linkages by taking advantage of portions of an already-in-place Hank Aaron trail system that serves the larger urban region?

Meaning

How can the site design…

* evoke the area's rich history, in the shadow of a new industrial development?

* immerse site users in a landscape whose comprehensive form is based on stormwater process?

* describe the site's natural history through landscape restoration?

Purpose

How can the site design…

* manage stormwater while serving as community open space?

* successfully integrate industrial, infrastructure, and open space site uses?

* create a site that will be a model for future developments?

Efficiency

How can the site design…

* optimize the 20 acres to share space between recreational, habitat, and stormwater treatment functions?

* ensure a low-maintenance landscape?

* make the site serve as a vital and multifaceted gateway to downtown Milwaukee?

Stewardship

How can the site design…

- minimize public expenditure on open space maintenance through a program of volunteer management?

- foster public stewardship by inviting public participation throughout the design process?

- create a new ethic of industrial sustainability?

Program/Site/Context Comparison

Program development is an evolving process that occurs in push and pulls between design ideas, client and regulatory requirements, and site and context restrictions. Like the chicken and egg dilemma, landscape analysis and programming both seem to need to come first. In reality, their evolution occurs simultaneously. To clarify the program, it is helpful to understand the relationship between the site, the context, and the program by looking at a side-by-side comparison of issues such as site health, access, parking, or meaning. This serves to reveal where issues overlap or are divergent—where opportunities exist or challenges need resolution.

In the case of Menomonee Valley Industrial Center, three sustainable factors—environmental factors, cultural factors, and economic/social factors—are compared vis-à-vis program mandates and the site/context analysis. Specifically, this comparison for the Menomonee Valley Industrial Center reveals a "need and response" relationship where the program, site, and context take turns initiating program development and landscape analysis responses. Again, this is a back and forth activity where new conditions in the site reveal the need for augmenting the program, or conversely, where the client has a change of heart and the site must be reanalyzed against new possibilities. The examples below show how all three aided in the goals of sustainability and moved the program forward.

Environmentally Initiated

Site Need: The long fenced-off site needed remediation in order to be safely utilized for stormwater management and public access.

Program Response: Despite the initial intention to connect site hydrology to the river on this floodplain site, extensive evaluation of the soil revealed the only feasible and safe solution to the arsenic and petroleum contamination was to cap the site. The capping nevertheless allowed the site to be accessed and usable for surface stormwater cleansing.

Culturally Initiated

Program Need: In order for the site to be useable and sustainable it required access from people in the surrounding valley. Site access was complicated by three factors: by insufficient roadway infrastructure, the construction of a new highway that bisects adjacent neighborhoods, and steep grades.

Contextual Design Response: The city improved site access by building new roadways into and through the site. A new visually intriguing "gateway" bridge improves not only access but injects an exciting element to traverse between downtown and the long-inaccessible valley.

Economically/Socially Initiated

Contextual Need: Urban joblessness was a problem in Milwaukee as job opportunities migrated out of the city to the suburban fringes.

Site Design Response: The site selection for this project was perfectly suited to the contextual need. Flat and ready to build on, this brownfield was prime real estate in the heart of Milwaukee that lay fallow and degraded for over 20 years. The new industry offered thousands of jobs and needed the workforce found in adjacent neighborhoods.

	INITIAL PROGRAM GOALS	SITE CHARACTER	CONTEXT CHARACTER
ENVIRONMENTAL	Remediation of contaminated land	Blank, flat, sterile landscape	Riparian corridors have long history of degradation related to industrial use
	Biological stormwater treatment for industrial development pads	Site contamination with arsenic and petroleum. Debris fill to depth of 21' in some areas.	
	Creation of habitat	Degraded Menomonee River edge	Floodplain filled to accommodate development. Impeded flood control, water quality, and habitat.
			Stormwater triggered large-scale contamination of drinking water supply
CULTURAL	Acknowledgment of site and neighborhood industrial history	Remaining industrial chimneys from Milwaukee Road rail yard days	Influences of historic industrial infrastructure, river dependence, and remnants of rail yard forms
	Consideration of aesthetic and spatial improvements to define public/ private uses	Historic use of site for largest rail yard in United States	Native American influences
ECONOMIC/SOCIAL	Need for local light-industrial job creation	Former industrial site provided local jobs	Current high unemployment levels
	Desire for neighborhood revitalization	Centrally located site lies fallow and unusable	"Dead" area sandwiched between lakefront downtown and stadium
	Make riverfront available as public open space	Site inaccessible to public and separates neighborhoods	Culturally diverse historic working-class neighborhoods

CASE STUDY— MENOMONEE VALLEY INDUSTRIAL CENTER

LOCATION: Milwaukee, Wisconsin, USA
SITE SIZE: 140 acres total (70 acres open space/70 acres development. The park discussed here is 20 acres.)
CLIENT: City of Milwaukee
DESIGNERS: Landscape Architect—Wenk Associates, Inc., Denver, Colorado
  Ecological Consultant—Applied Ecological Services, Brodhead, Wisconsin
  Engineers/Planners—HNTB, Milwaukee, Wisconsin
FORMER SITE USES: Industrial, then abandoned
LANDSCAPE BUDGET: $1.75 million
DATE OF COMPLETION: 2007

(Credit: Historicaerials.com)

Overview

Sited along the Menomonee River, this brownfield is an example of a sustainable design that developed from a spectrum of factors and needs—environmental, social, and economic within the neighborhood, city, and region of Milwaukee, Wisconsin. The initial programming was defined by a not-for-profit health center, the Sixteenth Street Community Health Center, who called for a competition to **master plan** an industrial site along the river. Alongside this objective, stormwater management was also a key goal of Milwaukee's mayor because of recent devastating floods that took lives, cost the city millions of dollars in damage, and contaminated the drinking supply. The winning landscape architectural firm, Wenk Associates Inc., drew upon the requirements outlined by a team of experts as to what elements to include in the competition program. Thereafter the landscape architects developed that vision further into an uncommon use of stormwater basins, not as elements to be hidden, but as the primary form-making features of what was to become a public park. The adjacent, densely developed industrial complex has its stormwater piped to this 20-acre park into successively larger and deeper basins that lead to the river. The very park would not exist if visioning for the building development had not valued the need for a balance between development and open space. A conventional design would have spaced the buildings evenly across the entire site and inaccessible basins at its remotest point. This

Figure 2.1 Industrial Ruins. By the 1980s the Menomonee River Valley's industrial activity had severely diminished, leaving large sites abandoned and contaminated, such as the Milwaukee Roads rail car factory site, pictured here.
(Credit: City of Milwaukee)

project, however, combined these seemingly incompatible uses to provide open space and access to the river to the surrounding neighborhoods and greater region of Milwaukee.

Project Inception

The Menomonee Valley Industrial Center project is part of a larger redevelopment area that extends westward from downtown Milwaukee along the Menomonee River Valley. The area's heavy industrial history left it contaminated with a variety of materials and compounds that rendered it a **brownfield** site following its large-scale abandonment in the 1980s (see Figure 2.1). Prior to redevelopment, the city of Milwaukee worked to secure federal and state brownfield grants to study and address the contaminated soil, old foundations, and miles of relic brick sewers left from the former industrial uses. The site was unusable for any redevelopment **program** without a plan for **environmental remediation** that would isolate or remove the contamination, protect the groundwater and human inhabitants from potential exposure, and restore ecological health to the site.

After lying fallow for many years, the valley is being redeveloped in response to regional economic need and the desire for community revitalization. The site developer, Menomonee Valley Partners, and many other public and private partners in the Milwaukee area collaborated in the visioning and planning for the valley as a whole (see Figure 2.2). After extensive study and outreach, a design charrette

in 1999 resulted in a blueprint for **smart growth** in the area. Then in 2002, on the former site of the country's largest rail car manufacturer, a national master plan design competition was launched. The basic components of the redevelopment were new parcels and infrastructure for light industrial use that would provide desired economic impacts, and open space that would provide environmental improvement and community connections (Sixteenth Street Community Health Center 2004). Another important goal was to inspire other projects of its kind throughout the region. The availability of this vast former industrial property in the center of Milwaukee surrounded by communities in need of employment provided the right ingredients for a unique development of this kind.

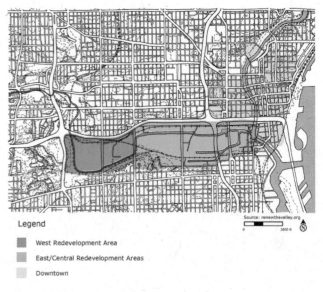

Legend

▪ West Redevelopment Area

▪ East/Central Redevelopment Areas

▪ Downtown

Figure 2.2 Menomonee Valley Redevelopment Areas.

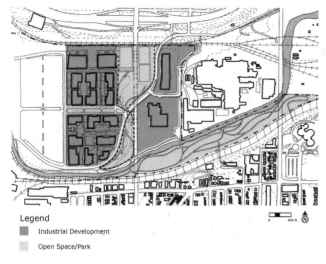

Legend

■ Industrial Development

░ Open Space/Park

Figure 2.3 Menomonee Valley Industrial Center Land Uses.

Design Concept

The design conceived and developed by Wenk Associates, the winner of the design competition, is built around the concept of multifunctional stormwater management, where a stormwater park becomes a civic recreational and ecological centerpiece for industrial development sites that are raised out of the floodplain. The concerns of water quality and detention are integrated with active and passive recreation and smart growth development. The stormwater management scheme, based on the need to cap the contaminated site, provides progressive levels of stormwater storage/open space flooding and biological filtration. Placement of the park is intended to allow the open space to function as both a destination spot and a node along the larger river greenway. The concept calls for reinforcement of the focus on this open space through dense development of the surrounding industrial parcels (see Figure 2.3).

This concept integrates the programmatic concerns of industrial development with those of park development, unlike conventional approaches, which treat these two land uses as at odds with one another. Within the park itself, a seamless integration of the stormwater, recreational, and habitat functions of the open space was envisioned.

For purposes of this case study, the redevelopment project is discussed as a whole, but the focus is the design of the open space (or park space known as the Menomonee Valley Community Park) portion of the site. The park itself has several subareas, the majority of which are identified in Figure 2.4. Although the riverfront Airline Yards is a critical planned park area, we further focus on the Chimney Park and River Lawn portions as the main body of the park that has been built to date and where the majority of the intensive program is carried out. These two park areas cover approximately 40 acres, while the Airline Yards area and other planned segments are about 30 acres, for a total of 70 acres of open space.

Project Philosophies and Approach

The design program emanated from the three basic goals of the competition mandate: economic impact, environmental improvement, and community connections. The direction taken in realizing these program goals was a direct product of the design philosophy and approach of both the client and the landscape architect.

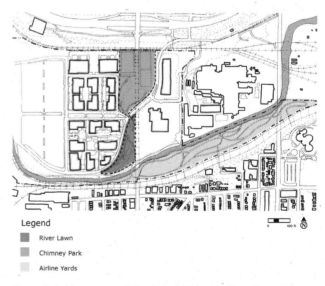

Legend

■ River Lawn

▓ Chimney Park

░ Airline Yards

Figure 2.4 Menomonee Valley Industrial Center Open Space Zones.

The Menomonee Valley Partners, Inc. (MVP) organization was created in 1999 in response to a recommendation in the Menomonee Valley Land Use Plan calling for a public-private partnership to guide a redevelopment effort. The mission of MVP is to promote redevelopment of the Menomonee Valley for the benefit of the entire Milwaukee community. The Menomonee Valley Redevelopment approach has centered on public involvement and collaboration in charting the project's direction from the outset. An initial design **charrette** held in 1999 and the subse-quent 2002 national design competition were central among the many opportunities for public engagement which have continued as the project has been implemented in stages. A diverse group of community partners, including design professionals, government agencies, business leaders, and nonprofit organizations have worked together to create and realize a new vision for the valley.

The Menomonee River Valley National Design Competition: *Natural Landscapes for Living Communities* was

Areas Addressed in Menomonee Valley Sustainable Design Guidelines

Site Design

Site Analysis and Planning

Stormwater Management

Natural Landscape

Parking and Transportation

Exterior Site Lighting

Building Design and Energy Use

Building Design

Energy Efficiency

Daylighting and Interior Lighting

Alternative Energy

Building Commissioning

Materials and Resources

Exterior and Interior Materials

Water Conservation

Construction and Demolition

Waste and Recycling

Erosion and Dust Control

Preoccupancy Controls for Indoor Air Quality

Indoor Environmental Quality

Indoor Air Quality

Acoustic Quality

Operations and Maintenance

Operations Manual and Monitoring

Facility Maintenance

Maintenance and Stewardship of Site and Landscape Elements

Appendix 1—U.S. Green Building Council and the LEEDTM Green Building Rating System

Appendix 2—Environmental and Geotechnical Considerations in the Menomonee River Valley

Appendix 3—Site-Specific Stormwater Requirements and Opportunities

Appendix 4—Considerations to Guide Landscape Installations

Appendix 5—Achieving a 25 Percent Reduction in Energy Consumption in Your Office, Assembly and Manufacturing, and Warehouse Space

Appendix 6—Construction and Demolition Debris Management

(Menomonee Valley Partners, Inc.)

Program Type and Development Trend

Program Type: The New Industrial Park and Industrial Ecology

Community gathering spaces and access to nature are not typically synonymous with industrial park development where the norm is private lots dominated by buildings, parking lots, and single-use stormwater management ponds. There is a distinction to be made between business industrial parks that have a community park component versus decommissioned industrial sites repurposed as parks. While the latter is becoming more common—for example, the Acid Mine Drainage in Pennsylvania, Gas Works Park in Washington, and Park Duisburg Nord in Germany—this New Industrial Park program is being envisioned as a way to build in formerly off-limits areas for reasons such as site contamination or sensitive ecological features. New industrial developments are being pressed to provide both economic and environmental benefits to the greater community to stay competitive and ecologically viable. The New Industrial Park provides several functions: It must provide jobs to an area in need of economic opportunities; it must establish a network of green infrastructure; and it must provide community open space linkages and access to nature.

Eco-industrial parks are emerging as an important testing ground for **industrial ecology.** Similar in some respects to standard industrial parks, eco-industrial parks are designed to encourage businesses to share infrastructure as a strategy for enhancing production, minimizing costs, and managing environmental issues. In an eco-industrial park, the concerns of industrial production and overall park maintenance are integrated to follow the principles of natural systems through cycling of resources, working within the carrying capacity of local and global ecosystems, and optimizing energy use. The idea of "industrial ecology" originated with a development in Kalundborg, Sweden. The *industrial symbiosis* of Kalundborg is built as a network between six processing companies, one waste-handling company, and the Municipality of Kalundborg. The philosophy behind the symbiosis is that the six companies—a power station, a plasterboard factory, a pharmaceutical plant, an enzyme producer, an oil refinery, and a waste company—along with the Kalundborg Municipality each utilize one another's byproducts for commercial benefit. The outcome is reduced resource consumption and reduction in environmental degradation. The collaborating partners also benefit financially from the cooperation because the symbiosis is based on commercial principles (Kalundborg Center for Industrial Symbiosis).

The concept of industrial ecology has spread from the transformation of the industrial process itself, to the transformation of site development and landscape infrastructure that support such industry. Cape Charles, Virginia, a small town on the southern tip of Virginia's eastern shore, is an apt illustration of the eco-industrial park concept. An EPA Brownfields Assessment Pilot award funded environmental assessments of a 25-acre former junkyard targeted as the center of a new 200-acre eco-industrial park. Selected by the President's Council for Sustainable Development as a demonstration project site for eco-industrial development, the Cape Charles Eco-Industrial Park hosts an ecological infrastructure that restores and regenerates the region's threatened wetlands and limited groundwater—environmental issues that had previously restricted development. The keystone of a concept plan developed in a public design charrette organized and facilitated by William McDonough + Partners, the park's greenway and wetland corridor provides natural storm drainage, retention, and aquifer recharge while enhancing wildlife habitat in and around the site. The plan considers a range of issues, including the relationship between the park and the town, the interrelationship of industrial and recreational economies, multimodal access to the site, and the region's ecological fragility. The park's first building, a 31,000-square-foot facility that includes North America's largest solar electric roof system among its green features, houses tenants such as Solar Building Systems, a company that manufactures the same photovoltaic panels used in the roof system. In addition to the economic benefits of this project, nearly one-half of the land in the park was set aside as natural habitat, including a 30-acre Coastal Dune Natural Area Preserve and approximately 60 acres of other natural areas (William McDonough + Partners).

Development Trend: Urban Infill

Over the last 40 years, many industrial park developments have been located in areas along the urban fringe in former agricultural areas and were therefore major contributors to suburban sprawl. After the advent of the urban flight phenomenon in the 1960s and 1970s, where many factors including the expansion of suburban infrastructure contributed to urban decline, downtowns across the United States were seen as problem areas where renewal was difficult or impossible. Soils contaminated by industrial waste, discriminatory real estate and political policies, and abandonment fostered further neglect and decline. Beginning around 1990, however, cities in the United States began to question whether previously abandoned industrial areas could be re-visioned as opportunities for economic development, environmental restoration, and much needed open space. Today, in part because of economic, cultural, and environmental pressures, these abandoned locations are seen as *sources* of economic competitiveness and social cohesion (Communities and Local Government 2000). Tanner Springs Park in Portland, Oregon, a case study in this book, is an example of a former industrial site where a renewed interest in high-density urban living created the pressure to rebuild the long-fallow district. On the Menomonee Valley site, however, the pressure to build was not preceded by property value escalation, but from a need for economic renewal and the desire for environmental remediation and restoration (Sixteenth Street Community Health Center 2004).

hosted by a collection of public and nonprofit agencies, including a neighboring health center, Menomonee Valley Partners, the City of Milwaukee, the Milwaukee Metropolitan Sewerage District, Wisconsin Department of Natural Resources, and Milwaukee County. The National Endowment for the Arts New Public Works Initiative was the major sponsor. Four finalists were invited to Milwaukee to meet with agency representatives, community-based organizations, valley stakeholders, and other interested parties. A panel of nationally recognized jurists reviewed the finalists' designs after they were evaluated by a Technical Advisory Committee. The winning design by Wenk Associates was well-informed by the public process, and this process did much to garner the enthusiasm, education, and support for the project.

The specific charge the designers were given by the client for the open space was to achieve functional goals—including restoration of native species, filtering stormwater runoff, and providing community access—as well as aesthetic goals. As a client, the City and MVP supported and, in fact, prescribed an integrated approach to the industrial and open space development. According to landscape architect Bill Wenk, what makes this project unique and visionary in comparison to the many other sites on the Great Lakes with similar issues is "Milwaukee's set of values: integrating the civic open space and redevelopment for the best interest of the entire city."

Along with public involvement, the Menomonee Valley Partnership's philosophy and approach has emphasized other sustainable development strategies, such as a comprehensive set of sustainable design guidelines to be followed in all site and building development taking place in the larger redevelopment area. These guidelines are adapted from the LEED program, but are tailored to the unique use and context of the project, including the area's brownfield issues.

Wenk Associates is a firm that has developed a focus on the sustainable management and design of water systems in the landscape. Within their portfolio, over half their projects fall within the categories of urban waterways, water quality planning and design, and greenways and stream restoration. Their body of work ranges from small sites, such as their own former office with its water harvesting and stormwater gardens, to mid-size sites such Shop Creek Wetlands, a municipal wetlands/stormwater treatment project, to very large multiple-parcel projects such as Stapleton Redevelopment in which they created a master plan and design guidelines for a new public stormwater treatment system (Wenk Associates). These projects reflect a design philosophy that recognizes the integral role and value of water to all landscapes, its operation at and connections through a variety of scales, and the aesthetic potential it presents for form-giving. This background and philosophy made them particularly well-qualified for and suited to the needs of the Menomonee Valley Redevelopment project.

Figure 2.5 Menomonee Valley Industrial Center, national context.

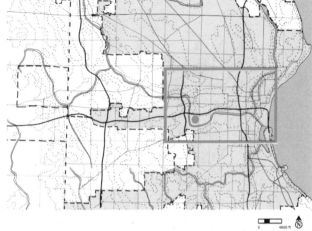

Figure 2.7 Menomonee Valley Industrial Center, local context (shaded area is within the Milwaukee city limits).

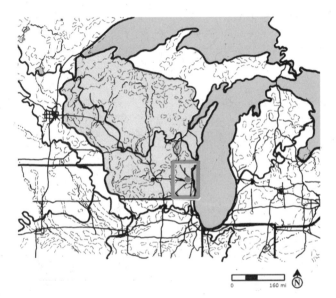

Figure 2.6 Menomonee Valley Industrial Center, state region context.

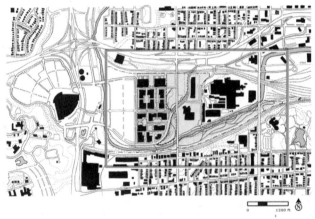

Figure 2.8 Menomonee Valley Industrial Center, neighborhood context.

Context

Menomonee Valley Industrial Center's context—beginning with the site within the region and ending with a site plan—is shown at various scaled maps in Figures 2.5, 2.6, 2.7, and 2.8. Through regional context analysis, the design process was infused with an understanding of site and regional potentials and challenges. That analysis situated the site relative to area history, regional attitudes and ecological health. Following is a description of landscape form, function, and philosophy of this area of Milwaukee that explores the setting and combination of sustainable factors to which the project design uniquely responds.

Legend

Highlands

Central Plains

Lowlands

Figure 2.9 Landform areas of Wisconsin.

Regional Form

Natural Patterns

The state of Wisconsin is roughly divided into three major landform areas: the western and northern uplands or Highlands, the glaciated areas of northwestern and north central Wisconsin, or Central Plains, and the coastal plains along Lakes Superior and Michigan, or Lowlands, where the Menomonee River Valley lies (see Figure 2.9). In the coastal plains of the Menomonee River Valley, glacial action formed the Eastern Ridges and Lowlands that slope down to meet Lake Michigan. Many of the numerous lakes and wetlands in the state were formed by the melting glaciers. The prominent geologic formations are underlain by 200 feet of calcareous glacial drift deposits that produce the region's characteristic limestone formations.

Development Patterns

The overall development pattern of Milwaukee is densely urban. Surrounding the Menomonee Valley are close-knit, single-family neighborhoods such as Merrill Park and Piggsville (reflecting the area's early agricultural uses). Established during the boom years of the 19th century industrial revolution, these neighborhoods and others lie to the north and south just above the valley basin. They are the most dense, ethnically diverse, and lowest-income neighborhoods within the entire state of Wisconsin (Dorolek 2007). See Figure 2.10.

During its heyday, Milwaukee was distinguished as one of the heaviest industrialized cities in the United States (see Figure 2.11). While today it is perhaps best known as the birthplace of Harley Davidson Motorcycles and breweries such as Schlitz, Pabst Blue Ribbon, and the Miller Brewing Company, between 1920 and 1970 it was the center of booming railroad-manufacturers.

Prior to European settlement, Milwaukee was inhabited by Native American tribes such as the Winnebago, Santee Dakota, and Menomini. The Menomonee Valley is the namesake of the Menomini, the Native American name for wild rice *manomin*. While there had been a presence of native tribes for as long as 12,000 years, many moved into the Milwaukee area in the mid-1800s to take refuge as they fled areas farther east. Native American presence per-

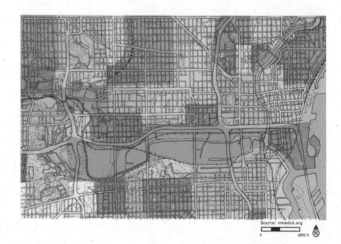

Figure 2.10   Dense, well-defined neighborhoods surround the Menomonee River Valley.

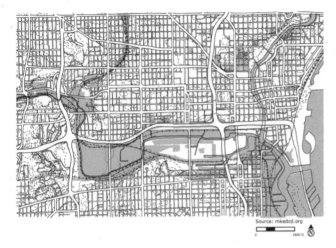

Figure 2.11 *The primary core of Milwaukee's historic community structure is now being viewed as a source of green infrastructure and economic development.*

sisted and the Winnebagos had a site overlooking the Menomonee Valley as late as 1875. As European settlers arrived, southeastern Wisconsin became the most populated area in the state because of its level topography, fertile soil, temperate climate, and river access (Wisconsin Department of Natural Resources). In 1800, fur trade was the predominant economic activity across Wisconsin. By 1840, much of the fertile lower Menomonee Valley was used for agriculture. Later, lead mining, agriculture, wheat growing, and lumber took over as leading industries. Around 1870, 60 acres of marshland adjacent to the Menomonee River were filled to make way for develop-

ment such as tanneries, meatpacking, and the Milwaukee Road rail yard. On the Menomonee Valley Industrial Center site itself, the Milwaukee Road rail company built rail cars, which during the height of Milwaukee's industrial period employed more than 50,000 people (Sixteenth Street Community Health Center). Figure 2.12 shows the active rail yard, which persisted until it was decommissioned in the mid-1980s.

Regional Function

Natural Systems

The state of Wisconsin is uniquely located on the dividing line of two major U.S. hydrologic areas; the western portion of the state which drains into the Mississippi River and eventually into the Gulf of Mexico, and the eastern portion which drains into Lakes Michigan and Superior and eventually into the Atlantic Ocean. The Milwaukee River Basin, which includes the Menomonee River, consists of six watersheds, and covers 900 square miles (see Figure 2.13). It contains approximately 400 miles of perennial streams and more than 85 natural glacial lakes and ponds. Today, many of the rivers in the Milwaukee area are contaminated due to industrial pollution, large areas of imperviousness, river channeling to control flooding, and combined sewers. In recent years, improvement of the water system has become a priority.

Upstream of the Menomonee Valley Industrial Center, much of the river is buffered with forest or included with-

Figure 2.12 *The Milwaukee Road Rail Company, shown here looking east toward downtown Milwaukee and Lake Michigan, toward the end of its active period during the 1960s.*
(Credit: City of Milwaukee)

in a network of parks, although there are some former industrial areas that have contributed to river quality degradation such as the Moss Superfund site. As seen in Figure 2.14, the majority of land area in the Menomonee River watershed is covered by urban uses (42 percent), while most of the remainder is grasslands (22 percent), agriculture (17 percent), forests (8 percent), and wetlands (7 percent) (The State of the Milwaukee River Basin 2001). Flooding has been problematic in the Milwaukee area, and in recent years the Milwaukee Metropolitan Sewerage District has implemented several flood-control projects, channelizing and straightening the river to convey flood-

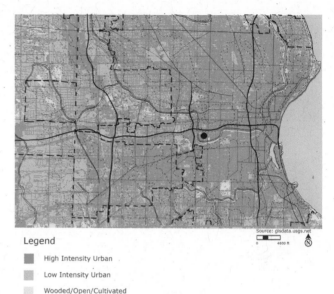

Legend

■ High Intensity Urban

■ Low Intensity Urban

■ Wooded/Open/Cultivated

Figure 2.14 Milwaukee area land cover.

waters off the land more quickly. Even so, a slim fringe of vegetation persists along the Menomonee River's south side as it runs through the city (Milwaukee River Basin Partnership).

While the state is known for its pristine streams and clear lakes, the southeastern portion of the state was heavily industrialized and its waters are largely polluted. Because the natural estuary of the Menomonee Valley had been filled to provide a buildable surface for industry (see Figure 2.15), groundwater there has been contaminated for years. Stream and wetland filling, runoff, overland erosion, and industrial point sources of pollution are major contributors to degraded water and habitat quality within this watershed. Real or perceived contaminants have proven a daunting roadblock for potential developers of the Menomonee Valley until recent years when studies found that the soil and groundwater contaminants could largely be mitigated with **natural attenuation**.

The project area lies in the National Forest Service vegetation classification system's Southern Great Lakes Province (see Figure 2.16). Prior to European settlement around 1850, three primary vegetative biome regions covered the state of Wisconsin—the Coniferous Forest biome, the Deciduous Forest biome, and the Prairie biome. The Deciduous Forest

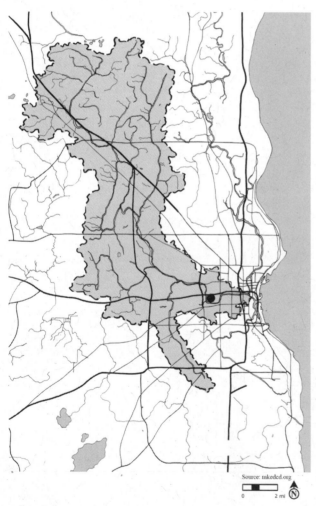

Figure 2.13 Milwaukee River Basin.

Program Development

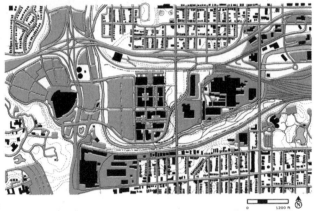

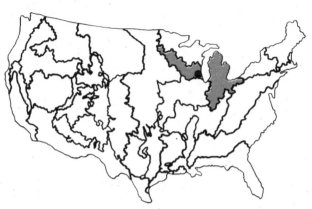

Figure 2.16 U.S. Natural Regions: The Southern Great Lakes. (Harker 1999)

Figure 2.15 The Miller Stadium parking lot pavement significantly increased impervious land cover in the valley watershed, further exacerbating stormwater management and water quality challenges for the area.

biome which predominated in the Milwaukee area is characterized as Maple/Basswood Forest (shown in Figure 2.17) and consists of species such as American basswood (*Tilia americana*), sugar maple (*Acer·saccharum*), and northern red oak (*Quercus rubra*). This area, most of which is no longer forested, exhibited the westernmost U.S. range of these plants. Former areas of flat prairie biome have been converted to agriculture and much of the area has been urbanized (Barnhill 2005).

Human Systems

During the industrial period, the valley was accessible by railroad and was connected to the surrounding urban fabric. Later, roadways and bridges that cut across part of the valley fell short of accessing the Western Valley, while steep

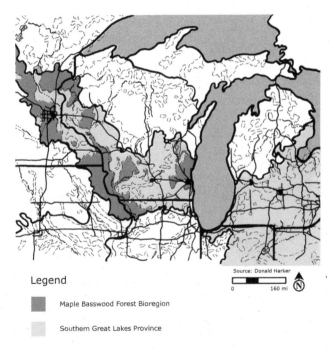

Legend

Maple Basswood Forest Bioregion

Southern Great Lakes Province

Figure 2.17 Maple Basswood Forest Locations. Within the Southern Great Lakes region, the Menomonee Valley lies within an area that would have originally been dominated by vegetation of the Maple Basswood Forest plant community. (Harker 1999)

grades, private property, fencing, and fears of contamination kept people from accessing the site and the river. Interstate highway development along the northern edge of the valley during the 1950s further cut the valley off from its northern neighbors. In servicing more recently developed citywide attractions in the valley, such as the Potawatomi Casino and Miller Park Stadium, Canal Street stopped short of connecting a continuous road along its floor. Thus, the Western Valley, just three miles to the east, was not accessible by road or by foot from the surrounding neighborhoods or the downtown. To remedy this, two features, the Canal Street Extension Road and a new Sixth Street Bridge shown in Figure 2.18 were added as a first priority in the site development to make the entire valley accessible from the east, west, and north. In addition, a regional trail system, the Hank Aaron State Trail, was expanded from Lake Michigan into the valley to Miller Park Stadium. Used for cycling, walking, jogging, and commuting to work, when finalized, this trail (shown in Figure 2.19) will extend from the Summerfest grounds on Lake Michigan and connect via other trails to western Wisconsin's Prairie du Chien on the Mississippi River, passing through the site (Paulsen 2003).

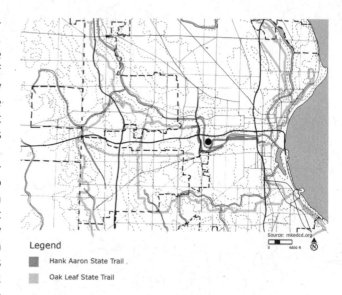

Legend

- Hank Aaron State Trail
- Oak Leaf State Trail

Figure 2.19 The Hank Aaron State Trail provides vital connection through the valley to other regional trails such as the Oak Leaf trail system.

Regional Philosophy

Conservation versus Development

The natural systems of the Milwaukee area experienced years of encroachment and declining health during a time when little attention was given to the social and environmental benefits of quality hydrologic, vegetative, air, or soil systems. Relatively few natural areas, outside of the lake area fringes, and a network of parks remain within the urban fabric. Natural waterways have been channelized and contaminated by years of industrialization. Recently, nonprofit organizations and government offices have begun to plan open space overlay districts, community garden initiatives, and tree planting programs in a grassroots effort to improve and enhance the urban green spaces. Still, the area could be said to have low biodiversity and poor ecological health.

Nevertheless, Wisconsin has fostered several early pioneers in the field of environmental awareness and stewardship. One is the oft cited Aldo Leopold, often called the "Father of Wildlife Ecology." As an employee of the U.S. Forest Service and later an advisor on conservation to the United

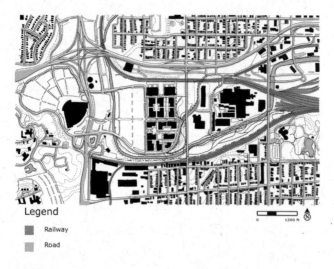

Legend

- Railway
- Road

Figure 2.18 The gridded road network of the surrounding urban fabric was extended and curved down the valley slopes into the former industrial area.

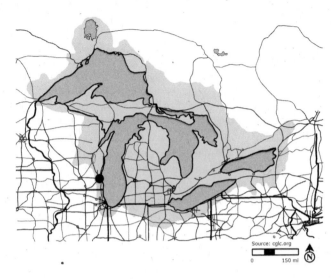

Figure 2.20 *The Great Lakes Conservation Zone.*

the world's fresh water and the region's companies manufacture 60 percent of the continent's steel and 60 percent of automobiles made in North America" (Council of Great Lakes Governors). Wisconsin and seven other U.S. states as well as the Canadian Provinces of Ontario and Quebec (outlined in Figure 2.20) have galvanized around sustainable practices that strive to improve the water quality, wildlife diversity, native vegetative species, and protect the tourist and fishing economies.

While the state of Wisconsin can be said to have contributed to sustainable thought and vision for the region and country, the Menomonee Valley Industrial Center largely remains a maverick sustainable development project in the state.

The focus on development in Milwaukee is primarily driven by unemployment produced by the collapse of old industries and the need for new industry and business. Recent studies found substantial racial gaps in Milwaukee joblessness rates. Between 1970 and 2003 the percentage of joblessness for African Americans, the population that fueled Milwaukee's industrial period, increased from 15 percent to an alarming 50 percent. This was due to deindustrialization, suburbanization of jobs, and housing segregation, which separated urban populations from the exurban job markets. Today, the city is addressing these economic challenges by stimulating workforce development, encouraging minority entrepreneurship, and addressing regionalism such as transportation, access, and housing where jobs are located. The Menomonee Valley Redevelopment Project was conceived of specifically to address these very concerns.

Cultural Resources

During the late 1800s and early 1900s many U.S. cities, including Milwaukee, recognized that parks were necessary for passive and active recreation and acted as reprieves from the harsh urban conditions. The purchase of open space began in 1860 when Milwaukee leaders desired more exposure to nature in this fast-growing urban center. At first, the parks were called "gardens for the poor" and were conceived as areas of natural beauty for those who could not afford their own gardens. In 1889, the city of Milwaukee created its park commission and three Frederick

Nations, Leopold was widely recognized for his local message that resonated with larger concepts of the ecological world. His book, *A Sand County Almanac,* in which he outlines a land ethic framework, posits, "Quit thinking about decent land-use as solely an economic problem. Examine each question in terms of what is ethically and esthetically right, as well as what is economically expedient. A thing is right when it tends to preserve the integrity, stability and beauty of the biotic community. It is wrong when it tends otherwise" (Leopold 1949). His belief that the same tools people used to disrupt the landscape could also be used to rebuild it is widely cited today (Aldo Leopold Nature Center).

In the 1950s, Wisconsin's intact natural landscape was recognized as a key vacation destination for nearby Chicagoans. Under the *Outdoor Resources Action* program established in 1961, Wisconsin legislators used **conservation easements** to acquire land throughout the state to retain the integrity of the state's natural resources. Gaylord Nelson, a Wisconsin U.S. Senator who founded Earth Day in 1970, was a prominent environmental leader of that era in the state.

A broad initiative begun in the 1980s sought to preserve the single largest fresh water source in the world, the Great Lakes Basin. "The Great Lakes contain one-fifth of

Figure 2.21 Milwaukee area open space and parks.

Law Olmsted parks were implemented: Lake Park, Washington Park, and Riverside Park, all three of which remain the framework of Milwaukee's present-day park system (see Figure 2.21). Alongside these fragments of open space in Milwaukee are pockets of historically significant links to the city's past industrial identity. Artifacts such as the sand hopper shown in Figure 2.22, factory ruins, rusting railroad trestles, and viaducts dot the city as visually powerful reminders of Milwaukee's thriving past as it transitions to a new future.

Regional Setting for Pioneer Site

In summary, the site context for the Menomonee Valley Industrial Center project is largely unsustainable—it is still recovering from its industrial heyday where the environment was not a consideration. With the building of this project, the Milwaukee area has taken a significant step toward becoming more sustainable. Awareness of the importance of healthy ecological systems, cultural needs, open space assessment, and urban revitalization is beginning to take shape. As an example of a *sustainable pioneer*, this project's local context exhibits few aspects of cultural or ecological sustainability in the built environment. The project itself, however, exerts influence as a demonstration to inspire future development within the Milwaukee area and beyond.

Site

Design Considerations

Existing Site

The project site is a 140-acre area located at the western end of the Menomonee Valley. It is bordered by the Miller Park Stadium to the west, the Menomonee River and valley wall to the south, an interstate highway and valley wall to the north, and a mix of existing industrial sites to the east. This site covers approximately half of the entire planned redevelopment area. To facilitate industrial development, including the site's main use as the Milwaukee Shops rail yard, the original floodplain had been filled over time.

Figure 2.22 Sand hoppers have been incorporated into the riverfront grounds of downtown Milwaukee's new Harley Davidson Museum as reminders of the city's industrial heritage and the site's former use as a sand processor.

Figure 2.23   Intact industrial chimneys.
(Credit: Wenk Associates, Inc.)

Though most of the historic buildings, rails, and other industrial artifacts were removed from the site as they fell into disuse and deteriorated, two large chimneys survived the decay. The iconic scale and location of these structures near the raised viaduct roadway that crosses through the site and connects the two sides of the valley (see Figures 2.23 and 2.24) provided some of the only remaining site character from which to draw visual meaning and a link to the site's past.

As a brownfield, the site's contamination, while invisible, provided severe usage restrictions. The subsurface would need to be capped, which would eliminate the opportunity for stormwater infiltration and necessitate large areas for stormwater detention. The site's inaccessible and functionless condition created a major block, which separated Miller Park Stadium from downtown Milwaukee, and the neighborhoods on either side of the valley.

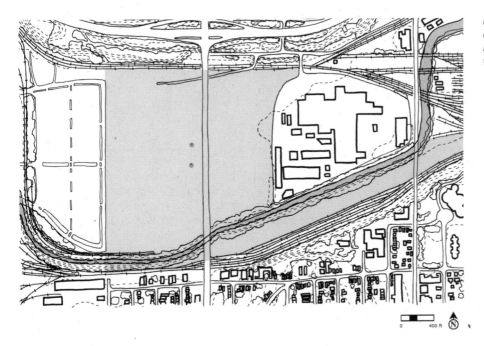

Figure 2.24   By the time of the site design competition in 2002, all that remained above-grade on the site were the two chimneys.

	ECO-REGION	COMMUNITY	NEIGHBORHOOD	SITE
SCALES OF LANDSCAPE INFLUENCE				

Program Development

This project is strongly embedded within the history of larger planning efforts that preceded and gave impetus to it. The Menomonee Valley Land Use Plan and early design charrettes were instrumental in creating a vision for integrated industrial development and community open space. This project created site-specific opportunities to apply these planning concepts and guidelines through site planning, site design, and detail design. While all three of these scales of design were important to the realization of a sustainable outcome, the site planning decisions that organized the major spaces, and the stormwater and related vegetative systems, produced the most critical program elements:

The program addresses four major environmental goals. First, the restoration and creation of natural landscapes within the community park space and along the river corridor was a priority for habitat and biodiversity improvement. Second, the use of ecological methods for stormwater management through biological and subsurface filtra-

tion was favored as an alternative to conventional detention methods. Third, an approach to flood control that integrates the needs of commercial function and recreational use was envisioned to maximize the use of the land. Finally, the brownfield needs associated with capping of the site and the protection of the groundwater created specific parameters for how the site could be used and structured.

The cultural aspects of the program revolved around interpretation, recreation, and the creation of a civic identity for the site. The chimneys presented a physical opportunity to interpret the site and region's industrial past, while the riverfront offered a connection to its natural history. Visual emphasis on the site's stormwater function provided another level of interpretation. A recreational program emphasis was included to provide the desired community connections to the site, through the use of linked bike paths and community play fields. The concept of dense blocks of industrial development sites around a central open space, borrowed from the idea of a village commons surrounded by individual sites, provided programmatic direction for the project's civic identity.

A Conventional Industrial Park Design

Falk Corporation, Milwaukee, Wisconsin, USA

The Falk Corporation, located directly east of the project site, is one of the oldest remaining industrial complexes in the Menomonee Valley, as well as the whole Milwaukee

region. Since 1850 it has operated on this site, over time producing a variety of products beginning first as a brewery and then as a manufacturer of precision mechanical equipment that began through its association in making gears used in the production of the neighboring Milwaukee Shops' rail cars. It has outlived the Shops' existence as it has adapted its production to newer needs. Its small stature and location along the river was essential to its early days, but later it occupied a larger and larger footprint of the site and no longer depended on the river for power. Now the site is covered with structures and paving, having developed prior to the institution of site planning regulations. In its proximity to the river, it now poses difficulties in maintaining water quality, which is at the heart of the valley's redevelopment challenge.

In conventional contemporary approaches to industrial site design, ironically referred to as industrial parks, open space per se is not considered as part of the program. However, the realization of the effects of large impervious surface ratios has resulted in the requirement of large stormwater detention areas. These detention basins are typically treated as sterile, utilitarian elements rather than ecological elements and are located in remote areas of the site, not integrated with other programmatic elements or with the surrounding lands and neighborhoods. This is exemplified in Figure 2.25, an aerial photograph of a recently built industrial facility in Ann Arbor, Michigan. Built on this type of model, industrial development and its stormwater infrastructure has traditionally been purposefully segregated and screened from the surrounding neighborhoods as a visually undesirable land use.

In conventional approaches to park design—a second element of the Menomonee Valley Industrial Center—infrastructural needs such as stormwater management are rarely considered as driving programmatic elements; rather, they have been considered in conflict with the

human recreational activity around which parks are traditionally built. When water is included in the design, it is typically introduced to the site through artificial means or contained in limited areas, with little or no connection to the ecological function or history of the site, and used primarily as visual focal points.

Figure 2.25 Conventional industrial development. (Credit: John Sullivan Aerial Assoc.)

Site Design Form

The Menomonee Valley Industrial Center design outcome is illustrated in Figures 2.26, 2.27, 2.28, and 2.29, through site plan, sections, and detail views. The project is analyzed with respect to two critical dimensions of sustainable site design: landscape form and landscape function.

Patterns

As seen in Figure 2.30, the park layout reflects two major pattern themes: the grid of the old and new development, and the organic ribbon-like lines of the river and former rail lines.

The park's primary form-giving reflects the flowing lines of the river and rails through the sculpted landform created to

provide the stormwater management function of the park. Deep pools around the stormwater outfall areas and spreading basins gain intensity as they get closer to the river as shown in Figure 2.31, while the pedestrian paths, shown in Figure 2.32, create ribs that define the basins. Canal Street, which provides an east-west connection through the site from downtown Milwaukee to Miller Park and defines the subspaces of the park, further reflects the organic influence.

The industrial development parcels are oriented to a new valley grid with a structure and density that reflects the pattern of surrounding neighborhoods and a more compact arrangement of industrial use than historically found in the area. One of the first industrial parcels being developed is for Badger Railing, seen in Figure 2.33 from the Miller Stadium parking lot. The smallest lot is 1.5 acres and

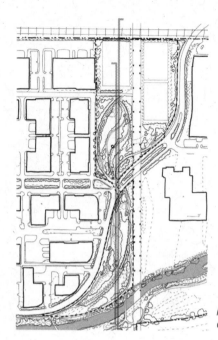

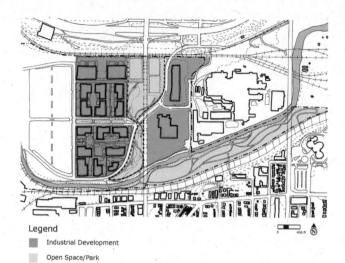

Legend

Industrial Development

Open Space/Park

Figure 2.26 Menomonee Valley Industrial Center Site Plan.

*Figure 2.27 Menomonee Valley
Community Park Site Cross Sections.*

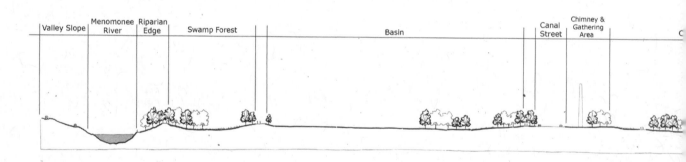

| Valley Slope | Menomonee River | Riparian Edge | Swamp Forest | | Basin | | Canal Street | Chimney & Gathering Area | C |

| Neighborhood | Valley Slope | Play Field | Basin | Basin | Canal Street | | Basin |

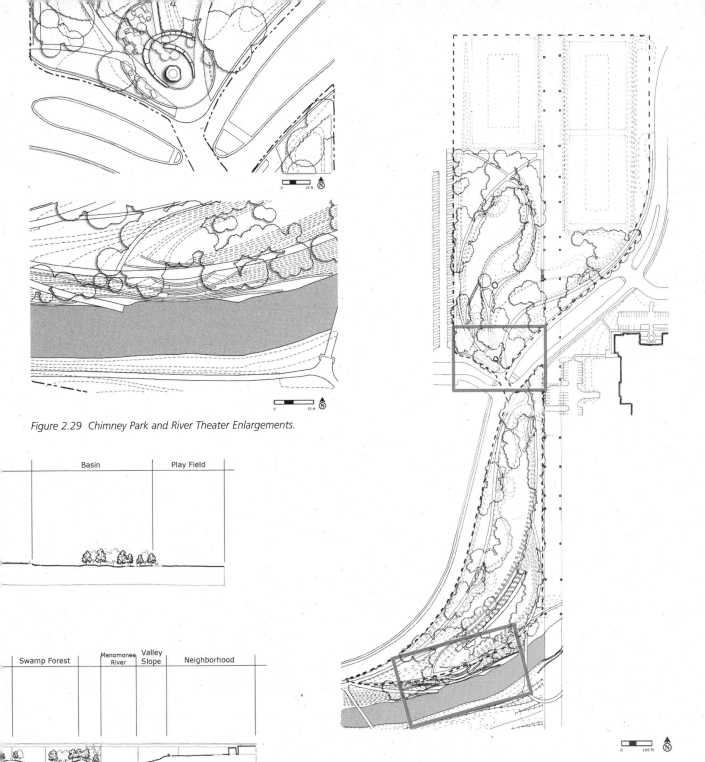

Figure 2.29 Chimney Park and River Theater Enlargements.

Basin | Play Field

Swamp Forest | Menomonee River | Valley Slope | Neighborhood

Figure 2.28 Menomonee Valley Community Park Site Plan.

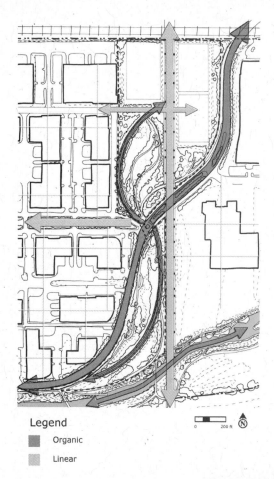

Legend

■ Organic

■ Linear

Figure 2.30 Site organization derivations.

larger lots can be assembled from this module. In total there are 70 acres for development, with 20 to 30 acres of allowable building coverage. The grid of the development extends into the park at its northern end with the placement of the playing fields, the planned park building, and the Wheelhouse Road walkway extension. The 35th Street viaduct, with its soaring linear presence, gives a dramatic view into the site from above and a layered structure to the site from below. The Parkway, which reaches from the park through the industrial parcels to the Miller Park parking lot, integrates the park into the grid of the development and connects to a major sports entertainment venue.

The site's location in the valley, underscored by the valley slopes and the viaduct's vertical datum that meets the neighborhoods above, creates a primary definition of the site. Unlike other design competition proposals, which concentrated open space along the river, Wenk's plan situates the open space to span across the valley. As such the park forms a linear open space spine that is perpendicular to the river, connecting the north and south sides of the city to the valley, through a sequence of areas that transition from more active human use in the northern Chimney Park section, to more passive uses in the southern River Lawn section and the Airline Yards riverfront area. These areas use planting density, vegetative surface variation, and landform to define this transition.

Figure 2.31 The lower spreading basins closest to the river are shown during both a dryer period on left and following a heavy rainfall on right, illustrating the site's flexibility and multipurpose capacity. (Credit: Nancy M. Aten (left), Paul Boersma (right))

Figure 2.32 Section drawings of the park illustrate the progression of water treatment and the integrated relationship of pedestrian and vehicular circulation to the park's stormwater functions.

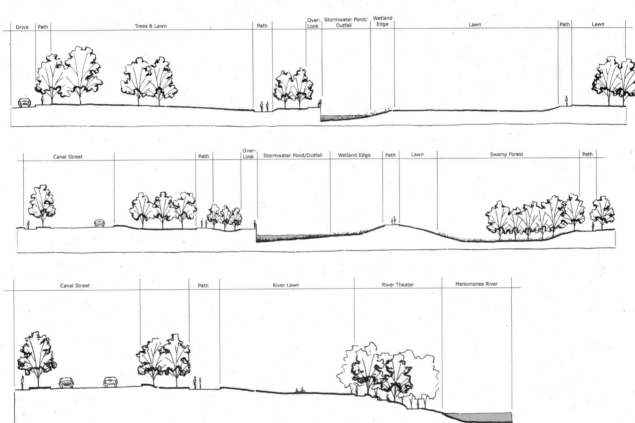

Figure 2.33 One of the first industrial parcels developed is for Badger Railing, seen here from the Miller Stadium parking lot, looking east toward Chimney Park.

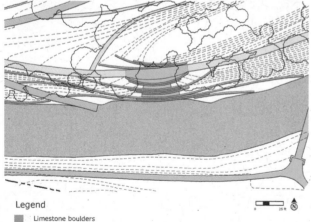

Legend
■ Limestone boulders
■ Concrete
■ Gravel

Figure 2.34 Limestone block terraces are placed in arched alignments along the riverfront to provide shore stabilization and a node for congregation and access.
(Credit: Nancy M. Aten)

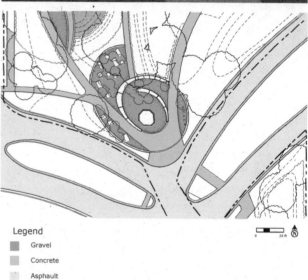

Legend
■ Gravel
■ Concrete
■ Asphault

Figure 2.35 Materials used include granular surfacing concrete for curved seat walls that mimic pathway alignments and enclose the space, and elliptical pipe for benches.

Materials

The site is primarily vegetated with small isolated paved nodes for gathering. The constructed materials consist of:

• concrete paving at the stormwater outfall nodes with metal railings inset with glass interpretive panels. These have a modern industrial feel.

Legend

◼ 2 Year Flood Event

▨ 5 Year Flood Event

▫ 100 Year Flood Event

Figure 2.36 The site design and engineering allows for a series of stormwater events to distribute runoff to park areas that provide bio-treatment and detention while still allowing access and use of the park.

(Credit: Wenk Associates Inc.)

- large, locally obtained rough-cut stone terracing at the river amphitheater that gives rustic structure at the natural river edge, shown in Figure 2.34.

- 8-foot and 6-foot asphalt pathways.

- granular surfacing, curved linear concrete seat walls, and elliptical pipe benches at the Chimney common area, as shown in Figure 2.35.

Much of the site's intensive construction is invisible—making use of highway rubble for the subsurface constructed soil system created to satisfy fertility, filtration, and drainage needs for the extensive stormwater basin planting scheme.

Site Design Function

Natural Systems

The site is contaminated primarily with free petroleum and arsenic from its former industrial use. Early in the scoping of the redevelopment project, a geotechnical site feasibility study of the Milwaukee Road Shops Property was prepared for the City of Milwaukee. The test borings encountered historic fill to depths as shallow as 1 foot to greater than 21 feet below grade. Fill material consisting of reworked silt, clay, sand, and organic rich materials was discovered, as well as nonsoil fill including cinders, slag, coal, debris, ash, and building materials (wood, bricks, wire, concrete) and domestic refuse (glass, bottles, rubber, ash). The City removed rubble and consolidated contaminated materials in 2004 in preparation for construction. As part of the redevelopment project, seven distinct approaches to capping contaminated soils were used to assure public safety, support stormwater management

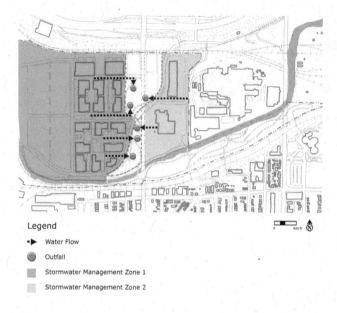

Legend

- ▪▶ Water Flow
- ● Outfall
- ▨ Stormwater Management Zone 1
- ▨ Stormwater Management Zone 2

Figure 2.37 Stormwater basins are fed from the two developed sides of the site.

goals, and support the reintroduction of indigenous landscapes. Approximately 8 feet of fill has raised the land out of the original floodplain. The Menomonee Valley Partners, who are working with industrial businesses in developing their sites, have prepared guidelines to assist with special geotechnical concerns for working in this sensitive area.

As a primary function of the park, stormwater management occurs in nearly every area of the park. As the images in Figure 2.36 depict, a series of successively larger and deeper basins, or **stormwater treatment train** (STT), is designed into the landform of the park land, providing storage for 2-year, 5-year and 100-year storm events. The treatment areas are divided into two stormwater management

areas (SMA) by the crossing of Canal Street through the park. The lowest SMA leads to a "swamp forest" outlet at the river's edge. At the 100-year storm event all of the park landscape except for one playing field would be inundated. Because the park has been capped due to brownfield contamination, these areas provide detention and water quality treatment, but do not allow for infiltration of the stormwater. They are designed to remove 80 percent of the total suspended solids (TSS) contained in stormwater runoff (Wenk Associates).

The SMAs and the Swamp Forest treat water in three steps:

1. Stormwater is collected and piped from the industrial redevelopment areas and Canal Street to the storm outfalls located in the park. Here large particulates settle in small pools.

2. Storm flows spread out across broad shallow wetland meadows. The subgrade layer, called an "infiltration gallery," consists of coarse-textured, crushed concrete that allows stormwater to infiltrate below the surface, above the capped soils.

3. Infiltrated storm flows will be collected and transpired through the plant material at the Swamp Forest as shown in Figures 2.37 and 2.38. The system both removes particulates and pollutants, and detains the 100-year storm, eliminating the need for traditional detention basins within the industrial development parcels themselves.

The park's vegetation is designed to bring back natural ecological function to the valley (Figure 2.39), while also providing active recreational use. There are limited lawn areas of varying scale interspersed with natural areas that mainly correspond with the areas of the site used for stormwater management. On balance, the northern, high-

Figure 2.38 Layered components include the subgrade cap (bottom), drainage infiltration gallery (middle), and growing medium for plants that provide biological treatment (top).

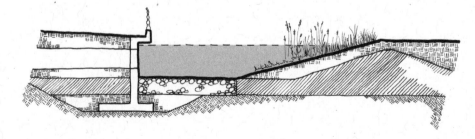

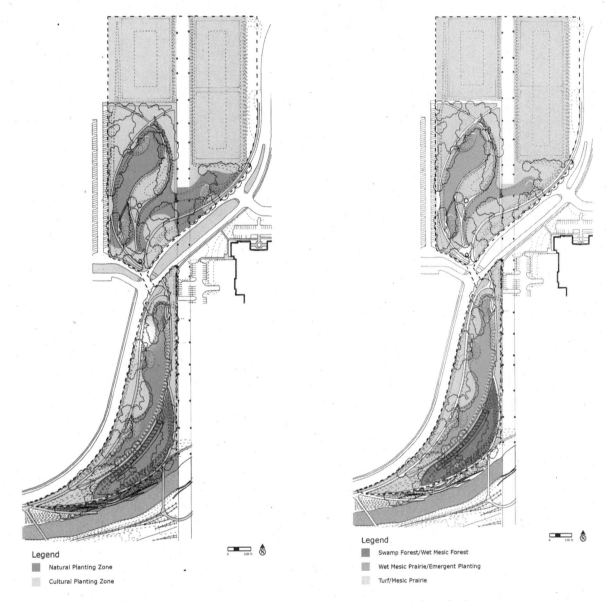

Legend

■ Natural Planting Zone

▨ Cultural Planting Zone

Figure 2.39 Planting zones.

Legend

■ Swamp Forest/Wet Mesic Forest

▨ Wet Mesic Prairie/Emergent Planting

▨ Turf/Mesic Prairie

Figure 2.40 Ground plane planting zones.

er elevations of the park have more lawn, including the three play fields, while closer to the river there is a greater emphasis on biofiltration and a diversity of planting. As noted in Figure 2.40, the ground plane planting for the natural areas consists of a variety of seeding types includ-

ing mesic prairie, wet prairie, and emergent planting mixes. The pool areas immediately surrounding the stormwater outfalls are not planted but are ringed with the emergent seed mix, which transitions to the wet prairie and then to mesic prairie.

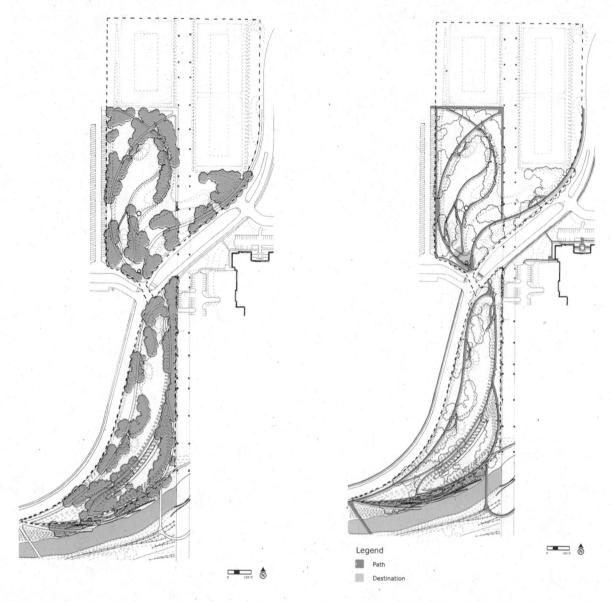

Figure 2.41 Mature canopy coverage.

Figure 2.42 Pathways system includes internal loops and connections to external routes and a variety of congregation areas.

Legend

■ Path

■ Destination

Figure 2.41 shows that canopy plantings are grouped in clusters along the paths, leaving large expanses of open pool, wetland, prairie, and lawn. The canopy plantings consist of two groups of species: one of deciduous natives that respond to mesic conditions and another of mixed deciduous and evergreen species suited to the wetter conditions of the lowest basin, approximating a swamp environment. Specified tree sizes are varied within most species, from 1.5-inch caliper to four-year transplants, to mimic natural growth. The installation of the plant materi-

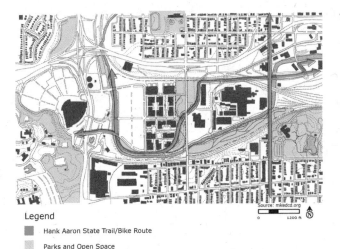

Legend

██ Hank Aaron State Trail/Bike Route

░░ Parks and Open Space

Figure 2.43 Hank Aaron Trail and Bikeway. Regional connections through the site are well integrated with the new open space.

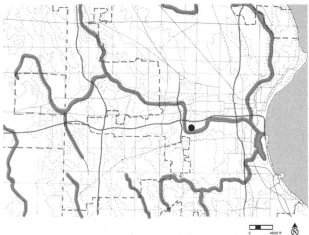

Figure 2.44 River and Rail Inspirations. Spatial and temporal context provide inspiration for park forms through river meander patterns at the regional scale and the historic rail line organization of the site. (Credit: City of Milwaukee)

al was performed in part by volunteers, which cut costs and provided an important community connection to the implementation of the park.

Human Systems

Movement is an essential function of the site: movement both of people and of water. The carefully planned movement of stormwater through the site, as discussed earlier, provides important ecological function to the development; as the site cannot infiltrate the water, it must spread out and slowly move over the entire park area as it makes its way to the Menomonee River. This movement of water is integral to the movement of people through the park.

Despite a few destination spots, such as the play fields, the majority of the spaces encourage movement through their flowing, braided form and pattern, suggested by the former use of the site as a rail yard and the presence of the river as seen in Figures 2.42, 2.43, and 2.44. The park is primarily designed for biking and walking within and through the site. In addition to active recreational opportunities, the site is programmed to provide educational opportunities for community users as depicted in the images of Figure 2.45.

Maintenance

The project's emphasis on public involvement has continued through the critical stages of implementation and establishment and management of the built development. This has been accomplished through such efforts as community tree planting (as shown in Figure 2.46) and a Stewardship Crew Challenge, where new businesses in the development are encouraged to involve employees in park stewardship activities. The open space, by virtue of its focus on natural landscapes, is intended to be low maintenance/low input.

Figure 2.45 Biking and kayaking are among the active recreational uses of the park, while educational programming on the site's cultural and natural dimensions are provided on an ongoing basis.
(Credit: Nancy M. Aten, Dan Collins (bottom left))

Site Design Engagements

Engagements are specific site design elements that take advantage of natural phenomenon, site activities, and amenities that engage the user with site and regional ecological and cultural systems. This project exhibits two types of ecological engagements: regeneration through large-scale stormwater treatment basins and the creation of a new vegetation matrix. The following cultural engagements are categorized into elements, views, and nodes (see Figure 2.47).

Node: River Theater/Canoe Launch. As one of the primary "River Points" located along the Hank Aaron Trail, this node provides the park users with a multifaceted exposure to the Menomonee River, which was not possible in the past due to industrial riverfront use. As can be seen in Figure 2.48, the "theater" provides a low shelf for performers and tiered stone seating that overlooks both the performer and the larger backdrop of the river. A nearby trail ramp provides river access either for boating or simply for a refreshing wade.

Figure 2.46 Community involvement in planting and maintenance is critical to the ongoing improvement and management of the park, as well as the sense of community ownership and stewardship of the open space.
(Credit: Nancy M. Aten)

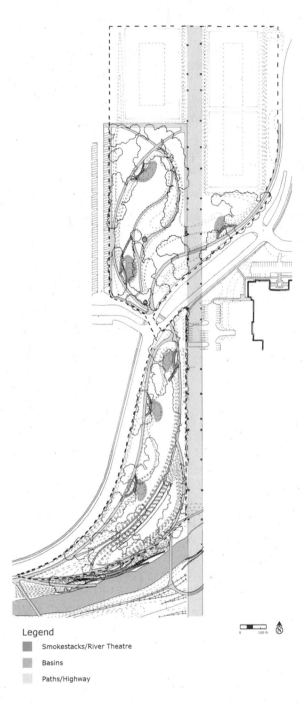

Legend

■ Smokestacks/River Theatre

■ Basins

▢ Paths/Highway

Figure 2.47 Special elements, nodes, and views encourage user experience and understanding of the park's sustainable design on both conscious and subconscious levels.

Figure 2.48 River Theater/Canoe Launch. (Credit: Nancy M. Aten)

Node: Stormwater Outfall/Overlook. In six locations throughout the site, stormwater outfall pipes release water from adjacent industrial development sites into ponds that hold the water and slowly release it toward the river. At these areas, natural wetland vegetation provides biofiltration of the stormwater and wetland habitat. (Figure 2.49) Each outfall has a pedestrian path spur that comes off the main path and ends in a brow that forms an overlook toward the pond, as a deliberate endpoint. As shown in Figure 2.50, the overlook has a railing that is inset with glass art panels that depict various plant and animal species found in the park's habitat areas.

Element: Paths. The pathway system not only provides connectivity throughout the park, but its flowing, braided, and branched shape evokes the form of the river and its tributaries. They are not placed onto the landscape, but actually give form to the landscape, and create the ridges that separate the water treatment basins. The park path system connects to a larger regional network as well as neighborhoods to the north and south sides of the valley.

Element: Industrial Chimneys. Two 80-foot-tall smokestacks shown in Figure 2.51 are the only remnants of the site's long history as one of the nation's largest rail yards. They once served the rail yard power house and are now the focus of the central green area of the

Figure 2.50 Glass Art Panel at Overlooks.

Figure 2.49 Stormwater Treatment Progression.
(Credit: Nancy M. Aten)

park, which is the site's main gathering space. The southern chimney is grounded in a paved area with several benches and the northern chimney is in the main lawn area. The chimney hearths create a frame that is eye level and planned for art installations.

Element: Benches. Figure 2.52 shows the benches in the gathering area that are created from precast concrete in the form of half-buried culvert pipes. This form evokes the water theme and relates to the nearby overlook outfall points where water flows from adjacent development into the park.

Element: Interpretive Signage. As seen in Figure 2.53, throughout the park interpretive signs and other elements discuss the site's cultural history, including industrial and Native American influences, as well as the natural flora and fauna which the project has restored.

Element and View: 35th Street Viaduct. The 35th Street Viaduct, an elevated roadway, is a visible thread of connection across the valley. The deliberate place-

Program Development

Figure 2.51 Industrial Chimneys.

Figure 2.52 Elliptical Pipe Bench.
(Credit: Nancy M. Aten of Menomonee Valley Partners)

Figure 2.53 Interpretive Signage.

ment of the park area in alignment with the viaduct was a dramatic move on the designer's part to engage the park user with the massive piece of infrastructure and use it to define the park spaces and organization. It also affords panoramic views for pedestrians and drivers on the viaduct down to the park and the Menomonee River, with the new industrial area, the valley slopes, and Miller Stadium as background.

Outcomes

The Program/Site/Context Comparison

Predesign Site/Context Conditions

The sustainable outcome of a project is determined largely by the design team's approach at the project outset toward three areas of design decision-making: (1) the selection of program goals, (2) the judgments made in the assessment of site character, and (3) the judgments made in the assessment of the context. The relationship of these decisions can be demonstrated via the three common aspects of sustainability: environmental, cultural, and social.

The view of the predesign relationship between site, context, and program for the Menomonee Valley Industrial Center project is summarized with these factors in mind as follows. It shows that the initial program goals drafted by the client developed largely from regional conditions. Later, the landscape architect refined the program to develop specific site responses to these broader regional issues.

Postdesign Site/Context Impacts

The site design solution developed by Wenk Associates, has its most significant sustainable design impact primarily at the community level, although probably more than any of the other projects studied, it has also had sustainable impact at the metropolitan region level.

At the community level, the project provides economic development and needed local jobs for surrounding neighborhood residents. The park component of the site provides a civic gathering place and recreational amenity that now unifies the community rather dividing it as the site did in the past. An area with high levels of impervious surface now has stormwater treatment to improve local water quality and flood control.

At the metropolitan region level, the project serves as a model for the remaking of the heavily industrialized regional landscape. The remediation of brownfields, the regenerative treatment of stormwater, the renewal of riparian habitat, and the reconnection of the urban fabric provide benefits that are highly visible and centralized within the entire region.

	INITIAL PROGRAM GOALS	SITE CHARACTER	CONTEXT CHARACTER
ENVIRONMENTAL	Contaminated land remediation	Blank, flat, sterile surface	Riparian corridors have long history of degradation related to industrial use
	Biological stormwater treatment for industrial development pads	Debris fill to depth of 21' in some areas, contamination with arsenic and petroleum	
	Habitat creation	Degraded Menomonee River edge	Floodplain has been filled to accommodate development and inhibit flood control, water quality, and habitat capacity
CULTURAL	Site and neighborhood industrial history acknowledgment	Historic industrial chimneys from Milwaukee Road rail yard	Historic industrial architecture and rail form remnants, influences
	Aesthetic, spatial considerations to improve character and define public/private use	Historic use of site for largest rail yard in United States	Native American influences
SOCIAL	Neighborhood connection/ revitalization	Site inaccessible to public and separates neighborhoods	Current problems with crime and unemployment
	Local light industrial businesses and jobs	Centrally located site lies fallow and unusable	"Dead" area sandwiched between lakefront downtown and stadium
	Public recreational open space		Culturally diverse historic working-class neighborhoods

The scales of context that most significantly influenced the development of this design are the community scale and the neighborhood scale. The significant identity of the whole metropolitan Milwaukee area with its industrial past and the effects of its collapse are channeled through this one site. As a *sustainable pioneer*, the redevelopment is hoped to provide a model for a sustainable future for the entire city, and the program, with its emphasis on the integration of job development and environmental quality and community connectivity, comes from that community level of interest.

At the neighborhood scale, the juxtaposition of the valley and its surrounding neighborhoods creates a physical pattern that was critical to the site planning decisions that were suggested and implemented by the designer (see Figure 2.54).

Improving Site Sustainability

The specific details and techniques of this site design are critical to site function, spatial quality, and user experience. The following design techniques were used to improve the site, mitigate the impact of development, and create a compelling, functional site design regardless of the conditions of the context.

A Multi-use site: Park, Industrial Development, and Infrastructure

Brownfield remediation

Naturalized landscape: Meadow, Wet Meadow, Swamp Forest, Riparian edge

Biotreatment of stormwater

Improving Regional Sustainability

Despite being a "sustainable pioneer," this design made moves to improve and to take into account the landscape and natural processes that occur outside the site. The design captures some of the goals and impacts of the larger region. The following design techniques helped improve the region's sustainability.

Trail system linkage

Preservation of historic artifacts

Public open space

Linking hydrology of open space to adjacent development/open space

Plant community restoration

Sustainability Criteria Met?

Five landscape sustainability criteria were presented in Chapter 1 as a means for evaluating landscape sustainability: *Connectivity, Meaning, Purpose, Efficiency,* and *Stewardship*. Our discussion now turns to the design outcome of Menomonee Valley Industrial Center as it is evaluated in relation to these criteria.

Connectivity

The site design:

* reconnects the valley to its place along the river with a biodiverse, repaired landscape.

	METROPOLITAN REGION	COMMUNITY	NEIGHBORHOOD	SITE
SUSTAINABILITY IMPACTS				

Figure 2.54 Postdesign and predesign in context. Adjacent to the massive stadium parking lot in foreground, the final site plan is shown above, with new industrial buildings and braided park layout and below, prior to redevelopment. (Credit: Wenk Associates Inc.)

- models a healthy, visibly connected flow of stormwater from development, including upstream off-site parcels, through a filtering open space and into the larger watershed.

- creates a vital and multifaceted connection between downtown Milwaukee and the city's stadium and out-skirts beyond.

- links two sets of neighborhoods, which had previously been separated by fallow and contaminated land, with recreational pathways and open space as well as economic opportunity.

- integrates industrial, infrastructure, and open space site uses.

Meaning

The site design:

- evokes the area's rich industrial history, while actively renewing a productive and sustainable industrial life for the site.

- immerses site users in a landscape whose comprehensive form is based on stormwater process, integrating human paths and nodes with water paths and nodes.

- describes the site's natural history through landscape restoration, artistic interpretation, and educational signage.

Purpose

The site design:

- creates stormwater infrastructure, which would normally be hidden or separated from usable open space, that takes on civic identity and a centralized place in the development.

- takes a land use—industrial—that would typically be driven by the creation of individual autonomous private parcels, and uses the landscape as a central organizing, unifying, and functional entity.

Efficiency

The site design:

- optimizes usefulness of open space by integrating recreational, habitat, and stormwater treatment functions.

- minimizes public expenditure on open space maintenance through a program of volunteer management.

- boasts low-maintenance landscape zones.

Stewardship

The site design:

- fosters public stewardship of the land through a strong program of public participation throughout scoping, design, implementation, and management phases of the project.

- creates a new ethic of industrial sustainability through connections of industrial site function to public open space, in contrast to conventional relationships where industry neither relies on, nor is responsible for its effects upon public open space.

Parallel Projects
Thomson Factory, France

The Thomson Factory site, shown in Figure 2.55, was designed by French landscape architects Desvigny and Dalnoky, who recognized that their landscape approach must address function that endures long beyond the lifespan of its use as a factory. The site and regional assessment revealed a rapidly changing landscape with low ecological value. Their approach to site development sought to improve site ecological function and ensure ecosystem viability in the greater landscape over time. Despite the site's poor soil drainage and the addition of pavement and buildings, the team improved the compacted and depleted soil structure and permeability by planting nitrogen-fixing short-lived trees while improving site identity and integrity by establishing groves of long-lived oak trees. This strategy acknowledged both the need for immediate site repair and the needs of the greater landscape long after its current industrial use becomes obsolete. Site repair and fostering of longterm landscape viability provides ecological benefits to the greater environment by improving the soil, bypassing the need for costly piping, and eliminating intensive maintenance regimes by intending plants to mature without unnecessary control. This forward-thinking strategy anticipates the future site health despite changes in land-use, economy, and ecology.

Figure 2.55 Parallel Project: Thomson Factory. Quick growing leguminous plants absorb runoff from parking areas while improving soil chemistry. The dense planting begins a new landscape typology in this agricultural region where changing land uses and plant succession occur in unison.
(Credit: Michel Denancé.)

Herman Miller Factory, Georgia, USA

The now decommissioned Herman Miller furniture manufacturing and assembly plant was situated on a 70-acre site in rural Georgia. Michael Van Valkenburgh Associates, Inc., approached the project with a simple strategy: They graded the 22-acre development footprint at 5 percent to place the factory on a level base, so that water would sheet drain from impervious areas into wetlands they constructed for the purpose, thereby eliminating the need for curbs, pipes, and manholes. The parking lot was divided into three bays that drain into wetlands planted with grasses, forbs, and sedges. When dry, these areas become meadows. The edges of these wetland trays transition to 10- to 15-foot-wide thickets of floodplain trees that abut the undeveloped portions of the site.

Using hydrologic management as an engine of this project's design, the landscape architects showed the client how to redirect money from the engineer's budget and use grading, planting, environmental stewardship, and site organization to integrate stormwater management into a vast industrial development. In their scheme, parking becomes part of a thriving ecological system that neutralizes the impacts of runoff, provides habitat for wildlife, and offers a compelling arrival and departure experience to the factory's employees.

The project's modest building and site budget included no provision for landscape architecture before the architects invited Michael Van Valkenburgh Associates to join the design team. The client required parking for 550 cars and 120 semi-trailers—a total area of 10 acres. Runoff from the parking surfaces, the roadway, and the roof of the 330,000-square-foot facility would have had a devastating impact on the surrounding fragile creek ecosystems. The landscape architects determined that treating and slowly releasing large volumes of runoff into the landscape must become an essential priority for the project. By elegantly integrating ecology into acres of hardscape (seen in Figure 2.56), this project is a model for low-cost, low-maintenance, sustainable industrial landscapes, which can be applied with equal success in suburban and urban areas (Michael Van Valkenburgh Associates).

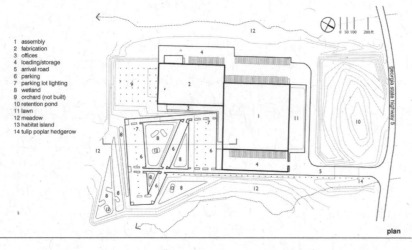

1 assembly
2 fabrication
3 offices
4 loading/storage
5 arrival road
6 parking
7 parking lot lighting
8 wetland
9 orchard (not built)
10 retention pond
11 lawn
12 meadow
13 habitat island
14 tulip poplar hedgerow

Figure 2.56 Parallel Project: Herman Miller Factory. (Credit: Michael Van Valkenburgh Associates, Inc.)

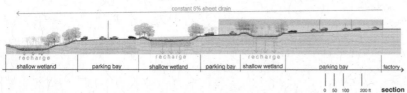

3 STAKEHOLDER INFLUENCE

How are the philosophies and needs of neighbors, community members, and other project stakeholders purposefully incorporated into project scoping and direction?

Whitney Water Purification Facility

When (citizen) participation in the design process is successful, the resulting physical environment integrates and expresses the unique goals of the residents. The places reflect what the residents want them to be, not just the designer's values.

—Randolph T. Hester

BACKGROUND

When a design project is conceived, the parties with the most direct control over the design's direction and outcome are the client, the design professional, and the required regulatory agencies. The American emphasis on property rights and individual autonomy promoted by the free market system has created an atmosphere that de-emphasizes community values and civic responsibility, even on public projects, which are often sold on the basis of their economic development potential. As interest in sustainability rises, the need for cooperative decision-making and consensus building must extend past those with direct control to effectively and proactively involve those stakeholders with a broader and more removed yet no less real interest in a site's development. The external stakeholder is an important, but often disregarded, part of the "population" considered in design programming and throughout the life of the site—and one that can contribute greatly to a project's sustainability. This book's emphasis on a site's positive response to and influence on its context, includes the innovative consideration of multiple viewpoints.

External stakeholders may be end users in the project, as in the case of parks and other public facilities. These users may come from direct neighboring adjacencies, such as in the Whitney Water Purification Facility, or they may be drawn from city-wide, regional, or even larger geographic areas, such as in the Sandstone Visitor Center. External stakeholders also may be public agencies or nonprofit organizations, who may not have a direct interest in the property, but have important programmatic ideas that benefit the project. This was the case with the Menomonee Valley Industrial Center's involvement of a local health agency as a partner whose interest in public health bolstered the community open space component of the project.

Even in residential or other types of private design projects, where neighbors may not be implicit users of the site, sustainable design must consider the concerns of adjacent and nearby property holders, in the interest of neighborhood character and function, both social and ecological. While it is clearly more critical and relevant to actively involve external stakeholders in the sustainable design process on public projects, private projects have their own sustainability needs for such involvement, not the least of which is just being a good neighbor. Robert Frost's poem "Mending Wall," an exploration of the idea that "good fences make good neighbors," recognizes the human urge to separate oneself from neighbors, but to also work toward mending the fences together.

The involvement stakeholders can have ranges from intensive *community* or *participatory design*, where end users for a public project actually build or participate in the creation of the design itself, to more minimal involvement where stakeholders are allowed access to and input on the design direction via public meetings, workshops, and other efforts. The idea of participatory design, called "Take Part" planning by landscape architect Lawrence Halprin, who developed it in the 1970s, differed from the norm of design process at the time because it was "participatory and cyclical rather than hierarchical and linear" (Macy 2008). It incorporated the use of hands-on interactions around developing awareness and understanding of the community's sense of place. Halprin conceived of this process in association with his work in urban planning, when it became important to heal the wounds of urban renewal in which massive planning efforts were conducted without consulting stakeholders in the process. The resulting wholesale destruction of entire districts of old and valued urban areas prompted the development of new planning processes that would be open, participatory, and democratic as well as energizing, rewarding, and engaging. The transfer of such planning-based methods to site-level design has become more commonplace over the past 30 years, as its benefits related to social and environmental justice and community buy-in and stewardship have become clear.

While participatory design methods were initially aimed at mending social fabric and forging relationships, the emphasis now recognizes the shared natural resource interests of disparate groups across watersheds, ecosystems, and bioregions. In the Menomonee Valley Industrial Center project, for instance, renewed health and biodiversity of the river corridor was a common interest that united neighbors, environmental groups, recreation groups, and businesses alike.

Although there is some overlap, it is important to make the clear distinction between the nature of *community design* efforts, where citizens design their own "everyday" environments with assistance and facilitation from design experts, and *stakeholder-influenced design* efforts, where design professionals gain and apply stakeholder insight to a more complex design challenge. While many of the same concepts and benefits apply, this book is geared to the latter situation, where the need for professional expertise and collaboration limits the level to which citizens may or ought to participate in the actual design, but for which appropriate involvement and participation can be critical.

While involving external stakeholders can be critical to the sustainability of a project, it is not without its potential pitfalls. Without strong leadership, participatory processes can become muddled and confusing, lacking clear goals and outcomes. Sometimes participants are asked to make contributions that are beyond their abilities or knowledge as laypeople, or input that is asked for and given in good faith is not utilized as expected. The term *design by committée* is the unfortunate description attached to the outcome of poorly executed participatory design processes that are characterized by needless complexity or the lack of a unifying vision. It takes extra time and effort to involve stakeholders well and avoid these pitfalls, but if planned carefully, such processes can be invaluable. The following strategies for stakeholder involvement are aimed at maximizing the benefits of participatory design processes by carefully identifying the *who, what, when, why*, and *how* of participation.

STRATEGIES FOR STAKEHOLDER INVOLVEMENT

1. Recognize stakeholder needs that differ between public and private projects. The type and extent of participation for public projects is very different than that for private projects. Increasingly, projects are being pursued as public/private partnerships, such as the Menomonee Valley Industrial Center, where economic development is fueled by the private industrial development of part of the project and community development is fostered by the common open space/green infrastructure aspects of the project.

2. Assess the identity of the stakeholders. Who are the groups and individuals that are relevant stakeholders and why? Have they identified themselves already through the project inception, as in the case of the Whitney Water Purification Facility, or are they being brought into the project following its inception? Should you treat them as one group or involve them in smaller groups in different ways?

3. Determine the extent and timing of participation. How will you involve the stakeholders? What do you hope to accomplish with the participation? How can it contribute to sustainable design outcomes?

4. Plan roles in facilitating participation. Participatory processes often benefit from involving a neutral facilitator who is neither the client nor the design team. This practice is followed by John Monroe with the National Park Service Rivers and Trails Program for community park development. In his role as facilitator, he provides the important mix of leadership, organization, and trust-building, while the design team is free to guide with their expertise.

5. Communicate clearly and listen to participants. What is the purpose of this process? What are the rules and procedures you will follow? What can you realistically guarantee will result in their participation? How will you show that you are hearing what they say?

6. Determine each stakeholder's sustainability needs for the project. While stakeholders may identify "sustainability" as a goal, many times that goal means different things to different constituents.

7. Determine how stakeholders feel about the existing condition of the project site. What do they value about it? What do they not like about it? For the Whitney Water Purification Facility site, the neighbors had a high value for the open space use of the site and the industrial history of the site, though they hoped the form and character of it could be improved.

8. Determine how stakeholders feel about the context of the site. Relative to the project site, are they generally positive about the state of their neighborhood or community or are they looking for this project to somehow catalyze improvements? What contextual places are memorable and meaningful to them? What resource systems do they value?

9. *Identify the general issues that are of concern.* Is the project generally favored or is it generally not favored by stakeholders? Why? What types of impacts are of greatest concern—economic, environmental, visual?

10. *Envision participation as a two-way opportunity.* You are learning valuable things from the participants that will help you make sustainable design decisions, and they can learn things from you about design, new thinking, and innovation about sustainability.

11. *Involve stewardship to insure that the design intent is preserved over time.* What mechanisms can you set in place to actively involve stakeholders in the establishment and ongoing care of the new landscape?

METHODS FOR STAKEHOLDER INVOLVEMENT

Specific methods for involving stakeholders in sustainable site design nearly all involve group activities that may address one or more of the following levels or stages of participation.

Attitudes and values: establishing general group makeup and perspectives

Visioning: development of common goals and direction

Designing: decision-making on how to implement goals

Postdesign: evaluation and care of designed landscapes

Attitudes and Values Activities

Prior to the beginning of thinking directly about design or decision-making, it is useful to engage in activities that introduce the stakeholders and the design team and establish their individual perspectives. The design team can introduce their work and their approach to sustainability and design. General stakeholder attitudes, experiences, and perceptions about places or problems can be estab-

lished through surveys conducted prior to workshop events. Introducing sustainable precedent studies provides stakeholders with an image to concretize the concepts being discussed. Walking the site or its neighborhood, having stakeholders describe their sense and elements of place, recording stakeholder knowledge and memory, and surveying environmental attitudes or visual preferences are all ways of establishing a base of information about the place and the people. Technological methods, such as key pad polling where visual images are shown and participants use hand-held remote key pads to vote on their preferences, are creating workshops with critical surveying that is instant, anonymous, and interactive.

Visioning Participation

This is the more focused period of project direction and goal setting. National Park Service community design facilitator John Monroe describes his visioning process through the concept of the hourglass: beginning with broad brainstorming and developing "wish lists," followed by narrowing of possibilities through analysis and consensus building to create clarity and focus in direction, followed by another broadening of the vision to develop the focus into different dimensions for the project.

To manage expectations and begin their projects with a common understanding of terms and goals, the firm Atelier Dreiseitl holds weekend-long workshops where divergent stakeholders partake in a project visioning process. The firm's Tanner Springs Park project goals were initially defined by the client—the city of Portland, Oregon—to promote sustainability in the built environment. But including the public in the front end of the site design process helped define how sustainability might be applied in this context, with these users. Dreiseitl's visioning process is aimed at establishing consensus on a philosophy or a general sensibility for a project, and initially avoids getting too specific with the detailed form it might take. In addition to asking questions about what is wrong or what is missing in the current environment, Dreiseitl presents users with broad possibilities for project direction and involves them, through art-making, music, food, and experimentation, in a festive and noncombative process for creating a vision.

Designing Activities

With more focus on sustainable solutions, design activities that involve stakeholders can take a range of forms. It is at this point that it becomes especially important to define the proper role of laypeople in relation to the design professional, and for the designer to firmly guide the direction with his or her expertise, while allowing the participants open access to the process and opportunities for meaningful, considered input.

Design Charrettes

A *charrette* is a collaborative session in which a group of people drafts a solution to a problem. Charrettes often involve several groups working simultaneously, each coming up with different solutions, and then coming together at the end of the session to share results as a means of generating dialogue, a variety of perspectives, and eventual consensus about design direction. The intent is not to generate an absolute or detailed solution, but to identify issues and narrow the possible alternatives. Charrettes can be done with groups of designers and others with professional perspectives on the project, or they can involve nonprofessional stakeholders led by professionals.

Involving stakeholders in this type of hands-on problem solving can be aided by structuring the process in a way that makes it easier for them to contribute as nondesigners. A "kit of parts" approach, where scaled building units, parking units, play-field units, landscape units (woodlands, gardens, wetlands, etc.), and other program elements are provided as moving pieces, is a useful method, especially when used in conjunction with goals or site planning rules that come out of the visioning process.

Design Review and Advisory Committees

A less hands-on but equally useful way of involving stakeholders can be employed through citizen design review and advisory roles for a site design project. The design for the Whitney Water Purification Facility in Connecticut was developed through a design competition that the Water Authority client and neighborhood stakeholder group conceived together. The neighborhood group was integrally involved in the process of developing the parameters for the competition and its emphasis on landscape-based solutions. The group also was involved in reviewing the submitted design entries and selecting the team of Michael Van Valkenburgh Associates landscape architects and Stephen Holl Architects. The Menomonee Valley Industrial Center project employed a similar use of design competition and citizen review, through their highly organized stakeholder group, Menomonee Valley Partners. This type of nonprofit organization that brings together stakeholders is increasingly utilized on large complex sites where multi-use development is being pursued in public/private partnerships.

Postdesign Participation

Postoccupancy Evaluation

The concept of postoccupancy evaluation was developed as a way to determine whether a designed environment—a building or a landscape—is meeting the needs of the people and design goals. It can be used to improve and fine tune a project design and its maintenance, which is often of interest to the client and the designer, as well as the site user and other project stakeholders. But it also can be used as a benchmark to inform the design of future projects with similar features and functions. Sustainable design techniques often use innovative or unfamiliar materials, functions, or elements, so the relevance of postconstruction evaluation is especially high. Revisiting project goals and how they were realized in the implemented design is useful to reinforcing why certain things were done, why they may look different than a conventional landscape, how they can be expected to change over time, and how they can be used differently.

Postconstruction evaluation can take the form of organized stakeholder gatherings, or they can be done through informal observation and recording conditions and activities via photography, filming, as-built plan notes and drawings, and conversations with site users. It is a good idea to plan this aspect of the project in advance and consider revisiting the evaluation at regular intervals. While a client may not be willing to include these as paid services of the designer on conventional projects, sustainable design clients may be more interested in the benefits of this type of service if well structured.

Stewardship Activities

Landscapes are alive and dynamic. From the moment of construction, cycles of growth, natural events, and cultural attitudes can subtly or dramatically change the design and its intent. The site conditions at any given time are as John Dixon Hunts puts it, "an infinitesimally small part of its existence." The designer must anticipate landscape changes over time through programming strategies but also prepare to hand off responsibility of project maintenance to site users. Because landscape values shift and the site/user relationship changes over time, the life expectancy of any landscape design is strongly dependent on the attitudes of the community that cares for it and how the designer provides for long-term management plans.

Community support established from the onset of the design process often carries through to the postconstruction maintenance of the site. The Pearl District in downtown Portland, Oregon, has a community organization called Friends of Tanner Springs Park that helps care for the park and ensures that site users are informed as to the design intent. At the Central Park Conservancy, working with the city of New York, volunteers are assigned specific areas to maintain so that each understands the unique requirements of that particular area (Cranz 2004). The Menomonee Valley Industrial Center has established a "Stew Crew" comprised of employees of the development's new manufacturing businesses and other neighborhood volunteers, who have been instrumental in planting areas not covered by the project construction budget and ongoing stewardship of the community park, which is not a part of the municipally maintained park system.

Landscape architects must assist the community or constituent body with ongoing site maintenance and stewardship after project installation, and provide maintenance guidelines and descriptions of what to expect over time. The designer must plan for and communicate early in the design process the type, quality, and quantity of maintenance and change to expect on a site. A maintenance plan can very simply provide management guidelines to accompany the planting and seeding plans, or in some cases show 10-year, 20-year, or 30-year succession forecasts and prescriptive direction.

Sustainable site management trends reflect shifting environmental values, where old maintenance approaches such as lawn mowing, fertilization, and irrigation are being displaced by less mechanized care involved in naturalized landscapes. This shift accommodates a volunteer component for landscape management, where machinery and chemical inputs are replaced by hands-on participation.

CASE STUDY— WHITNEY WATER PURIFICATION FACILITY

LOCATION: Hamden, Connecticut, USA
SITE SIZE: 14 acres
CLIENT: South Central Connecticut Regional Water Authority
DESIGNERS: Landscape Architect—Michael Van Valkenburgh
  Associates, New York, New York
  Architect—Steven Holl Associates, New York, New York
  Civil Engineer—Tighe and Bond Consulting Engineers, Inc.,
  Westfield, Massachusetts
  Sustainable Design Consultant—The Bioengineering Group Inc.,
  Salem, Massachusetts
FORMER SITE USES: Water Purification Facility and Open Space
LANDSCAPE BUDGET: $2.88 million
DATE OF COMPLETION: 2005

(Credit: Historicaerials.com)

Overview

The Whitney Water Purification Facility is a prime example of the power and effectiveness that stakeholder involvement can have in a sustainable project outcome. The case study that follows chronicles the lead taken by a residential neighborhood in fostering a community-minded, ecologically vibrant solution for the redevelopment of an infrastructure site.

Project Inception

Due to upstream development and the ensuing water pollution, as well as increasing demand on the Whitney Reservoir, a redevelopment and upgrade of the 85-year-old Whitney Water Purification Facility was required. Increasingly stricter standards for the quality of purified drinking water, beyond what the original sand filter could provide, also contributed to this need.

In planning for the 14-acre site redevelopment, moving the facility to a new location was considered. But instead, when the South Central Connecticut Regional Water Authority (SCCRWA), a nonprofit utility that owns the public water supply, decided to redevelop the existing site, they sent out more than 1,000 notices to surrounding neighbors

asking for their input and involvement. The redesign of the facility was directed in part by this interest group whose concerns were quality open space, improved real estate values, restored ecosystems, and enhanced neighborhood character in keeping with the innovative spirit of the area's historic association with Eli Whitney.

Design Concept

The new state-of-the-art facility is largely underground but includes a sculptural architectural presence above ground. Both moves by the architect allow the landscape to be the dominant feature of the renovation. The landscape design concept, seen in Figure 3.1, is based on a set of sequential landscape spaces that interpret aspects of the water treatment processes being performed by the facility as well as hydrological processes and forms found in the larger landscape. Mathew Urbanski, lead landscape architect for the project with Michael Van Valkenburgh Associates, characterizes the design as a "microcosm of a **watershed**." The progression of spaces has both horizontal and vertical order and variety from pond to hill landscapes as the site topography progresses from east to west across the landscape. The sequence contrasts larger areas of exuberant, wild spaces against smaller areas of more controlled, mini-

malist cultural spaces. The spaces are linked with each other and with the surrounding neighborhood through an interwoven system of water flow, vegetative cover, and pedestrian circulation. As can be seen in Figure 3.2, the site land cover is over 75 percent vegetated, with the majority of the plantings designed with native meadow and woodland plant communities. This project was chosen as an AIA Committee on the Environment Top Ten Green Project for 2007.

Philosophies and Approach

Development of the program emanated from two basic needs: the need for expanded water purification capabilities and the desire to create a state-of-the-art process for water purification, which reflected the ingenuity and innovation of the original 1906 sand filtration system.

The site's historic treatment facility form, with extensive open lawn panels atop raised sand filtration beds, had long functioned as open space for the neighborhood (see Figure 3.3). In developing the program, strong identity and function of the facility as an open space was identified as a second basic need. This is a dramatic departure from the conventional program for infrastructure sites.

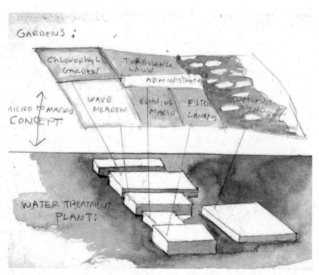

Figure 3.1 Architect's Concept Sketch.
(Credit: Steven Holl)

Figure 3.2 Landscape Architect's Concept Diagram.
(Credit: Michael Van Valkenburgh Associates Inc.)

Figure 3.3 Original Whitneyville Slow Sand Filter. Designed by Civil Engineer Charles Ferry and built between 1904 and 1908, this water filtration facility was the first in Connecticut and operated until the 1990s. Its open and accessible character invited neighborhood use as an open space.
(Credit: Michael Van Valkenburgh Associates Inc.)

In the Whitney Water Purification Facility project the philosophies of both the client and the designers, in addition to the active stakeholder group, centered on sustainability. A key member of the selected design team, the Bioengineering Group, acted as the sustainable design consultant. A sustainable approach to design of infrastructure sites begins with a basic philosophical shift in land use and landscape potential. In this case, the landscape was seen as the primary vehicle for sustainable site development that would address and interpret the water treatment function as well as neighborhood open space needs.

The South Central Connecticut Regional Water Authority is proactively concerned with engaging the community in responsible stewardship of regional water resources. Through a watershed protection program that has strong outreach components, the Authority provides information and education regarding wise land management practices for the public as well as the authority's own activities, facilities, and land resources. Their commitment to high-quality site planning and design for the facility reflects their integrated attitudes about land use and water quality.

The Water Authority's close work with the neighborhood in the development of plans for the upgraded purification facility exemplifies their philosophy about the importance of engaging the community in sustainable resource development. The participation and leadership of project stakeholders—neighboring landowners and community members—was instrumental in the program direction and design quality this project was able to achieve. Not only were members of the public involved and consulted throughout the design process, but they actively encouraged and participated in the initiative to select a highly creative design team and develop an innovative and visionary program for the facility. The project benefited from the consensus that existed among the public and the level to which they were able to influence the development.

The selection of the design team was accomplished through a process whereby designers were invited to prepare and present concepts for satisfying programmatic requirements of the water purification needs combined with an open space component. The winning team of Steven Holl Associates and Michael Van Valkenburgh Associates was ultimately selected because their concept treated the building expression, although contemporary in nature, as subservient to the site (Urbanski 2008). Michael Van Valkenburgh Associates has a strong reputation for high-quality design blended with ecology, as evidenced through such projects as the Wellesley campus's Alumnae Valley Landscape, the University of Iowa's Athletic Center, and the Herman Miller Factory (MVVA). The firm's strong functional design and technical capabilities, combined with its well-developed use of landscape medium for artistic expression, have not been compromised as they have increasingly layered sustainability concerns into their approach.

Program Type and Development Trend

Program Type: Community-Focused Utility

Public utilities such as electric, water, gas, or sewer, are typically off limits to the public often due to safety and regulation concerns. Many times these facilities have been a part of a community for decades but have not contributed to the vibrancy of the area. Their primary focus has been providing services, facility maintenance, and managing resources. The properties themselves are often hidden from sight behind dense vegetation or chain-link fencing—not open spaces for interaction.

Increasingly, nonprofit as well as municipal utilities are fostering community outreach and education programs that protect their resources, reduce processing costs, and forge community partnerships. The Sacramento Municipal Utility District in California, for example, is a customer-owned electricity utility whose focus is energy efficiency, cost effectiveness, and renewable resources. Likewise, the Whitney Water Purification Facility, even prior to retrofit, was an integrated part of the neighborhood's cultural fabric both physically as open space or parkland, and through education, resource protection, and a transparent design process. According to the Trust for Public Land, "the South Central Connecticut Regional Water Authority is one of the most progressive suppliers in the state when it comes to protecting source water, and investing in land conservation and watershed management strategies."

Development Trend: Rebuilding versus Relocating

Businesses and organizations, due to growth, consolidation, or obsolescence, partake in the unsustainable practice of relocating to accommodate their changing needs. This practice leads to sprawl as well as leaves employment and derelict land gaps in the communities left behind. In addition to the tax revenues, philanthropic endeavors, and jobs, these companies often provide stability and a sense of identity to a community that is lost upon relocation. Some businesses and organizations, like the Whitney Water Purification Facility, are committed to investing in their communities by renovating or rebuilding rather than relocating.

Context

The Whitney Water Purification Facility's context—beginning with locating the site within the region and ending with a site plan—is shown at various scales in Figures 3.4, 3.5, 3.6, and 3.7. Through regional context analysis, the design process was infused with an understanding of site and regional potentials and challenges. This analysis situates the site relative to area history, regional attitudes, and ecological health. Following is a description of landscape form, function, and philosophy of this area of Connecticut that explores a setting and combination of sustainable factors to which the project design uniquely responds.

Regional Form

Natural Patterns

The primary **physiography** of the immediate project area is characterized by trap rock ridges that define the skyline of nearby New Haven. These uniquely shaped geologic ridges formed by glacial action, due to their unbuildable steep cliffs and thin soils, were developed into park systems such as the vast urban East Rock Park. East Rock Park's 360-foot red cliff face, which offers overlooks to New Haven, Hamden, and the Long Island Sound, is the most prominent geologic landmark in the region. As shown in Figure 3.8, this feature is visible from portions of the site.

Figure 3.4 Whitney Water Purification Facility—National Context.

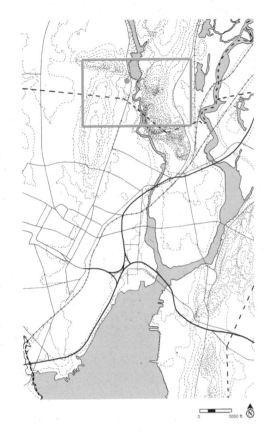

Figure 3.6 Whitney Water Purification Facility—Local Context.

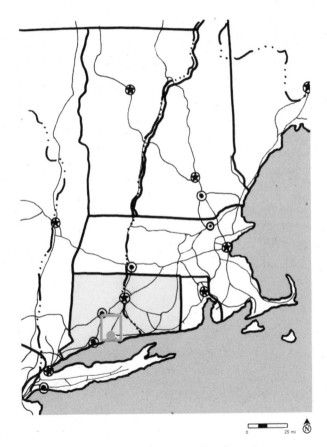

Figure 3.5 Whitney Water Purification Facility—State Context.

Figure 3.7 Whitney Water Purification Facility—Neighborhood Context.

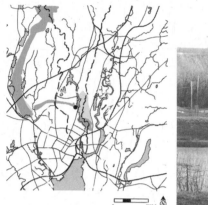

Figure 3.8 New Haven's Geological Trap Rock Ridge. East Rock is located in the Whitneyville neighborhood of New Haven.

Development Patterns

The history of the surrounding close-knit neighborhoods such as the Edgehill and Whitneyville neighborhoods, which many Yale University staff call home, is linked to the presence of the Mill River that runs near the site. It was here that Eli Whitney dammed the river to form Lake Whitney in 1806 to fuel a mill, employing mass production to supply munitions for the Civil War. During this time, the area was comprised of a mix of farms, worker housing,

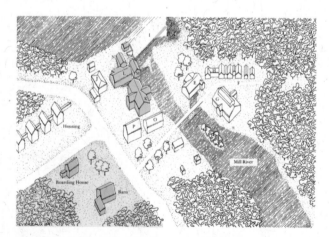

Figure 3.9 Historic rendering of Whitney Mill Buildings. The site, which still retains the mill's boarding house and barn, is shaded at lower left. The main factory building and dam along the Mill River are shaded at center.
(Credit: Eli Whitney Museum)

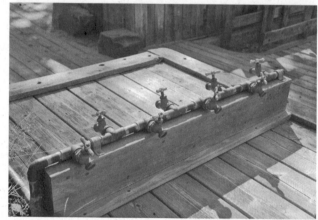

Figure 3.10 Remaining Historic Mill, Dam, and Facilities.

Figure 3.12 Barn and Boarding House on Site.

Figure 3.11 Intact Adjacent Estate Grounds.

and workshops for barrel making, forging, and dam-making, most of which are now gone (see Figure 3.9). A handful of buildings associated with this manufacturing remain both on and just off the Whitney Water Purification Facility site, as can be seen in Figures 3.10 through 3.12; to the north, a steam pump house with its 90-foot chimney built by Eli Whitney, Jr. still stands from when he started the New Haven Water Company. At that time, he raised the Whitney dam in the Mill River from 6 to 35 feet in order to draw water for New Haven's drinking supply and to provide energy to run the factories. To the south, the site borders the 27-acre historic Edgerton Park, a former estate of Eli Whitney's family. The Edgerton Park Conservancy's mission to preserve the park, support environmental awareness, and enhance connections between nature and the arts matches other such sensibilities in the larger region.

While the area has changed dramatically from its early industrial focus from large block delineations to a community of medium-density, single-family clusters of "hamlets" with a mix of historic uses and park networks, it has retained historic features that are reminders of its early beginnings.

In the larger urban pattern, Hamden's neighborhoods and hamlets surround the central city of New Haven (see Figure 3.13). New Haven is a classic northeastern city with a dense and well-preserved body of historic architecture, and a strong infrastructure of **cultural landscapes** that contribute to the public realm, such as the New Haven Green, shown in Figure 3.14, and the many courtyards of the surrounding Yale campus.

Regional Function

Natural Systems

The site lies three miles north of the Connecticut coastline where the Mill River and the Quinnipiac River flow together into the Long Island Sound Tributary. The 165-square-mile Mill River watershed, outlined in Figure 3.15, includes 15 towns and the majority is a regulated system of dammed lakes and controlled flow. Although highly

Source: The Hamden Historical Society
cityofnewhaven.com
0   3000 ft N

Figure 3.13 Historic Districts and Sites.

Figure 3.14 The New Haven Green and Yale University. The famed courtyards of Yale's campus are shown here as integral with the larger historic street grid and central green, which form a strong system of cultural landscapes.
(Credit: Robert Perron)

urbanized in the lower reaches, the upper reaches are largely forested. As the land use map in Figure 3.16 shows, within the lower reaches, where the site lies, increased development and imperviousness adversely impact Lake Whitney and the Mill River with discharge from over 60 outfalls. Despite recent improvements, the biological quality of this hydrologic system remains low due to stormwater runoff, landfill leachate, and dams, which create a lack of sensitive species, low degree of

diversity, and poor water quality during weather events (DEP 2001). While there is little evidence of anadromous fish passage, sea otters have been spotted inhabiting the Mill River up to the point of Whitney Dam, near the Water Purification Facility site (Lichtenfeld 1999).

The dominant landscape vegetative type in Connecticut is the deciduous forest. The site lies within the broadly defined ecological community called the Appalachian Oak Forest (the shaded area of Figure 3.17) covering many

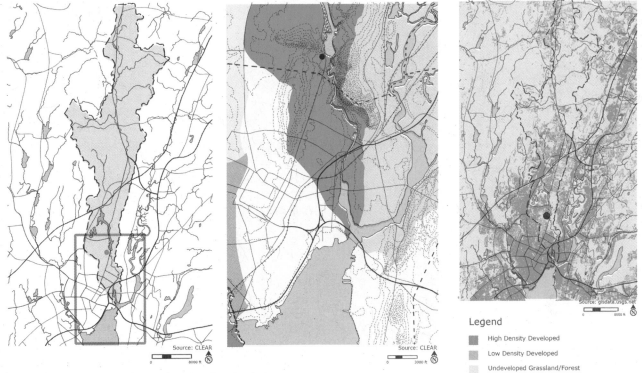

Figure 3.15 Entire Mill River Watershed on Left and Enlargement on Right.

Figure 3.16 Land Use at the Watershed Scale.

Legend

- High Density Developed
- Low Density Developed
- Undeveloped Grassland/Forest

states from New England to Alabama. Locally, this vegetation type is called the Eastern Broadleaf Forest, characterized by a temperate coast-hugging climate of cold winters and warm summers and tall broadleaf forests with dense canopies that shed their leaves in winter. The natural inclination of the region is to succeed to a mature forest condition consisting of deciduous canopy trees, understory trees, a shrubby layer, and a thin herbaceous layer that varies depending on **microclimatic** soil type, moisture, and elevation.

Within the ecological community covering much of New England, the last 400 years of land uses have changed the landscape dramatically. Prior to this change, New England had been old-growth forest somewhat managed by the Native American populations of the area. Then during English settlement beginning around 1635, the forests were cleared for building structures, fences, and for fuel (Favretti 1976). Later they were cleared further for agricul-

tural uses. By the early 19th century, nearly 60 percent of Connecticut's forests were cleared for production. Since this time, with the gradual disappearance of agriculture in the state, this landscape has transitioned back to deciduous forest in undeveloped areas. In southern New England, this **succession**—the sequence of dominating plant species over a period of time—relies on moisture, elevation, soil type, and seed availability, but in general proceeds from annual weeds, to native warm season grasses, to the invasion of red cedar and gray birch and finally to red maples, oaks, and hickories (Jorgensen 1981).

Wetlands are a prominent feature of northeastern landscapes. Figure 3.18 provides a cross-section of the vegetated wetlands, which provide critical water quality, habitat, and flood control benefits. By the mid-1980s, Connecticut, under heavy development pressure as part of the industrialized corridor between Boston and New York City, had lost approximately 74 percent of its estimated original wetlands

Figure 3.17 U.S. Natural Regions: Appalachian Plateaus and Mountains. (Harker 1999)

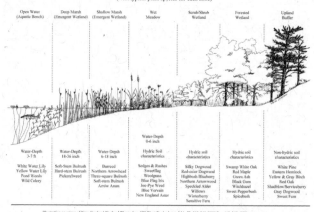

Figure 3.18 Wetland Plant Communities Cross Section. (Credit: New England Wetland Plants Inc.)

base, a higher rate of wetland loss than any other New England state.

Human Systems

Although often associated with New Haven, the cultural center of Connecticut, the site is located on the town boundary in the small suburb of Hamden (see Figure 3.19). Hamden was originally settled by Puritans and today remains a series of small distinct hamlets that originated in the mid-18th century. Whitney Avenue, the primary through-street in Hamden is an historic spine that houses the Eli Whitney Museum as well as other historic sites. New Haven is largely a series of gridded streets that in Hamden begin to curve in response to the rivers and topography, as can be seen in Figure 3.20.

Residents here enjoy substantial areas of open space set aside as parks and natural preserves (shaded areas of Figure 3.21). Thousands visit annually to hike, canoe, and bird watch in Sleeping Giant State Park and East Rock and West Rock Parks, which are each hundreds of acres in size and provide miles of hiking trails within Hamden and New Haven. The Farmington Canal Greenway, used for biking, covers approximately 85 miles and extends from New Haven and Hamden, Connecticut, to North Hampton, Massachusetts. Hamden's Natural Resources and Open Space Advisory board has focused purchases and preserves in ecologically sensitive areas.

Regional Philosophy

Conservation versus Development

Lake Whitney, while off-limits to recreation, is viewed as an aesthetic asset in the town of Hamden. Its beauty is evident in Figure 3.22. During the water purification facility design process, neighboring residents were very knowledgeable, concerned, and pro-active about environmental and cultural issues that would affect the lake. Their interest in ensuring that the water level of the lake did not decrease with the additional "take" by the increased capacity of the Whitney Water Purification Facility in part fueled the direction of the project scope. A high-profile lawsuit, settled out of court, brought by the cities of New Haven and Hamden during the predesign phases, questioned the new facility's impact on the health of the hydrology systems of the Whitney Reservoir and Mill River. Further publicity generated from the building of the Whitney Water Purification Facility has spurred continuing local interest in stormwater runoff issues in the area, such as a nearby commercial development in Hamden that employs **green infrastructure** (EPA).

The presence of the internationally renowned Yale School of Forestry and Environmental Studies is a strong force for

Legend

■ High Density Developed

▨ Low Density Developed

▨ Undeveloped

Figure 3.19 The Dashed Line Shows New Haven/Hamden Relationship.

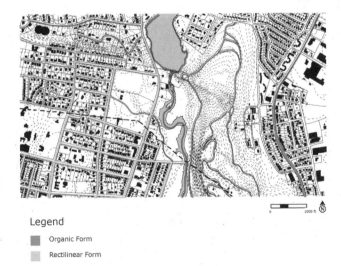

Legend

■ Organic Form

▨ Rectilinear Form

Figure 3.20 Infrastructure Patterns.

Source: cityofnewhaven.com
greenway.org

Legend

▬ Farmington Canal Greenway

▨ Open Space

Figure 3.21 Local Open Space.

conservation in the area, with its research and outreach resources efforts often focused on local issues and landscapes.

The Hamden area is a well-established and stable community of small commercial centers, residential neighborhoods, parks, and institutions. Commercial development or development of any kind is not of significant concern because of its status as built-out suburb of the centralized city of New Haven. The community is focused on the

Figure 3.22 Lake Whitney Reservoir. This image is looking south toward the dam from a park area north of the site.

Figure 3.23 Notable Architecture of New Haven. Area architecture includes buildings by notable architects such as Marcel Breuer, Louis Kahn, Frank Gehry, and Eero Sarinnen.

preservation of the character of its neighborhoods and town centers rather than the promotion of large-scale change and development.

Cultural Resources

Preservation of historic character of the neighborhood and area is important to the community identity and is one of the primary attractions of the neighborhood, both to prospective residents and tourists. The site lies within a suburban mix of neighborhoods and small town centers, a network of public open space, and extensive Long Island Sound shoreline. The presence of the Yale School of Architecture in New Haven has fostered an uncommonly rich building tradition by well-known architects such as Louis Kahn, Eero Sarinnen, Marcel Breuer, and Frank Gehry, examples of whose work can be seen in Figure 3.23. The area also has dozens of colleges, universities, and museums including the Peabody Museum and the Yale Center for British Art.

Threaded throughout the neighborhood and area are preserved remnants of the original character of the area. The Water Purification Facility site itself retains two original buildings from the Whitney manufacturing complex—an historic barn that hosts programs for the Eli Whitney Museum across the street, and the original Whitney Munitions Factory boarding house that aptly houses the

offices of the Connecticut Trust for Historic Preservation. Because of the Whitney family's long-time influence and enduring historic structures, the neighborhood is known as Whitneyville.

Regional Setting for Integrator Site

As an example of a "sustainable integrator," this project's local context exhibits several aspects of cultural or ecological sustainability in the built and natural environments. The project design connects both physically and conceptually to these existing sustainable influences. The sustainable site design of this project came about not only because of high expectations of the neighboring community but from the rich cultural context, extensive natural areas, and efforts to preserve the health of the surrounding regional features such as East Rock Park and the Mill River. In this way, the context inspired the community and design team to reach beyond immediate site program needs to fit within the existing fabric. The resulting site design, a sustainable integrator, reciprocates by reinforcing and improving the regional character.

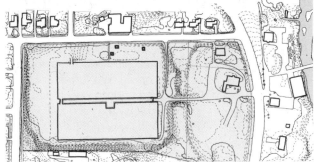

Figure 3.24 Predesign Site.
(Credit: Michael Van Valkenburgh Associates Inc.)

Site

Design Considerations

Existing Site

Built in 1905, the original Whitney Water Purification Facility was ahead of its time in its use of sustainable technology for community water treatment and in its evolved shared neighborhood use as an open space. As such, the site had functioned as an integral part of its larger Whitneyville neighborhood for many years. As can be seen in Figure 3.24, the site is bordered on three sides by streets, two of them residential side streets and one a major arterial connector leading from the heart of New Haven northward, loosely following the alignment of the Mill River and Lake Whitney. This street, Whitney Avenue, separates the site from the Eli Whitney Museum, located in his historic munitions factory, and the dam and Lake Whitney, built to power the factory. To the south of the site is Edgerton Park, the historic grounds of a former Victorian mansion that

belonged to Whitney's niece and later to industrialist Frederick Brewster, who called the estate Edgerton for its location at the edge of New Haven, where it was intended to act as a retreat from the industrial city (Edgerton Park).

Prior to its 2005 redevelopment the site existed as originally built, as a large, open expanse of lawn that covered underground sand water filtration structures that protruded only slightly above the natural grade. There were two small areas of wetlands—remnants of its former natural condition in which the site was occupied by fresh water and brackish wetlands. Several buildings dotted the site, some industrial brick structures related to the water treatment and distribution functions and the previously mentioned older wood structures—the barn and dormitory—associated with the 19th century Whitney family farm and munitions factory. Although clearly utilitarian in its structural features and sparseness, the site was open and accessible to the surrounding neighborhood.

Program Development

The primary scale of sustainable design influence for this project is the neighborhood. This is due both to the intimate involvement and interest shown by neighboring residents, as well as the highly defined and evolved neighborhood structure of the New Haven and Hamden communities. While there has been relatively little recent comprehensive planning at the neighborhood level that influenced the direction of the project, the built-out nature and maturity of the area created strong patterns for contextual reference (see Figure 3.25).

While the patterns and identity of the neighborhood were important contextual influences, the primary scales of design program focus for this project were at the site planning, site design, and detail levels of design. Site planning decisions facilitated the basic program goal of having the landscape act as the primary subject of the site through placement of the utilitarian water treatment structures on the internal edge of the site and surrounded by open space landscapes on all three of the site's street edges. Site design decisions created the identity and function of the landscape portion of the site with a program of sequenced zones that represent elevational, landform, and vegetation zones of a watershed. Detail design decisions developed

Source: cityofnewhaven.com

Legend

■ Open Space

░ Developed

Figure 3.25 Neighborhood Influence.

the cultural and ecological identity of program elements within these zones.

A central tenet of the site design program is to create a **naturalized landscape** over the majority of the site. This is a dramatic departure from the predesign site conditions, which had only very small remnants of natural landscape, which is the norm for conventional infrastructure sites. This landscape is not meant to re-create the primarily forested landscape that would have been on the site originally, but was envisioned as an open meadow landscape that would provide contrast to the surrounding open spaces in the area and open views within and to distant features. The focus of this natural landscape is to interpret elevational and landform changes in the larger watershed and the associated presence or absence of water, providing a full range of created landforms from hill to hummock to pond. This landform manipulation was suggested by the need to use excavated site material. Further naturalization of the site is built into the program by covering a large portion of the water purification structure with an **extensive green roof**.

Interpretation of the site and neighborhood's industrial history is the primary cultural aim for the program. The use of environmental art and industrial materials and forms in the site and facility architecture are employed to accomplish this without the use of signage. The contrastingly modern form of the main building introduces an element of newness, excitement, and high technology. A looping pathway element that links all zones of the site provides for the primary recreational use of the site, while a small area of lawn acknowledges the heart of the residential neighborhood and allows for picnicking and lounging.

The Whitney Water Purification Facility design outcome is introduced in Figures 3.26 and 3.27.

	ECOREGION	COMMUNITY	NEIGHBORHOOD	SITE
SCALES OF LANDSCAPE INFLUENCE			Enduring historic character Involved neighbors Valued open space	

	REGIONAL PLANNING	DISTRICT PLANNING	SITE PLANNING	SITE DESIGN	DETAIL DESIGN
SCALES OF PROGRAM FOCUS					

A Conventional Water Infrastructure Facility Design

Mill Rock Water Storage Site, Hamden, Connecticut

The distinction between a conventional and sustainable site design varies in program, design philosophy, and the design outcomes of landscape form and function. Conventional water treatment plants, along with nearly every form of infrastructure, have not typically been seen as landscape projects, but as mechanical projects. A water treatment facility design program, whether for waste water or water purification, usually produces the classic "not in my backyard" (NIMBY) response from neighbors of a proposed facility site. With its sterile character, industrial scale and materials, and fenced perimeter, it is disconnected from its context by design. The main use of vegetation is in screening the facility from neighbors. Though it provides a basic human necessity—clean drinking water—it is viewed as a burdensome land use and even with some suspicion as to the need for its sequestration.

The single-use focus programming and philosophy of these facilities eliminates the potential for shared uses and relationships with the neighborhoods and local areas which they serve. This conventional approach extends to nearly all forms of infrastructural land use programs, such as highways, utility corridors, and drainage systems. Dominated by highly engineered architectural and landscape treatments that serve only one utilitarian function, they wipe out imprints of the former landscape, cultural and natural. More damaging than producing sterile or hidden character for single sites, this approach creates fragmentation and division in the larger landscape.

A water storage facility just a few blocks from the site provides a good example of the conventional approach to design of water treatment infrastructure sites. This site, which is perched along the wooded ridge of Mill Rock, houses two large covered reservoirs that store treated water from the Whitney Purification Facility. Here, the surrounding residential neighborhood is fenced off from the facility and heavy vegetative screening further separates it from surrounding land uses. The reservoir, sited on this knoll-top elevation to produce gravity flow of the water, has no apparent relationship to the site or neighborhood landscape.

Site Design Form

Patterns

The pattern of the site derives from both cultural and natural influences. The overall site is organized by a grid taken from the neighborhood street pattern into quadrants that contain the varied landscape and water treatment zones. A line that skews off the grid acknowledges an important diagonal force that comes from the street corner where neighboring pedestrians enter the site. The line is emphasized by the placement of low inkberry (*Ilex glabra*) hedges running perpendicular across the axis in the garden entry landscape. These are the only plantings that have strict linear order.

The pattern of the waterways, landform, and the majority of plantings and pedestrian pathways is based on the curved and undulating forms created by the forces of nature. As the water gathers intensity and volume, so too does the vegetation swell and gain mass, while the land-

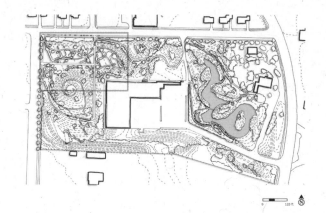

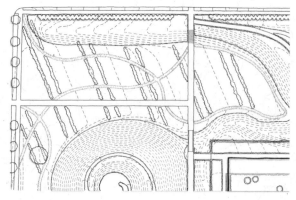

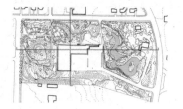

Figure 3.26 Whitney Water Purification Facility Site Plan and Plan Enlargement.

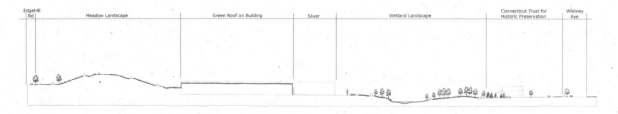

Figure 3.27 Site Section of transition between pathway on left and vegetated pond edge on right.

Figure 3.28 Site Organization: Local Pattern References. Organic and Rectilinear Patterns in Context (left) Informed the Site Patterns (right).

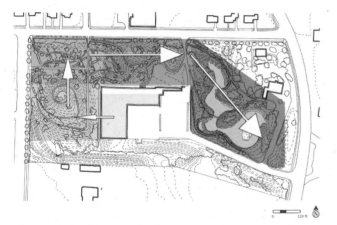

Figure 3.29 Spatial Zones. The site progresses from green roof to hill landscape to garden landscape, to stream landscape to pond landscape, each with its own distinct spatial character.

Legend

■ Steep Areas

■ Flat Areas

Figure 3.30 Landform Zones. Hilly, mounded, heavily vegetated zones contrast with flatter circulation areas.

form rises and dips in a fluid sequence. The landform, which provides the basis for the organic pattern, was created using material excavated for the water treatment structures and the ponds. Early drawings for the site design do not show the hill portion of the landform, which eventually took shape from the excavated soil and strengthens the watershed identity of the site.

While the organic pattern dominates the site, the linear elements provide an underlying structure. Both gridded and organic patterns are evident in the larger infrastructure of the local area and create interesting tension as they are brought into the site, as can be seen in Figure 3.28.

The varied spaces achieve legibility through their combined arrangement of topography, vegetation, and structures. Although the building is in the middle of the site, it effectively acts as an edge for active spaces around the three street-bordering sides, creating a large-scale definition of primary spaces.

Throughout the site, smaller-scale spaces are achieved through changes in canopy density, planting pattern, elevation, and degree of slope, which correspond to successional and hydrological landscape zones, depicted in Figures 3.29 and 3.30.

Materials

There are relatively few nonvegetative site materials used in the construction of the design. The overall feeling of the site is one of soft, organic forms, with splashes of drama and shiny contrast provided by exposed portions of the building/water treatment structure. A water droplet–shaped administrative building faces its glassed profile toward the stormwater pond and extends its 350-foot stainless steel edge along the stream landscape zone. The outdoor service court and filtration court are sheltered from the public by a 30-foot wire mesh wall that is planted with Virginia creeper (*Parthenocissus quinquefolia*), which provides a bright crimson backdrop for the pond in autumn.

Narrow pathways are constructed of stabilized gravel with concrete aprons and steps inserted at transition places. The parking area is also gravel. Site furnishings are minimal and include only three wood benches and two pedestrian bridges of concrete with metal rails that tie into the architectural materials (see Figure 3.31). A giant, weathered water pipe fitting is used as a site sculpture and adds an historic cultural counterpoint to the dominant softscape.

The former water treatment structure covered approximately two-thirds of the site. Although the structure was covered with grass and was therefore permeable, this surface was sterile and monocultural compared to the diverse zones of vegetation that replaced it. The facility footprint now has a concentrated area of only 2 acres devoted to the water treatment structure's footprint, with only a sliver of exposed building, a 30,000-square-foot green roof covering subsurface treatment chambers (Figure 3.32), a 30,000-square-foot area of paving to accommodate service areas, with the remaining 12 acres of the site converted to naturalized open space.

Figure 3.31 Site Materials.

Figure 3.32 Green Roof. (Credit: Michael Van Valkenburgh Associates Inc. (right image))

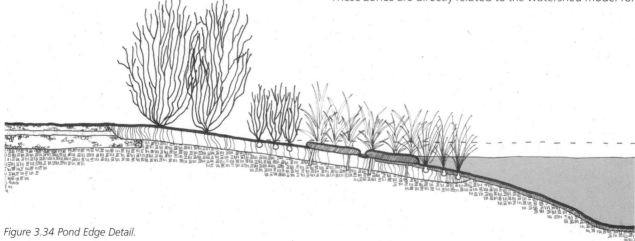

Figure 3.33 Site Elevations and Hydrology.

Legend

→ Surface Runoff Flow

⌇⌇ Swale

▨ Wetland

Figure 3.34 Pond Edge Detail.

Site Design Function

Natural Systems

As one of the primary site systems involved with the design concept, the hydrological regime gathers stormwater that falls on the site and the building and sends it through a vegetated swale that slows it while encouraging groundwater recharge. The swale starts as a small and nearly imperceptible runnel that begins at the summit of the hill and spirals down aside a ramped grass walkway. As it grows in volume, it takes on a more visible path of its own in the stream landscape. It culminates in the pond at the lowest end of the site, which is lined to retain an open water environment, as can be seen in Figure 3.33. Any emergency overflow from the pond, which has had the benefit of the site's **biotreatment**, eventually outlets into the Mill River downstream of the reservoir.

To achieve the dramatic topographic sequence, the site, which was already highly disturbed, was regraded to shift existing site soil from the pond and building excavation areas to the hill to create the watershed landform. Former existing small wetland patches on the site were retained and expanded with the new swale and pond environments (see Figures 3.34 and 3.35).

The planting design is keyed to the sequence of contrasting spaces. The hill, stream, border, and pond landscapes have largely natural plantings of meadow, woodland, wet meadow, and riparian plant communities, respectively. These zones are directly related to the watershed model for

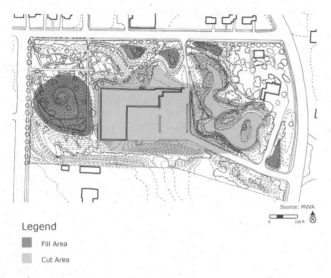

Legend
- Fill Area
- Cut Area

Figure 3.35 Site Cut & Fill Zones.

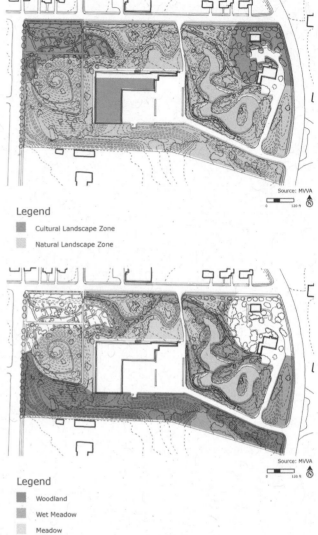

Legend
- Cultural Landscape Zone
- Natural Landscape Zone

Legend
- Woodland
- Wet Meadow
- Meadow

Figure 3.36 Vegetation Zones.

the site (see Figure 3.36). The building zone and the garden landscape have cultural plantings.

The landscape architect describes the planting design in terms of its temporal dimensions: "Unlike the design of a building that out of necessity resists change, the design of the planted landscape anticipates a slow and ongoing transformation of plant species and sizes that will come to fruition over time" (Urbanski 2008). The intention of the site to change seasonally and successionally is manifested by the planting design and the related management plan created for the project (see Figure 3.37).

- The natural planting zones create habitat for migrating birds, beneficial insects, and amphibious species. This new patch of habitat is linked to nearby woodland and wetland open space areas.

Human Systems

In addition to the vital water treatment the facility provides for the region, the project serves as both a neighborhood park where users enjoy strolling and stopping at well-placed benches to take in views of the site and beyond, as can be seen in the images of Figure 3.38. It also functions as an interpretive open space for the entire region that complements and links with the historic Eli Whitney Museum complex adjacent to the site as well as the Water Authority's own education mission. Unlike more conventional neighborhood parks where use is more social or recreational, the site's largely natural landscape and evocative cultural elements create opportunities for quiet observation and contemplation.

Use and identity of the site as a public landscape is facili-

Figure 3.37 Seasonal Change. The Meadow Exhibits Dramatic Spatial Changes Between Its 5 Foot Stature in Summer and it's Mown Winter State.

Figure 3.38 Human Uses of the Site.

tated by careful placement of fencing within the site to prohibit pedestrians from accessing the sensitive equipment and mechanical processes performed by the facility. The images of Figure 3.39 show that, although the build-

ing and associated above-ground treatment areas, including the green roof, are inaccessible to the public, the means of prohibiting access are innocuous. While early plans show a 6-foot fence around the perimeter, the final

Figure 3.39 Site Access.

Legend

Private

Public

configuration tucks the fence in close to the building, allowing visual and physical access throughout the site.

Pedestrian access to the site is gained at several entry points along the western, eastern, and northern street edges of the site, while vehicular traffic for the public is limited to a small gravel parking area shared with the Whitney dormitory historic building and barn, leased to an historic trust for educational use. There are two points of access for service vehicles related to the water treatment function, which are gated, though these gates are not tied to fences in the adjacent landscape, which is typically the case. Parking for the visitors to the outdoor grounds of the facility, which consists of a few dozen gravel spaces, is shared with the historic trust group that leases the barn and dormitory buildings.

Critical connections to context were achieved by looking beyond the strict boundaries of the site. Figure 3.40 shows a pedestrian and vehicular link to the Whitney Museum, which was secured with the addition of a traffic light and crosswalk on Whitney Avenue.

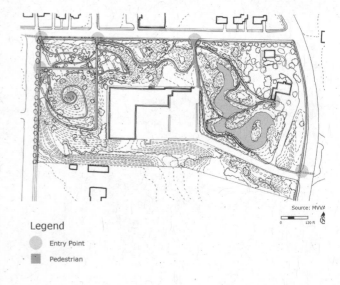

Source: MVVA

Legend

Entry Point

Pedestrian

Figure 3.40 Neighborhood Entry Points.

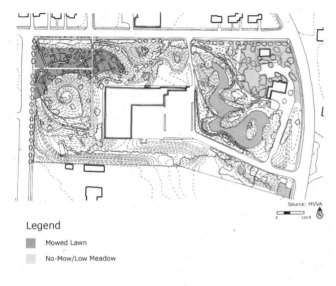

Legend

■ Mowed Lawn
▨ No-Mow/Low Meadow

Figure 3.41 Cultural Management Areas.

The site is designed to require minimal maintenance through the use of primarily naturalized plantings. Such landscapes, however, are not routinely encountered by landscape installation and maintenance crews, who are used to conventional ornamental landscape needs and expectations, and have very different establishment regimes and long-term maintenance methods. Required maintenance for plantings on the Whitney Water Purification Facility site is outlined in a Landscape Maintenance Manual developed by the design and construction team. This includes guidelines for mowed lawn areas, woody plant materials, seeded meadow areas, and bioengineered waterways (shown in Figure 3.41). It covers both establishment-period maintenance as well as long-term management intentions. In the meadow areas, annual September mowing is prescribed, as well as monitoring for soil quality and invasive species. The bioengineered areas along the swales, pond edges, and other basins, with a variety of perennial and woody plant material, are not mowed. These areas have important management instructions to ensure that vigilant monitoring and hand-removal of invasive species and dead plant material and control of goose disturbance will keep the waterways stable and functional.

Site Design Engagements

This project exhibits one primary type of ecological engagement, which is the *creation* of a new overall site vegetation matrix and a new stormwater sequence. From these natural systems, site meaning is derived through the element of **landscape narrative**. This narrative has dual sources and interpretations. The architect's initial vision for the site was that it would tell the story of the water purification process being performed by the several steps of treatment within the facility. As the landscape architect developed the landscape spaces and forms, the design evolved to take on the form of a "microcosm of a natural watershed," which allows the user to experience the workings of an environment that is typically too large to grasp within a single site. This water narrative can be seen in Figure 3.42.

The narrative emerges through visual drama produced by contrasts:

- controlled cultural expressions of structure and landscape contrasted against wild, ever-changing expressions of structure and landscape

- enclosed intimate spaces and framed views contrasted against wide-open spaces and panoramic views

- historic cultural elements contrasted against modern cultural elements

These contrasts can be seen in the images of Figures 3.43 through 3.45.

The theme of water-related technology links the site to its neighborhood context. The adjacent historic Eli Whitney Munitions Factory, which was the original reason for the dam, gives this design's emphasis on water and technology cultural meaning and fit. The use of the site as an educational resource for teaching about the science of producing clean water and linking this with ecological landscape health adds further sustainability to the project.

Other historic elements on and adjacent to the site provide further counterpoints and connections. The adjacent steam pump house and on-site Whitney dormitory and barn provide visual elements and uses that complement the cultural use of the site. The juxtaposition of the Water Treatment site and adjacent Edgerton Park provides an

Figure 3.42 Stages of Site Narrative Vegetated Swale, Meadow Basins, and Pond.

interesting contrast of the **pastoral** forms of historic open space and contemporary value for natural form in cultural landscapes.

The following elements and views engage the user with the integration of cultural and ecological site systems. They also engage the user with connection of the site and its qualities with the landscape beyond the site. These elements are outlined in Figure 3.46.

Element: Industrial Site Sculpture. The sculpture is a relic of the site's industrial history. The placement of this large-scale pipe fitting suggests the long use of the site while also evoking a deconstructed, successional quality (see Figure 3.47).

Element: Bridge over pond. Shown in Figure 3.48, the bridge provides access to the water that otherwise is quite limited due to the extensive traversing of the path along the water channels throughout the site. The bridge is an important opportunity to experience the water as it gains its fullest expression in the open pond.

Element: Benches at summit and pond. Benches, similar to the one pictured in Figure 3.49, serve as a contemplative landscape. Some of these benches placed within the site are lone and are focused on meaningful site and context elements.

Element: Hillside ramp. The path that winds around the hill provides an intimate exposure to the surrounding hillside meadow and water runnel and its grassed surface provides minimal visual interruption.

Element: Diagonal Hedgerows. The rigidity, linearity, and skewed alignment of the diagonal hedgerows calls attention to the highly contrasting patterns of cultural and natural form at play within the site. This creates site complexity and mystery, which engages the user in exploring the connections between nature and culture. These hillside paths and hedgerows can be seen in Figure 3.50.

Element: Water-drop-shaped building. The design and siting of the building in relation to the landscape zones heightens the understanding of the importance of water to the form and function of the larger landscape and offers evidence of the site's infrastructural function.

Figure 3.43 Controlled versus Wild Landscapes.
(Credit: Michael Van Valkenburgh Associates Inc. (left photo))

Figure 3.44 Intimate versus Open Spaces.

Figure 3.45 Historic versus Modern Elements.

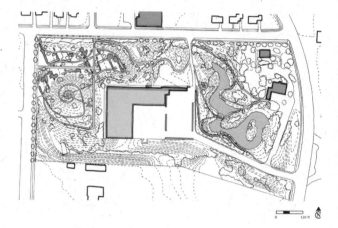

Figure 3.46 Site Engagements.

Figure 3.49 Engagement Element: Bench at Summit.

Figure 3.47 Engagement Element: Industrial Site Sculpture.

Figure 3.48 Engagement Element: Bridge over Pond.

Figure 3.50 Engagement Elements: Hillside Ramp and Diagonal Hedgerows.
(Credit: Michael Van Valkenburgh Associates Inc.)

Figure 3.51 Engagement Element: Pathways.

Element: Integration of Historic Buildings. The spatial and visual integration of historic buildings within the landscape zones define and give character to the sequence of spaces.

Element: Vine wall. A vine wall provides a permeable edge that is both organic and highly structural to separate the public open space from the nonpublic areas of the facility. With its prominent scale and view/watershed integration, it acknowledges the shared uses of the site.

Element: Paths. The series of pathways, shown in Figure 3.51, provide continuous engagement with the landscape and connection to the neighborhood.

View: Hilltop summit. From the summit of the hill one is rewarded with a view of East Rock, a local natural landmark that provided inspiration for the dramatic manmade landform features of the site (see Figure 3.52).

View: Pond. The culmination of the water path into a large, open pond environment engages the user fully in the hydrological emphasis of the site.

Figure 3.52 Engagement Element: Hilltop Summit Regional Topographic Transect.

Outcomes

The Program/Site/Context Comparison

Predesign Site/Context Conditions

The sustainable outcome of a project is determined largely by the design team's approach at the project outset toward three areas of design decision-making: (1) the selection of program goals, (2) the judgments made in the assessment of site character, and (3) the judgments made in the assessment of the context. The relationship of these decisions can be demonstrated via three groups of predesign factors: environmental factors, cultural factors, and social factors.

The view of the predesign relationship between site, context, and program for the Whitney Water Purification Facility project is summarized as follows. This analysis shows that the initial program goals drafted by the client developed largely from conditions within the neighborhood scale. In response to this the landscape architects refined the program to develop specific site responses to these contextual issues.

Postdesign Site/Context Impacts

The site design solution developed by Michael Van Valkenburgh Associates has its most significant sustainable design impact primarily at the site planning level, as opposed to a larger planning level or smaller detail level. While there was significant historic meaning and value to the site, physically speaking, there was little existing site character or resource value to consider in the site planning. As the majority of the site had been covered by lawn and the footprint of the old sand treatment facility, which needed to be removed, there were few existing site features to be retained and protected, aside from the small areas of remnant wetlands (see Figure 3.53). This created a significant opportunity to increase the site's natural and cultural sustainability and bring it into balance with the quality of the surrounding neighborhood and region.

Secondarily, the site design impacted the character and function of the neighborhood by creating a strong functional and visual association between the site and both the Whitney museum and dam complex, as well as its residential neighbors.

	INITIAL PROGRAM GOALS	SITE CHARACTER	CONTEXT CHARACTER
ENVIRONMENTAL FACTORS	Habitat creation	Monoculture of lawn	Well-protected system of of riparian corridors
	Biological stormwater treatment	Sand filtration beds to depth of 15' covering 2/3 of site	Network of intact geological formations and woodland landscape
CULTURAL FACTORS	Site and neighborhood industrial history acknowledgment	Historic barn and dormitory buildings	Rich, intact historic architecture and landscape
	Distinctive site architecture	Historic use of site for water treatment	Architectural distinction
			High concentration of cultural institutions such as museums and universities
SOCIAL FACTORS	Community open space	Unrestricted public access to site	Well-developed public realm
		Open-ended public use	Defined neighborhood structure

Figure 3.53 Predesign versus Postdesign View Toward East Rock. (Credit: Michael Van Valkenburgh Associates Inc.)

Improving Site Sustainability

Site-level sustainability has increased through the creation of new ecological function, human uses, and cultural character that improves on the former monoculture of the lawn. The facility accommodates a water treatment pro-

gram and an open space program in an integrated and seamless manner with the following techniques:

Naturalized landscape: Meadow, wet meadow, woodland, emergent pond edge

Green roof

Biotreatment of stormwater

Permeable surfacing

Multi-use site: Infrastructure and park

Site history reflection

Improving Regional Sustainability

In addition to increasing site-based sustainability, the Whitney Water Purification Facility design solution complements and enhances the high-quality ecological and cultural form and function of its contextual landscape. The design outcome links the site to important contextual resources contained in the rich history of Eli Whitney's local endeavors and artifacts and the striking ecological character and vitality of East Rock Park and the Mill River watershed. In this way the site goes much beyond the requirements of LEED to create sustainability in relation to its neighborhood, community, and bioregion through the following techniques:

Pathway system linkages

Natural vegetation linkages

Cultural character and meaning linkages

Site programming to complement and support adjacent land

Larger ecosystem modeling

	METRO REGION	COMMUNITY	NEIGHBORHOOD	SITE
SUSTAINABILITY IMPACTS				

Sustainability Criteria Met?

The five landscape sustainability criteria developed in Chapter 1 are reviewed in relation to their fulfillment by the Whitney Water Purification Facility project as follows:

Connectivity

The Whitney Water Purification Facility site design:

- links the site to its historic "Whitneyville" context through its industrially innovative form and function.

- connects to its residential neighborhood with quiet, contemplative, and accessible open space.

- replaces a monoculture of lawn with an ecologically rich natural landscape patch that relates to other nearby patches and corridors and models a larger watershed ecosystem.

- connects neighborhood, local, and regional uses through circulation that recognizes key nodes and transitions.

- links the function of the infrastructural use of the site with the open space use of the site.

Meaning

The Whitney Water Purification Facility site design:

- conveys the function and poetics of water and hydrological systems, and the importance of their health to overall environmental quality.

- layers historic and modern built forms to suggest value for both aspects.

- engages the visitor with views to the distant landscape to bring the site into relationship with its context.

- juxtaposes linear geometry with organic geometry to interpret an appropriate coexistence of cultural and natural landscapes.

- provides for contemplative experience and understanding of nature.

Purpose

The Whitney Water Purification Facility site design:

- creates the landscape as a place in its own right and with its own identity, not as screening or land cover as is typically the case with infrastructure-associated landscapes.

- forges a positive spatial relationship with architectural elements, where landscape and architecture are enmeshed with each other and play off each other to become one entity with several distinct zones.

- develops an alternative model for neighborhood park space that contrasts with conventional park landscapes of lawn and exotic plantings.

Efficiency

The Whitney Water Purification Facility site design:

- incurs low installation costs ($5 per square foot) and maintenance costs and inputs through its focus on regenerative plantings as opposed to inert constructed materials, and natural vegetation assemblages as opposed to ornamental assemblages.

- creates landform drama and hydrological movement on a previously disturbed site by utilizing cut material created by infrastructure excavation.

- redevelops the site for upgraded use rather than going to an undeveloped site and leaving this one fallow.

- creates a site that produces biodiversity, habitat, and stormwater processing capability, as opposed to consuming water, chemicals, and energy.

- allows for two uses to be fulfilled within one site— infrastructure and park.

Stewardship

The Whitney Water Purification Facility site design:

- extends the conventional role of public utilities to include active provision, innovative design, and focused management of open space land as part of its infrastructure mission, creating a cooperative partnership with community and neighbors.

- creates a sense of shared responsibility for and ownership of the site among the residential and institutional neighbors, as opposed to a typical adversarial or apathetic attitude toward an infrastructure site.

Parallel Projects
Waterworks Gardens; Renton, Washington, USA

A project comparable to the Whitney Water Purification Plant in its green infrastructure land use type and sustainable characteristics is Waterworks Gardens (shown in Figure 3.54), an environmental artwork built in 1996 within King County's existing East Division Reclamation Plant in Renton, Washington. The park is laced with trails and houses **native plant** communities while natural waterbodies filter and clean stormwater from the treatment plant's 50 acres of paved surface. Waterworks Gardens was designed by environmental artist Lorna Jordan in association with landscape architects Jones and Jones and engineers Brown and Caldwell as a series of garden "rooms." The environmental artwork's paths pass through a series of leaf-shaped ponds, an inlaid mosaic Grotto, and wetlands. After flowing through Waterworks Gardens, the treated stormwater discharges into nearby Springbrook Creek. The collaboration of environmental artist, landscape architect, and engineer is a notable aspect of the project, which resulted in a highly integrated expression of art, infrastructure, and ecology within the site spaces and forms.

Figure 3.54 Parallel Project: Waterworks Gardens. (Credit: Lorna Jordan)

Stormwater Pollution Control Laboratory; Portland, Oregon, USA

A second comparison project is Robert Murase's Portland Stormwater Pollution Control laboratory (see figure 3.55). Opened in 1997, the facility is now a landmark in the St. John's neighborhood of Portland. Once a brownfield, the site combines the important ecological requirement of treating stormwater produced on-site and throughout the neighborhood before it enters the Willamette River. It also functions as a park for public use and education about stewardship of the larger river corridor. Murase created a central pond as a sculptural form, with a curving rock swale leading to the pond that is defined by a striking stone wall. Wetland plantings create wildlife habitat areas, while also treating runoff contaminants before they enter the river. Oil and grease, heavy metals from tires and brake pads, animal waste, and fertilizer as well as chemicals used for lawns and gardens arrive in the pond and settle to the bottom or are treated by microorganisms.

The Water Pollution Control laboratory building, by Miller Hull Partnership architects, with its exposed steel frame skeleton, is well integrated with the landscape. The facility houses a laboratory, educational viewing areas, offices, and multipurpose conference rooms. To enhance a healthy environment, the facility uses operable windows, computerized window shades, and energy-efficient indirect lighting. Materials and colors found throughout the space reflect the strong character of the St. John's Bridge and the surrounding industrial context. Pedestrians can stroll past the laboratory building and its landscape to a section of the Willamette Greenway Trail that connects the lab grounds with neighboring Cathedral Park.

Figure 3.55 Parallel Project: Portland Stormwater Pollution Control Laboratory.
(Credit: Scott Murase)

4 REGIONAL AND SITE ASSESSMENT

What sustainable site design potentials are revealed by the consideration of context?

Sandstone Visitor Center

The virtual world will almost always extend beyond the original site boundaries, since a site depends on its context. The designer is suspicious of limits and yet cannot deal with the universe. Therefore he decides: Where shall my focus be? What shall be its context? How shall they connect? This is often a larger universe than the one first given and thus some tension arises. The design need not harmonize with its context should that be undesirable or ephemeral, but it must take it into account.

—Kevin Lynch

BACKGROUND

Functional and legible sustainable site design relies on the connections forged or maintained between a site and its context. A site may be required to function programmatically on its own due to strictly defined legal boundaries, and, in fact, sustainability is often thought of in terms of site self-reliance—like handling stormwater management on site, for instance. Yet each site is surrounded by a patchwork of others that have an effect simply because of their adjacency. Off-site factors that need to be included in the inventory are points of access, scale, views, uses, soils, hydrology, vegetation, and wildlife systems. Larger-scaled contexts beyond the site's immediate adjacency also influence the site design and, in turn, can be impacted by it. The scales of influence vary from project to project as shown in the six case studies presented in this text. As discussed in Chapter 1, *connectivity* is a critical dimension of sustainability. This chapter offers a list of natural and cultural resource issues to inventory and assess site-to-context connectivity. Leading questions about each issue provide further direction to drive design decision-making. This assessment creates overall designations for sites in relation to their contexts as either *Integrators* or *Pioneers,* and provides related guidelines for sustainable site design.

The ideas of site-to-context relationship in site design borrow from large-scale planning approaches. In the early part of the 20th century, visionary biologist and botanist Sir Patrick Geddes, who experienced Scotland's growth during its industrial era, was convinced that spatial form had social impacts and advocated that *region* be considered in the built environment. His ideas influenced a generation of thinkers and planners who followed, such as Lewis Mumford and Ian McHarg, who further developed the principles of balancing social and ecological factors within their own works. Today, Geddes's sentiment has been refined into a method of responding to resources that span site, town, state, and even country boundaries. Rather than artificial land boundaries driving development decisions, planners throughout the world are using bioregional and geographic character to define planning jurisdictions. This means that instead of the state of Wisconsin addressing the Great Lakes water quality concerns alone, all its bordering states—in the United States as well as in Canada—have joined efforts in their management. Likewise, individual sites contain small parts of broader concerns that often require cooperation and management between several entities. For instance, the site design of the one-acre Paradise Valley Residence in Arizona restored a segment of arroyo as part of larger neighborhood protection efforts. At the very least, the designer must consider these larger systems and address what is possible on the site at hand. Whereas its surrounding development disregards the greater stormwater issues, the Gannett/USA Today site design in Virginia improved not just visual attributes of the neighborhood stormwater pond located on its parcel but the quality and quantity of its outflow into Scott's Run. Cultural concerns also span multiple sites such as at the Whitney Water Purification Facility in Connecticut, which shares a portion of its site with historic barns and outbuildings owned by the neighboring Eli Whitney Museum. Landscape architects as well as planners are reaching across site boundaries to resolve environmental and cultural challenges and maximize opportunities for both in managing existing connections and shared resources.

Another benefit to looking beyond site boundaries is taking advantage of contiguous, congruent site and regional functions to forge new connections and shared resources—a technique also used in large-scale planning. In planning, this idea refers to clustering similar uses such as industrial, commercial, or residential together to function efficiently and to protect against incompatibilities. For site design, adding onto congruent functions means building upon the successes of neighboring intact systems. Fredrick Steiner addresses this in *The Living Landscape* through the inquiries of planner John Raintree, whose work helped create the foundation for sustainable site design theory. "In order to answer questions such as 'how does a system work?' and 'how does one improve site systems?' Raintree suggests that the site designer view the site as part of a larger network of processes. Raintree's approach includes a regional reconnaissance, from which sites are selected for diagnosis and design. That way, design at the site level represents appropriate interventions at the local level" (Steiner 2000). The best example of this from the case study projects is the Sandstone Visitor Center in West Virginia. To begin with, in keeping with the region's vision to maintain and maximize areas of natural scenic beauty, a previously developed site was chosen. Second, the barren site was located within an intact forest—two contrasting conditions. The design team subsequently chose to balance the new development with restored forest. This approach provided a mechanism for defining space—in densely planted tree copses—while using vegetation to facilitate a site stormwater strategy. Taking cues from the surrounding intact forest provided a cohesive vocabulary for the design. Contiguous ecologies such as this are important for wildlife habitat corridors, while continuous buffers maintain cool water temperatures that sustain stream health.

Similarly, the regional Hank Aaron Trail in Milwaukee connects to the Menomonee Valley Industrial Center site, which serves as one leg of the larger bike trail and provides cyclists and pedestrian linkages between towns and recreation areas. Building upon contextual linkages and intact systems within the context broadens landscape uses and brings more ecological function to the site design.

While some project sites contain useful or dramatic features, some are simply leftover areas with little internal function or character to fuel a sustainable use or form. How can each site be developed to draw from and contribute to the larger continuum of exciting, productive, living landscapes? This chapter provides strategies for inventory and assessment of and integrated thinking about site and contextual factors. It is important to distinguish between inventory, which is a non-evaluative accounting of existing conditions, and assessment—an evaluation of these conditions based on reasoned criteria. In this sense, inventory and assessment focus must be intimately connected with the program development process where project goals and criteria are established, as discussed in Chapter 2.

REGIONAL AND SITE ASSESSMENT STRATEGIES

Inventory Systems

Inventory site systems. Inventory both natural and cultural systems to provide the depth and breadth of information relevant to site planning and design decision-making. In contrast to the context, the site needs to be thoroughly and exhaustively inventoried. While a desert site has starkly different qualities than a tropical site, as shown in the parallel issues below, the same inquiries will serve to inform sustainable choices no matter the location.

Inventory regional systems. Site systems know no boundaries and a thorough contextual inventory is critical to informing site processes. It is therefore worth repeating: Inventory both natural and cultural systems to provide the depth and breadth of information relevant to site planning and design decision-making. Here, choosing *what* to inventory is important because not every factor will be relevant to the site. The factors for context may be different but related to those taken into consideration for the site design or the same issue at a larger scale.

Assess Qualities

Assess the stability of site systems. Unstable ecological relationships are out of balance while stable ecosystems are resilient. For example, erosion indicates disturbed soil; volatile invasive plants dominate vulnerable native vegetation; flooding reveals a hydrological system regaining balance. Recognize site system vulnerabilities and seek to balance them.

Assess the maturity of site systems. The designer must ask what values are critical to the site and how site development can improve these values. (Franklin 1997). Maturity is a measure of the long-term value of a factor. The gray-shingled clapboard architecture, for example, characterizes Cape Cod as a long-standing tradition. Mature vegetation has more value than newly planted vegetation. Most of the Northeastern U.S. vegetation "succeeds" (or transitions from one condition to the next) over a period of 80 years or so from grasses, shrub lands, understory woodlands to climax forest. Over time, this natural transitory progression becomes a mature system. Therefore, a lawn (first stage of succession) has much less value than a climax forest (final stage of succession). For building purposes, hardwoods are preferable to softwoods because of their long-term integrity. Assess the value of existing site factors for protection or enhancement by assessing their maturity.

Assess connectivity of site and regional systems. Systems are interdependent and thrive because of their connection with one another. For example, wildlife moves across habitats that range over a number of environmental conditions, such as the spotted salamander, which requires distinctly different habitats—upland woodlands and wetlands—during its life cycle. Disconnection of species habitat causes species decline. Development can impede or enable these connections. Likewise, greenways, pathways, and social corridors are more functional if connected and provide multiple uses and a higher-quality user experience than disconnected places that are difficult to access. Assess opportunities to restore or enable connectivity.

METHODS FOR REGIONAL AND SITE ASSESSMENT

The following is a list of systems to inventory and assess within the site and context. The list serves to (1) determine important factors to inventory both on and around the site, (2) identify critical natural and cultural needs of the larger region, and (3) identify opportunities to mend, improve, restore, and connect the surrounding natural and community systems. When matched with relevant questions below, these issues address parallel concerns that cross site boundaries.

Parallel Issues to Inventory and Assess

Site	Context
Site Hydrologic Cycle	Regional Watershed Issues
Site Vegetation Microclimates	Ecoregion and Vegetation Types
Site Vegetation Type and Maturity	Bioregional Vegetation Succession
Vegetation Associations	Regional Vegetative Communities
Wildlife Microclimates and Corridors	Wildlife Characteristics
Landform	Geologic Formations
Natural Opportunities to Build Upon	Natural Features in Abundance
Environmental Constraints	Natural Features in Decline
Natural Resources	Cultural Heritage
Microclimates	Climate Changes and Trends
Site Uses	Cultural Land Practices
Site Development	Development Practices
Site Infrastructure	Regional Infrastructure
Site History	Historic Growth Patterns
Attitude Toward Site	Attitude Toward Landscape

Below, each of these parallel issues is expanded with examples.

Site Hydrologic Cycle/Regional Watershed Issues

What drives the hydrologic regime at the regional and site scales? Is the site hydrologic regime functional or does a new one need to be manufactured?

Example: The program for the Menomonee Valley Industrial Center was to provide new industry in an economically depressed area within the floodplain of the Menomonee River. The proposal consolidated the stormwater basins of the new development into a 40-acre park. The project also stabilized and restored the site edge along the polluted Menomonee River, providing public access to the river. Requirements by the city, constraints of the site, and understanding of the regional and site hydrology issues were required to create a park that presents stormwater basins as an innovative solution to open space planning.

Site Vegetation Microclimates/Ecoregion and Vegetation Types

What is the quality and value of existing site vegetation? What natural processes are at work in the ecoregion? How are these relevant to site needs?

Example: The Tanner Springs Park planting design references the physical and historical context of the larger Oregon ecoregion. Prior to its 19th century development as a rail yard, the abandoned site was grassland, which the new site design translated into a wildflower and grassy meadow native to Oregon. Also, rather than using a street tree such as the ubiquitous Bradford pear municipalities often insist upon, the design uses the Garry oaks that reference Oregon's vanishing oak-savanna landscape. Without knowledge of the regional vegetation types, this design would not have been as functional or as interesting.

Site Vegetation Type and Maturity/Bioregional Vegetation Succession

How does regional vegetation change naturally over time? Can the site design accommodate this change?

Example: As a distinctive and unusual demonstration aspect of its program, the Sandstone Visitor Center design uses the natural phenomenon of vegetative succession to establish mature woodland that over time will blend with the surrounding forest. While change is inevitable in any landscape, in maintained landscapes succession is normally arrested, not encouraged.

Vegetation Associations/Regional Vegetative Communities

What plants are found growing together in this region and under what ecological conditions? What type of vegetative communities will the site soil and climate conditions support?

Example: Despite its suburban, city's edge location, the Gannett/USA Today Headquarters site design focuses inward, identifying unique zones of vegetation communities appropriate to each location—buffer, pond edge, woodland restoration, rooftop, and so on. Some of these communities were based on regional natural landscape types, but some were tailored to unique cultural conditions such as the rooftop. However, the concept of plant communities borrowed from the natural landscapes is present in all zones.

Wildlife Microclimates and Corridors/Wildlife Characteristics

What kinds of wildlife inhabit the region and under what conditions do they thrive? Does the site provide opportunities for establishing or preserving corridors?

Example: The Whitney Water Purification Facility considered that the site was located along a bird migratory route and provided habitat accordingly. The resulting meadow and wetland landscape emphasizes and integrates these habitat concerns with hydrology concerns of the program.

Landform/Geologic Formations

What natural functions formed the region? Are there landmark landforms to incorporate into the site design? How do the site's slope, elevation, and aspect aid in sustainable goals?

Example: While there is no significant landform on the site itself, the Paradise Valley Residence design oriented site structures to view surrounding landmark landforms to orient the viewer, to expand the garden experience beyond its boundaries, and to reinforce its location within the desert landscape.

Natural Opportunities to Build Upon/Natural Features in Abundance

What natural features are thriving? How can these systems be built upon?

Example: The context surrounding the Sandstone Visitor Center contains miles of intact forest. The design of this formerly fallow site built upon that precedent.

Environmental Constraints/Natural Features in Decline

What natural features are in decline and why? How can these systems be improved?

Example: The existing stormwater basin on the Gannett/USA Today Headquarters site was an inert system. By adding a forebay and buffer plantings, water quality was improved at a critical point in the heavily developed watershed, which sends runoff to the Potomac River and Chesapeake Bay system.

Natural Resources/Cultural Heritage

What natural resources contributed to the development of the region? How are these resources valued or consumed? What is the ecological and social history of the region in relation to these resources?

Example: Coal mining activities in West Virginia are a source of pride, providing 40,000 jobs in a state that produces 15 percent of U.S. coal. The local economy depends on this natural resource as well as on tourists interested in learning about it. The Sandstone Visitor Center, in interpreting the New River watershed information, broadens the story to include critical impacts the region's coal mining history had on the state's settlement patterns.

Microclimates/Climate Changes and Trends

How is development and climate change affecting regional natural systems and cultural attitudes? What are the existing and proposed microclimates on the designed site?

Example: The Phoenix metro area has experienced rapid growth and is troubled by a 30-year drought cycle. Water is a precious resource to be used minimally in the Paradise Valley Residence, where an existing natural arroyo is enhanced and new vegetation consists of hearty natives. In a region of irrigated, lawned neighborhoods, the focal point of the design is a sliver of reflective water that symbolizes its absence from the landscape within this xeriscape.

Site Uses/Cultural Land Practices

What are the predominant land uses in the area and how do they affect development practices and conservation initiatives? What uses will this site provide?

Example: The Whitney Water Purification Facility is located in an architecturally rich historic neighborhood with citizenry who care about the environment and cherish their open space. Prior to the redevelopment of the facility, these neighbors questioned the environmental, visual, and cultural impacts of the proposals and became active in the design assessment, which eventually included a site retrofit, open space, naturalized stormwater system, and high-profile architecture.

Site Development/Development Practices

What initiates development in the region? What factors initiated this site design in particular?

Example: The Menomonee Valley Industrial Center is located in a neighborhood in decline since the railroad industry closed. New development in Milwaukee, and specifically in the Menomonee River Valley, has focused on sustainable development that will first, provide jobs and stimulate the local economy, and second, improve the environment and provide cultural amenities.

Site Infrastructure/Regional Infrastructure

What transportation and infrastructure planning has occurred in the region? Does it serve the site? Could the site design benefit from being connected to the system?

Example: One connection between Tanner Springs Park in Portland's Pearl District to the rest of the city is the integration of a streetcar stop along its edge, made possible by the city's focus on providing multiple public transportation options within the downtown area. The *River District Park System Urban Design Framework* was developed hand-in-hand with the Portland Streetcar System that connects the downtown to the rapidly expanding Pearl District and its open space system.

Site History/Historic Growth Patterns

What is the cultural history of area settlement and how does it affect today's landscape? Where is the site couched within the spectrum of this regional history?

Example: Whitney Reservoir was dammed by Eli Whitney in 1806 to fuel his factories, which spurred growth in the area and then gave rise to the need for a managed water supply facility. This facility, begun by Whitney's son, occupied the site since the turn of the century. Today, at the Whitney Water Purification Facility, a state-of-the-art underground system, that site history is acknowledged with a pipe, its rusting hulk used as a sculpture to reference the site's former use and decommissioned technologies.

Attitude toward Site/Attitude toward Landscape

What is the regional attitude toward the landscape? What might it be to this project in particular?

Example: Portland, Oregon is proactive regarding sustainability in development of the city. This attitude, accepted and promoted by the municipality and the region, spearheads sustainable initiatives such as an urban growth boundary, *Green Streets,* and sustainable parks such as Tanner Springs Park. The site, so close to the city center, lay fallow for many years prior to this redevelopment. It was looked upon as an area of opportunity.

Is the Site Integrator or Pioneer?

Based on the qualities of its *context*, the site can be designated as either a *Sustainable Integrator* or a *Sustainable Pioneer*. If the context is cohesive then the site can *integrate* with, or add to it. If the context is fractured then the site must *pioneer* a sustainable approach. The terms "cohesive" and "fractured" refer to more than just physical connectivity but also overall stability, health, and value. These two designations, pioneer and integrator, provide direction for sustainable site design—in determining program, design development, and potentials for connectivity.

Following is a Context Evaluation Summary for the Sandstone Visitor Center that provides a graphic summary of the overall cohesive or fractured factors in the state of West Virginia, which is the primary scale of influence of this project. The evaluation concludes that the Sandstone Visitor Center site is an ecological *Integrator* because its contextual ecological systems are largely intact. Meanwhile it could be considered a cultural pioneer because the region provides little opportunity for visitors to orient themselves and is void of areas to stop and view the New River.

REGIONAL VEGETATION

Large, Adjacent, Contiguous, Mature Urban Forest

| Cohesive | | Fractured |

REGIONAL HYDROLOGY

Protected National Heritage Watershed

| Cohesive | | Fractured |

REGIONAL GEOLOGY/LANDFORM

Intact, Visually Rich Landforms

| Cohesive | | Fractured |

REGIONAL WILDLIFE HABITAT

Protected Contiguous Forest and River Network

| Cohesive | | Fractured |

REGIONAL HUMAN CONNECTIVITY

Few Roadways through Mountainous Region.
Pedestrian access ways exist only as hiking trails.

| Cohesive | | Fractured |

REGIONAL GATHERING NODES

Few Interpretation Visitor Centers for Tourists
and Interspersed Town Centers

| Cohesive | | Fractured |

REGIONAL HISTORIC REFERENCES

Few outlets for regional historic information dissemination.

| Cohesive | | Fractured |

Designing Integrator Sites

Integrator sites are found within cohesive regions where development practices are sustainable and where a sustainable "green" infrastructure is in place. Specifically, their contexts, or regions, have experienced development planning that took into consideration the preservation of open space, balanced resource use, stability of ecological resources, and a balance of developed versus built areas, and so on. These areas have intact natural and cultural systems and the prevailing attitudes strive toward achieving sustainability in the built environment. There may be an emphasis on either cultural or natural cohesiveness or richness, or there may be a relative balance of the two.

Context	Site Designation
Cohesive ——————————→	Sustainable Integrator

The integrator site design is context-responsive, in equilibrium with its surroundings, and its form is often a reflection of its surroundings. Integrator site designs are carefully crafted to fit within their regional systems. Through site and contextual analysis alongside informed and responsive program development, these projects are unique to one place. In other words with the same program in a different setting they would have been designed to look and function radically differently. These projects often invite negative contextual factors into the site, and the programs attempt to fix and improve them. In general, these projects tend to be collaborative. The designers seek answers to questions such as, "How can the site design best support its own needs as well as the needs of the context?" and "How do we build upon the success of the surrounding development?" An example is the Bloedel Reserve in Seattle, Washington. Within its property boundaries, this complex and beautiful landscape, despite its hard-edged and exotic gardens, is found within a natural, preserved woodland that extends seamlessly outward and blends with the biome of Bainbridge Island. The following list describes the predesign conditions of projects included within this book that represent integrator sites.

Sandstone Visitor Center	A fractured site + a cohesive context = Integrator
Whitney Water Purification Facility	A fractured site + a cohesive context = Integrator
Tanner Springs Park	A fractured site + a cohesive context = Integrator

Integrator Strategies

Successful integrator strategies:

- collaborate with regional entities with the same interests.
- blur site boundaries with ecological strategies or connections to other potentials within the region.
- determine the primary scale of influential context. Ask: "What is the critical context to connect to?" and "What scale of context benefits from connection?"
- improve upon already intact systems in the context such as stormwater/groundwater connections from off-site areas.
- introduce new function, engagement, and sustainable programs for other sites to connect to.
- expand and link to cultural networks such as paths and infrastructure.
- identify weaknesses in regional systems and improve them.
- further expand prevailing regional attitudes toward sustainable development.

Designing Pioneer Sites

Pioneer sites are found in fractured regions with little sustainable "green" infrastructure. These areas tend to have degraded natural systems and the prevailing attitudes toward the built environment lack an understanding or goal of sustainability. These regions are planned (or unplanned) in such a way as to allow ecosystems to be degraded, cultural systems undervalued, and economic systems depleted. The problems of the region may be more specific and focused on one issue or area, as in Milwaukee's Menomonee Valley, or they may be more generally present throughout the entire region, as in the larger metropolitan Phoenix area.

Context	Site Designation
Context	*Site Designation*

Fractured ———————➤ Sustainable Pioneer

Pioneer sites often stand in stark contrast as anomalies independent of their surroundings. Given the same program needs, these projects could be used as a basic framework for projects found anywhere regardless of context. In contrast to the surrounding development, these projects attempt to connect to systems. Often metaphorical connections, rather than physical ones, are created. These projects tend to be spearheaded by a single individual or entity. Pioneer sites focus on preservation, genius loci, and engaging the visitor in site phenomenon. An example of a pioneer site is the Kresge Headquarters in Troy, Michigan, whose small sustainable parcel sits within acres of paved parking lot along a suburban boulevard. The following list describes the predesign conditions of projects included within this book that represent pioneer sites.

Gannett/USA Today Headquarters	A fractured site + a fractured context = Pioneer
Paradise Valley Residence	A cohesive site + a fractured context = Pioneer
Menomonee Valley Industrial Center	A fractured site + a fractured context = Pioneer

Pioneer Strategies

The following are points to consider for successful pioneer strategies.

- When direct contextual connections are absent, make the sustainable connections you can.

- Despite limitations in planning and political spheres, what can you do to take into account the larger picture? How can you be proactive rather than reactive?

- Use the unique character of the site to inspire the design.

- Tap into local economy, ecology, history, culture, and natural phenomenon to make metaphorical site connections to the larger region.

- Revitalize a segment of lost or broken networks within the fractured region.

- Reintroduce forgotten heritage or invisible bioregional character of the area.

- Focus on restoring, creating, and establishing landscape ecologies.

- Make the site the model for new development.

- Inspire prevailing regional attitudes toward sustainable development.

CASE STUDY— SANDSTONE VISITOR CENTER

LOCATION: Sandstone, West Virginia, USA
SITE SIZE: 13 acres
CLIENT: United States National Park Service
DESIGNERS: Landscape Architect—Viridian Landscape Studio
  (formerly Rolf Sauer and Partners), Philadelphia, PA
 Architect—SMP Architects, Philadelphia, PA
 Civil Engineer—H. F. Lenz Company, Pittsburgh, PA
 Ecological Consultant—United States Department of Agriculture,
  Natural Resources Conservation Service
FORMER SITE USES: Quarry, public school, clean highway fill site
LANDSCAPE BUDGET: $2 Million
DATE OF COMPLETION: 2003

(Credit: United States Geological Survey)

Overview

The Sandstone Visitor Center was developed on a former quarry and highway fill site with manufactured slopes and little topsoil. As an example of an integrator site, this project is surrounded by a diverse, healthy, and mature forest that contrasted with the site's damaged, low-value landscape of invasive plants. Chosen in part because of its disturbance, the site was assessed for its potential to regenerate ecological function and reuse. Meanwhile, the context inventory and assessment revealed multiple dimensions of connection, maturity, and value for the purpose of integration into the site program. As a result, the design outcome had effects on the state, region, and community scales. The strategy to integrate this 13-acre site both ecologically and visually with the adjacent landscape was to reconnect its forested surroundings by planting a series of successional landscapes such as meadows, old fields, and copse woodlands. To integrate cultural elements the design introduced meaningful materials, signage, and form into the project such as boulder seating that referenced the site's former use as a quarry and interpretive programming that included regional cultural history.

Project Inception

This project came about as a part of two key economic development and preservation projects, the National Coal Heritage Area and the Coalfields Expressway Project. The New River Gorge National River, also a federal project, encompasses 70,000 acres along the New River and was established in 1978 to preserve, protect, and provide recreational access to the river corridor.

This remote region of southern West Virginia (seen in Figure 4.1) is characterized by its rugged hills, deep river gorge and flowing whitewater, and small communities developed around the area's coal mining heritage. Located at a strategic intersection of the southern end of the park and at the beginning of a major interstate highway built in the 1980s, the Sandstone Visitor Center site was considered a good opportunity to develop interpretive education for the region and the park. The plan is shown in Figure 4.2. With 50 miles of river, the area already had several

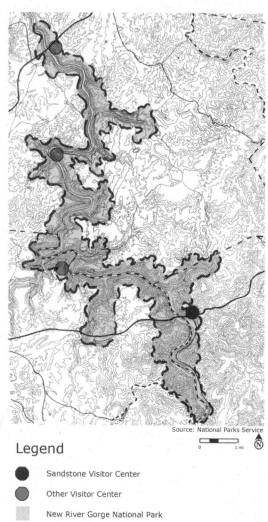

Source: National Parks Service

Legend

● Sandstone Visitor Center

● Other Visitor Center

New River Gorge National Park

Figure 4.2 New River Gorge National Park.

existing visitor centers at its central and northern reaches and the planned continuation of the interstate highway (the Coalfields Expressway) at the southern tip of the park presented an opportunity and need for another one.

The National Park Service's Sustainable Design Principles were used as a driving force for the development of this interpretive visitor center. The site selected for the project was a derelict property that had previously been used as a sandstone quarry and a school. The goal for the project

Figure 4.1 Sandstone West Virginia along the New River.

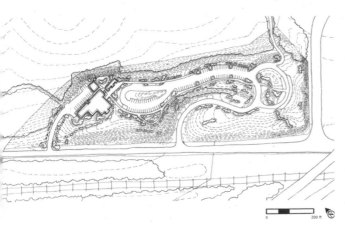

Figure 4.3 Sandstone Visitor Center Site Plan.

was to integrate the interpretive and functional aspects of the facility with the restoration of ecological function and identity of the site to reflect the larger ecosystem and watershed of the park landscape.

Figure 4.4 Inspiration. Surrounding wooded hillside landscapes of this portion of West Virginia served as inspiration for site restoration.

Design Concept

As the "southern gateway" to New River Gorge National River area, the visitor center building, conceived as a watershed education center for local schoolchildren and tourists, also was to serve as a rest area to orient visitors within the larger National River area. Cultural elements of the site and region would be showcased alongside watershed education programs both indoors and out. The basic elements of the program (shown in the site plan of Figure 4.3) were a sustainable site with a visitor center building, restroom building, parking for buses, RVs, and cars, and picnic areas.

Project Philosophies and Approach

The initial program goals for the project were determined by the National Park Service as well as others involved with the improvement of the local and regional Sandstone area. Then, as the design process unfolded, the design team further refined these goals.

The client and landscape architect's philosophies are critical in forming a site design's sustainable outcomes. The wooded hillside landscapes in Figure 4.4 served as inspiration for the design team. On this project, both the client and land-

scape architect shared a vision for sustainable design with this inspiration at the fore. With this approach in common from the onset, the design team intuitively assessed the site and context along many dimensions in order to understand the site's full potential for sustainability. The result was a forward-thinking integrated design process.

Several years ago, the client—the National Park Service—laid out guidelines that provided a sustainable framework for new development projects and with this focus, sought firms with working knowledge and experience with sustainability. These guidelines helped ensure, through innovation, broad collaboration, and experimentation that new development reached beyond conventional practices. On this particular project, the client was very in tune with the conditions of the site and context. Few sites were considered for this new visitor center because in this region of relative intact landscapes, the client team sought a site that had already been built upon—and those were few. The team pursued Leadership in Energy and Environmental Design (LEED) certification, allowing both the landscape and architecture to be visioned together, which helped both guide the design process and foster team coordination.

National Park Service: Guiding Principles of Sustainable Design

These Sustainable Guidelines outlined by the National Park Service serve as policy guidelines in site design for developed areas of national parklands and challenge the design of conventional tourism development.

Recognition of context. No site can be understood and evaluated without looking outward to the site context. Before planning and designing a project, fundamental questions must be asked in light of its impact on the larger community.

Treatment of landscapes as interdependent and interconnected. Conventional development often increases fragmentation of the landscape. The small remaining islands of natural landscape are typically surrounded by a fabric of development that diminishes their ability to support a variety of plant communities and habitats. This situation must be reversed. Larger whole systems must be created by reconnecting fragmented landscapes and establishing contiguous networks with other natural systems both within a site and beyond its boundaries.

Integration of the native landscape with development. Even the most developed landscapes, where every trace of nature seems to have been obliterated, are not self-contained. These areas should be redesigned to support some component of the natural landscape to provide critical connections to adjacent habitats.

Promotion of biodiversity. The environment is experiencing extinction of both plant and animal species. Sustaining even a fraction of the diversity known today will be very difficult. Development itself affords a tremendous opportunity to emphasize the establishment of biodiversity on a site. Site design must be directed to protect local plant and animal communities, and new landscape plantings must deliberately reestablish diverse natural habitats in organic patterns that reflect the processes of the site.

Reuse of already disturbed areas. Despite the declining availability of relatively unspoiled land and the wasteful way sites are conventionally developed, existing built areas are being abandoned and new development located on remaining rural and natural areas. This cycle must be reversed. Previously disturbed areas must be reinhabited and restored, especially urban landscapes.

Making a habit of restoration. Where the landscape fabric is damaged, it must be repaired and/or restored. As most of the ecosystems are increasingly disturbed, every development project should have a restoration component. When site disturbance is uncontrolled, ecological deterioration accelerates, and natural systems diminish in diversity and complexity. Effective restoration requires recognition of the interdependence of all site factors and must include repair of all site systems—soil, water, vegetation, and wildlife.

(National Park Service)

LEED for New Construction Site Design Checklist

Leadership in Energy and Environmental Design checklists are used to identify specific quantifiable planning and development techniques that contribute to sustainable design. Shown in bold are specific points that were considered in the design of the Sandstone Visitor Center landscape.

Alternative transportation; low-emitting and fuel-efficient vehicles

Construction activity; pollution prevention

Site selection

Development density and community connectivity

Brownfield redevelopment

Alternative transportation; public transportation

Alternative transportation; bicycle storage and changing rooms

Alternative transportation; parking capacity

Site development; protect or restore habitat

Site development; maximize open space

Stormwater design; quantity control

Stormwater design, quality control	Innovative wastewater technologies
Heat island effect, nonroof	Water use reduction, 20 percent reduction
Heat island effect, roof	Water use reduction, 30 percent reduction
Light pollution reduction	Innovation in design
Water efficient landscaping, reduce by 50 percent	Regional materials
Water efficient landscaping, no potable use or no irrigation	*(USGBC)*

The landscape architect Viridian Landscape Studio, then called Rolf Sauer and Partners, was hired as part of a design team for an indefinite quantities contract with the National Park Service. The firm's focus of sustainable design, ecological restoration, and environmental education aligned with the client's vision for the site. Collaboration between architects, engineers, and local scientific experts is a key ingredient in the success of their work. Starting with an understanding of the local biome, Viridian Landscape Studio identified and tapped local experts to supplement their knowledge of regional plant **ecotypes**. The design process for this project was far from autocratic where close collaboration between the landscape architects, the USDA, local botanists, and local and regional plant growers helped to decipher and develop a complex restoration process. The design programming was refined well into the construction documentation phase to ensure that all scales of design, from the overarching program goals of education and restoration to the details of material and plant communities, were additive to the project intent.

Program Type and Development Trend

Program Type: Interpretive Visitor Center

Conventional site design for visitor centers has been dominated in the past by circulation and other utilitarian concerns. Beyond locating trailheads for park hiking access, interpretive opportunities of such facilities have typically been realized through architectural program elements, where building design and indoor displays represent the outdoor environment. It is only in the last few decades that approaches to visitor center site design have embraced the notion that the visitor center site itself presents rich possibilities for integrating interpretation, circulation, and other programmatic needs such as ecological restoration or stormwater management with the programming and management of the greater landscape of the parks and landscapes they serve.

Development Trend: Regenerative-Based Site Selection

Traditionally park visitor centers have been developed on sites with a spectacular view or point of interest representing the larger landscape. As such, the location is driven by a single "hot spot" within the park. More recently, choosing degraded sites rather than building on greenfields has been seen as an opportunity that goes beyond cost savings for new infrastructure. These brownfields, or previously disturbed sites, are opportunities to dovetail sustainable building practices and site interpretation with regenerative design and environmental education goals. Sustainable development embraces the mending or restoration of disturbed sites and the preservation of pristine sites. The site selection process for visitor centers has shifted to consider the opportunities for degraded site reuse and restoration as a compelling rationale for siting and interpretive development that conveys a value for stewardship. An example of this trend is the Pinecote Pavilion, the restoration-focused visitor center and site at the Crosby Arboretum in Picayune, Mississippi.

Context

The regional context of the Sandstone Visitor Center is shown in a sequence of scales in Figures 4.5 through 4.9. Through regional context analysis, the site design process is infused with an understanding of potentials and challenges. It situates the site relative to area history, regional attitudes, and ecological health. Descriptions of landscape form, function, and philosophy of this area of West Virginia explore a setting and combination of sustainable factors to which the project design uniquely responds.

Regional Form

Natural Patterns

Nearly the entire state of West Virginia is traversed by the Appalachian Mountains, which stretch from New England to the southern states of Alabama and Georgia, as depicted in the shaded area of Figure 4.10. The New River Gorge is located on the western edge of this vast mountain chain, in the section known as the Appalachian Plateau, which is a series of dissected plateaus formed by uplifting and the

Figure 4.5   Sandstone Visitor Center—National Context.

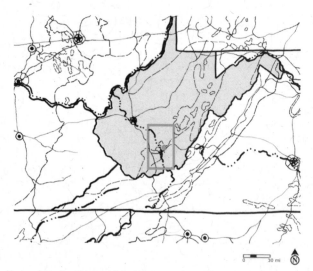

Figure 4.6   Sandstone Visitor Center—State Context.

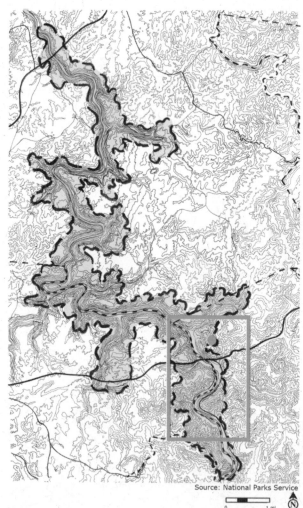

Source: National Parks Service

Figure 4.7   Sandstone Visitor Center—New River Gorge Park Context.

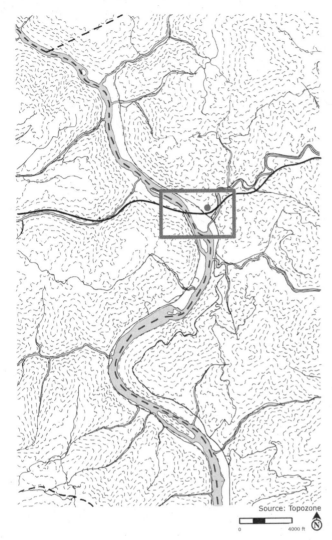

Figure 4.8 Sandstone Visitor Center—Local Context.

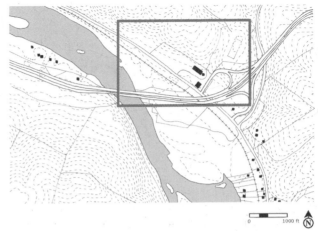

Figure 4.9 Sandstone Visitor Center—Neighborhood Context.

severe erosion that creates dramatic topography. This area of West Virginia is a landscape filled with an expanse of intimate valleys between uniform hill formations, as can be seen in Figure 4.11.

The New River Gorge cuts through the Appalachian Plateau, and exposes 3,200 feet of geological formation, much of which is sandstone and shale. As the gorge formed, the river exposed thick coal-bearing veins. Much of the New River Gorge National River area (though not the project site itself) lies within the New River Coalfield, one of seven major coal fields in southern West Virginia. The site location in relation to its surrounding coal heritage can be seen in Figure 4.12. Despite regional mining activity, the landform and soils are generally intact due to the well-connected matrix of vegetation and lack of other forms of intensive human development.

As the park name suggests, a central feature of the regional landscape and the force that created the gorge is the New River. Ironically, the New River is thought to be one of the oldest rivers in North America, belonging to the ancient Teays River system, which crossed the area prior to the ice age that wiped it away. Estimates suggest that the New River has been in its present course for at least 65 million years, making it second only to the Nile River in age. An indication of its age is that it flows across the Appalachian Plateau, not around or from it as do other waterways (see Figure 4.13). This suggests that the river was there before the Appalachians—which are themselves over a billion years old (National Park Service). The New River derived its name from early explorers who used rivers as corridors for travel and exploration of the New World. Prior to finding the New River, all waterways led them back to the Atlantic coast. Finally, the discovery of a "new" river led the explorers westward toward the Mississippi River. This route had been used by Native Americans prior to European settlement, and then became an important transport corridor aiding in the early settlement of the interior of the United States (Covington 2005).

Legend

▣ Appalachian Plateau
▤ Appalachian Valley & Ridge
▦ Blue Ridge Mountains

Figure 4.10 Appalachian Mountain Zones.

The New River's headwaters originate in North Carolina. As the river flows northward through southern West Virginia, it encounters the higher mountain ranges of the Appalachians, which attracts whitewater rafters, canoeists, and kayakers to the ancient gorge. North of the gorge, the New River joins the Gauley River, forming the Kanawha River, a tributary of the Ohio River that flows into the Mississippi. The watershed of the New River is divided into three subwatersheds formed by two dams in Virginia and West Virginia. The Sandstone Visitor Center site is located in the lower New River Watershed, shown in Figure 4.14. Though mining operations have affected nearby areas, this portion of the watershed has been largely protected due to its National River status.

The project area lies in the National Forest Service vegetation classification system's Appalachian Plateau area of the Eastern Broadleaf Forest Province. Mixed **mesophytic** vegetation, the province forest type with the greatest diversity

Figure 4.11 Elevation along the New River. The "mountains" of New River Gorge are actually dissected plateau formations as seen in the elevation diagram and photo of hills of equal height rather than hierarchical peaks of true mountains.

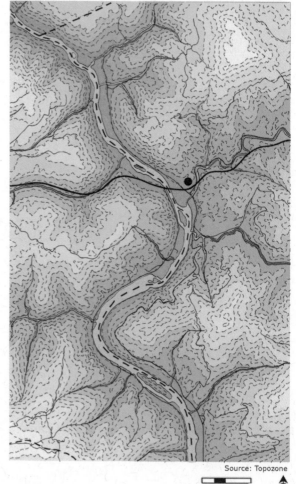

Source: Topozone

0   4000 ft

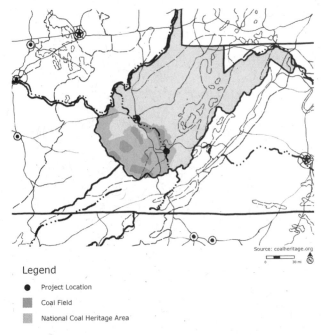

Legend

● Project Location

▮ Coal Field

▮ National Coal Heritage Area

Figure 4.12 National Coal Heritage Area.

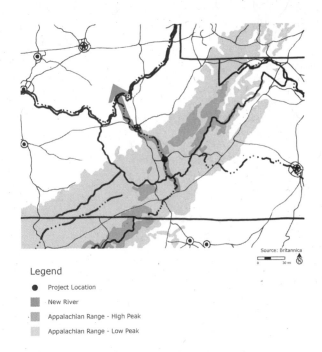

Legend

● Project Location

▮ New River

▮ Appalachian Range - High Peak

▮ Appalachian Range - Low Peak

Figure 4.13 The New River flows northwest across the Appalachians.

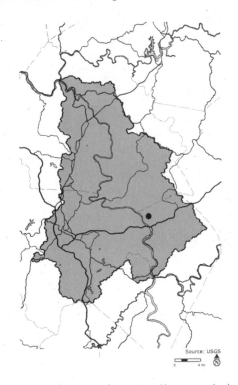

Figure 4.14 Project location in lower New River watershed.

in the United States, occupies moist, well-drained areas in the Appalachian Plateaus. Widespread dominants include American beech, tulip tree, basswood, sugar maple, buckeye, red oak, white oak, and eastern hemlock, in addition to two dozen other species. Figures 4.15 and 4.16 show areas where this vegetation classification occurs.

Recognized forest types in the New River Gorge River area are oak-hickory, mixed oak, oak-maple, oak-yellow pine, hemlock-hardwoods, northern hardwoods, cove hardwoods, and bottomland and floodplain hardwoods. The plateau contains some of the largest stretches of contiguous forest in the eastern United States and New River Gorge lies in the heart of the largest remaining unfragmented mid-latitude forest in the world (National Park Service).

Development Patterns

As the previous natural pattern description suggests, the predominant **landscape matrix** of the region is one of undeveloped forest. Therefore, in contrast to the strong

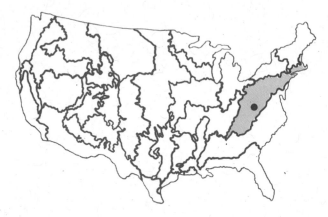

Figure 4.15   U.S. Natural Regions.

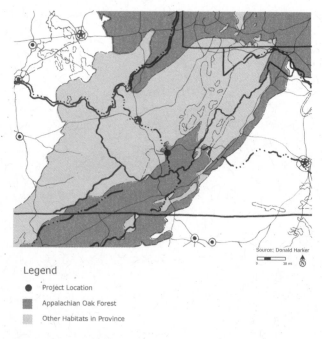

Legend

● Project Location

■ Appalachian Oak Forest

□ Other Habitats in Province

Figure 4.16   Appalachian Oak Forest.

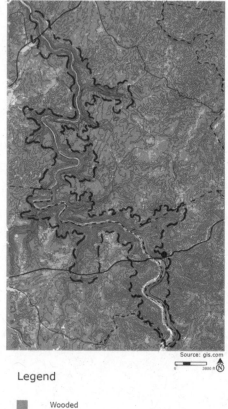

Legend

■ Wooded

■ Open Grassland/Cultivated Land

□ Developed

Figure 4.17   Regional Development Pattern. Largely forested, the region has isolated pockets of development located in valleys.

Regional and Site Assessment

Figure 4.18 Mountain-top Removal Mining. Advocates defend this practice as safer than underground mining and laud it as a way to create flat ground for development. (Credit: Vivian Stockman)

and intact natural landscape forms that characterize the region, the developed landscape has little presence, as can be seen in Figure 4.17. Historic development of the area began with agricultural activity in the early 1800s but soon was overtaken by the growth of mining operations spurred by the region's rich coal deposits and the nation's growing demand for fuel. Originally, the coalfields were mined primarily through underground operations but in the last 30 years practices have gravitated toward surface or mountain-top mining operations (see Figure 4.18). While both types of mines pose environmental problems, surface mining is highly visible in the landscape. Proponents of the practice point out that it creates cleared sites for other types of needed development, while opponents decry the ecological and scenic degradation that can result.

A rural pattern of development in the area has resulted in small patches of individual homestead and farm sites or clusters of sites located in unincorporated county areas rather than within town or city limits. Small village areas, such as the village of Sandstone, where the visitor center is located, developed as outposts for the mining and agricultural activities that brought settlers. However, as mining activity curtailed in the area, these villages have remained small or have even decreased in size. The community of Sandstone was first settled by the Richmond family, for which it was originally named, in the early 1800s. It began to boom at the beginning of the 20th century when a railroad was built along the river, providing important access for the agricultural, timber, stone quarry, and coal mining operations of the region. Although now little more than a highway off-ramp, a gas station, and several residences, Sandstone's former rail station activity had spawned a thriving commercial center and a population that supported its own school.

An important element of the landscape that provides an interesting cultural thread throughout the region is the system of rails, roads, and bridges that access this mountainous terrain. The Chesapeake and Ohio Railway was the first circulation route that entered the remote region in the early 1900s and, as shown in Figure 4.19, it hugs the layout of the river, closely following the eastern side and then both sides of the river in the northern reaches of the park. This railway now functions as a passenger rail line that provides an efficient and scenic mode of travel to the area. The forms of roads and railways provide distinctive elements as they traverse across slopes and the river, creating breathtaking overlooks and dramatic slope cuts, which often reveal geological stone formations. The New River Gorge Bridge, shown in Figure 4.20, is an engineering and transportation marvel that spans the New River over 800 feet above.

Figure 4.19 Roads, River, and Rail.

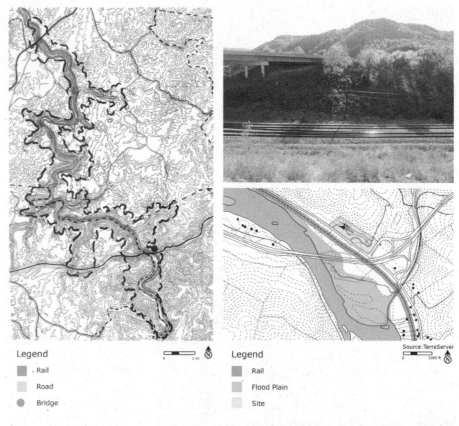

Legend

■ Rail
■ Road
● Bridge

Legend

■ Rail
■ Flood Plain
□ Site

Source: TerraServer

Figure 4.20 The New River Gorge Bridge. The highest vehicular bridge in the Americas, the New River Bridge rises over 800 feet above the river, allowing for spectacular views. (Credit: National Park Service)

Regional and Site Assessment

Regional Function

Natural Systems

The intact vegetative, hydrological, and landform systems of the New River Gorge area function as a rich and unfragmented habitat. The area supports the most diverse plant assemblage of any river gorge in the central and southern Appalachians and includes riparian areas, mixed hardwood forests, old fields, and high cliffs that provide for an array of bird habitats.

This gorge serves as a migration corridor, allowing wildlife and plant species more commonly found to the north or south to extend their ranges. This protected area has been used to reintroduce Peregrine falcon through special state-sponsored programs. There are also several **endemic species** that have become isolated from their populations by the steep rugged terrain and tumultuous rapids and waterfalls. Thus isolated, these animals evolved and adapted to the unique circumstances of New River Gorge. The cerulean warbler (*Dendroica cerulea*) makes its home here while in decline elsewhere within its range. Likewise, the area contains unique vegetative communities not found elsewhere such as the Appalachian Flatrock plant community that includes sedges, cedars, and pines and a rare Rim Rock Pine species. The New River itself is home to many species of freshwater game fish including bass, trout, walleye, carp, and channel catfish, several of which are also endemic to this region.

Human Systems

Coal mining, the major industry in the region for over a century, declined when oil replaced coal as a major fuel source. Concern over the environmental effects of mining and burning coal has risen, prices have fallen, and the more easily accessible coal deposits have become exhausted. While coal extraction still takes place in the United States, this activity is shifting away from the Appalachian and Illinois coal regions to the Rocky Mountain and Gulf Coast states (Milici 2006). These declines have left abandoned mines and slope instability high-priority issues in West Virginia. While coal mining has left environmental side effects such as acid mine drainage, the mining heritage is largely viewed as a source of livelihood, pride, and historic significance that is celebrated in the region.

More recently, use of the regional landscape has been focused on recreation and tourism. The New River falls 750 feet within 50 miles, which makes canoeing, kayaking, and whitewater rafting a primary attraction to the area. Some of the finest fishing in the state attracts anglers to its banks, while miles of trail segments bring hikers to scenic gorge vistas, forests, stone cliffs, and cultural sites such as historic coal mines and railroads. These activities provide an attractive combination of recreation and tourism for over one million tourists per year.

Regional Philosophy

Conservation versus Development

The ecological richness and the shift toward a recreation and tourism economy have encouraged a strong ethic and practice of conservation within the region. An important catalyst for this attitude was the 1978 designation of the New River as a National River. At present there are a total of five national rivers in the United States, as designated by the National Park Service (NPS). While the NPS nomenclature can be confusing—some are called national river and recreation areas, others are national scenic riverways, and still others are called wild rivers—this one is designated the New River Gorge National River. This designation includes protection of two of its tributaries, the Bluestone and the Gauley rivers. The area of land included alongside the rivers encompasses a mosaic of public and private properties, as well as both wilderness and historic areas. Through the NPS's management assistance, the area is promoted for recreational and interpretive use and managed for ecological health. The NPS works with local stakeholders and stewards to monitor and manage the river and recreation areas through management and master plan efforts.

In addition to its status with the National Park Service, the New River is one of only 14 rivers nationwide designated as an American Heritage River by the Environmental Protection Agency (EPA). This designation is intended to further three objectives: natural resource and environmental protection, economic development, and cultural and historic preservation. Rivers are selected for this designation according to the following criteria:

The characteristics of the natural, economic, agricultural, scenic, historic, cultural, or recreational resources of the river that render it distinctive or unique;

The effectiveness with which the community has defined its plan of action and the extent to which the plan addresses all three American Heritage Rivers objectives;

The strength and diversity of community support for the nomination of elected officials, landowners, private citizens, businesses, and state and local government;

Willingness and capability of the community to forge partnerships and agreements to implement their plan to meet their goals and objectives.

(EPA)

Although West Virginia's economy had shown improvement during the boom of the late 1990s and early 2000s, the southern portion of the state has had particular difficulty rebounding from the partial decommissioning of coal mining activities. Decline of the industry has led to heavy job and population losses. This is dramatically illustrated in recent census data showing the average household income to be under $15,000 with the average house value below $40,000.

Through the combined impact of the national programs and local grassroots efforts, the region has diversified its economic development options. The Coalfields Expressway project funded tourism development projects including the Sandstone Visitor Center. This highway project will provide easier commuting of the local population to areas with greater job opportunities. Eventually it will connect to the portion of Route 64 to provide an east-west transportation corridor linking southern West Virginia and Virginia and providing tourist access for populations in the metropolitan areas of Washington, D.C., Nashville, Cleveland, and Raleigh.

Cultural Resources

The coal-mining heritage, embodied by hardworking, resilient, and close-knit communities, is a source of regional pride and historic interest. West Virginia's National Coal Heritage Area is one of 22 Congress-designated geographic areas where natural, cultural, historic, and recreational resources combine to form a cohesive, nationally distinctive landscape arising from patterns of human activity shaped by geography. This designation is an effort to combine public and private partnerships—in this case the National Park Service and the state of West Virginia—rather than relying on assigning federally owned parkland. These areas help define and promote local identity and ownership and tell important stories uniquely representative of the national experience through both the physical features that remain and the traditions that have evolved within them. Federal financial assistance provides seed money for staffing, and leverages other money from state, local, and private sources (NPS). The Coal Heritage Area Strategic Plan, produced by the state, included a recommendation for the development of the Sandstone Visitor Center as one of its primary interpretive facilities.

In coordination with the National Heritage Area, the Coal Heritage Trail is a **national scenic by-way** that has been designated to the southeast of the Visitor's Center site to create a corridor that connects sites of historic interest such as a rail yards, country stores, county courthouses, historic village districts, and exhibition mines.

Regional Setting for Integrator Site

As an example of a setting for a *sustainable integrator*, the Sandstone Visitor Center regional context exhibits several dimensions of sustainability. It is located in a region where the landscape matrix is largely natural, intact, and unfragmented by extensive development. The numerous federal designations of regional landscapes as places of cultural and natural significance are strong evidence of environmental health and dedication to its stewardship. While the natural landscape has been impacted by mining activities, the shift toward economic development opportunities focused on tourism and landscape interpretation serves to protect and improve the region's outstanding scenic, recreational, and cultural resources.

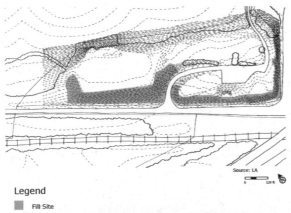

Legend

■ Fill Site

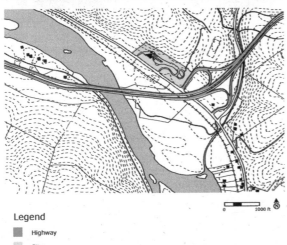

Legend

■ Highway
■ Site

Figure 4.21 Areas of Highway Fill. Mountainside cuts for highway construction reveal area geology adjacent to project and are the source of construction dumping on site.

Site

Design Considerations

Existing Site

The disturbed predesign condition of the Sandstone Visitor Center site was distinctive in relation to its pristine surroundings. Located within the New River Gorge National River in the small, unincorporated community of Sandstone, West Virginia, this 13-acre property was poor in ecological health but rich in local history. Previously owned by the Richmond family, the property had been quarried for sandstone in the late 1800s. This sandstone quarry, the source of the town name, is said to have contributed stone to the interior walls of the Washington Monument in Washington, D.C. Later, the Richmond family lent the site specifically for educational use for the building of the Sandstone High School. When local school consolidations forced the closing of the school, the building was abandoned and later demolished in 1999. The site was then used for the deposition of clean fill from the adjacent construction of Route 64 (as seen in Figure 4.21), further adding to its scarred form and lack of ecological function or cultural memory.

When the National Park Service planned this welcome center for the New River area, this property was selected because of its location and because, in comparison with other potential sites, it was already disturbed by former development, quarrying, and highway dumping. As before, the Richmond family, still interested in using the site for educational purposes, donated the property to the National Park Service, which identified watershed education as a key component of the new development.

The previous use of the site as a dumping ground for rubble from the nearby highway construction left nearly one-fourth of the site degraded and invasive plant-riddled. As shown in Figure 4.22, steep, man-made slopes and the graded former school site, provided an already existing plateau ready for new development. A shared access road to the local cemetery and an historic exposed quarry face were relics remaining from its past.

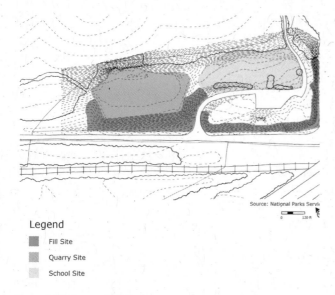

0   120 ft

Legend

■ Fill Site

▨ Quarry Site

░ School Site

Figure 4.22 Former Site Uses.

Figure 4.23 Indoor and Outdoor Exhibits.
(Credit: Viridian Landscape Studio LLC (bottom photo))

Program Development

The design of the Sandstone Visitor Center site, unlike conventional approaches, focused on achieving a balance between maximizing cultural amenities and mending the ecological impact of new and former site development. While basic site planning occurred in the initial design phases, development of two important design elements occurred later in the process. First, within the basic premise of landscape change, techniques were developed to repair and re-purpose the fallow, formerly developed site. This was done through vegetation regeneration. Second, cultural and educational factors were incorporated into all levels of the design outcome, from "active exhibits" both indoors and out to "landscape-based interpretative exhibits" such as building orientation. Examples of these exhibits are shown in Figure 4.23.

A central tenet of the landscape program, developed by the landscape architects, was to manage areas of the newly vegetated landscape to succeed (or change) over time into areas of forest. On this formerly barren site devoid of significant vegetation, areas of grassland are planted with thick woody **copses** maintained to develop into woodland. Other areas are established and main-

tained as meadow, and still other areas constitute a middle ground—areas in **arrested succession** such as old fields with tree groves. Site hydrology largely dictates two planting zones—dry areas established as grasslands and intermittently wet areas established with trees, shrubs, and perennials. These two patterns, a combination of stormwater flow and vegetation, form the core of the site's **green infrastructure**. Stormwater is managed at the source in sunken parking lot planting islands, along building facades, and along entry drives in swales. Site hydrology is addressed, not as a linear **landscape narrative,** as in the

Whitney Water Purification Plant in Connecticut or Tanner Springs Park in Oregon, both of which have minimal stormwater runoff areas, but as functional hydrologic systems that manage runoff as well as serve as points of engagement and focus in the landscape.

While intensive cultural interpretation of the region occurs primarily indoors through exhibits, the site landscape also provides clues to historic and cultural identity. Use of local stone and the reuse of the quarry area as a gathering space were introduced by the design team as a nod toward the site and the region's former uses. Signage, used sparingly, interprets the landscape design in multiple ways; individual plants are labeled, natural processes are called out, and "not to mow" meadow areas are delineated with signage. For the most part, these ideas were developed and incorporated quite far along in the design development and construction documentation phases.

The scales of sustainable planning and design that influenced the Sandstone Visitor Center design were **regional planning** and **site planning**. This means that the economic and environmental needs of the region as well as the degraded site conditions were the driving forces behind program decision-making. It is at these two scales where inspiration was derived and where the site design is most successful.

As mentioned, several statewide regional planning initiatives in West Virginia started this project, namely the National Coal Heritage Area, the Coalfields Expressway, and The New River Gorge National River. The broad needs of the region were manifold and largely dictated the project location, site amenities, and educational focus of the site design. The site's location in a sparsely populated area with few park service amenities was in need of economic incentives to boost the tourist industry and improve opportunities not just in the town of Sandstone but also within the larger region.

Meanwhile, site-planning opportunities were dictated largely by previous development of the property. With few intact resources for protection, the site's natural systems—its soils, slopes, vegetation, and hydrologic systems—needed restoration or improvement. New site damage could be minimized by developing previously used portions of the site. By reusing the existing entry drive, for example, the need for regrading the steep slopes along the site was spared.

As an extension of site planning influences, site design and detail design became influential in the final program configuration.

	REGIONAL PLANNING	DISTRICT PLANNING	SITE PLANNING	SITE DESIGN	DETAIL DESIGN
SCALES OF PROGRAM FOCUS					

A Conventional Visitor Center Design

Canyon Rim Visitor Center, Fayetteville, West Virginia, USA

The distinction between a conventional and a sustainable site design varies in program, design philosophy, and the form and function of the design outcome. Visitor center landscapes have typically been under-designed and have focused on indoor exhibits—largely ignoring the potentials of the landscape to carry through exhibit themes or contribute as ecological or cultural places of their own.

Most visitor destinations within the New River Gorge National River are located near spectacular views and thus the primary design focus of these destinations is to accommodate large volumes of visitors. Canyon Rim Visitor Center, pictured in Figure 4.24, is one such destination, located at the New River Gorge Bridge. This visitor center is the northern equivalent to the southerly-located Sandstone Visitor Center. Canyon Rim Visitor Center offers boardwalks to observation decks, loop trails, as well as indoor exhibits describing the area's history, industry, and recreation. As a former state park turned over to the National Park Service, Canyon Rim Visitor Center consists of conventional visitor center elements; the dominant landscape forms are parking lot and roadways, mown lawn, and wide pathways with benches. While the architecture uses local stone materials to blend with the geology of the sandstone ledge of the area, the landscape is designed and maintained as a static, ornamental backdrop for access to views and the building.

Figure 4.24 A Conventional Visitor Center. The Canyon Rim Visitor Center in Fayetteville, West Virginia.
(Credit: National Park Service)

The Canyon Rim Visitor Center has a similar regional character and basic site program as the Sandstone Visitor Center. The outcome of the former, however, is very different. Perhaps partially due to the size of the facility and the large crowds it must accommodate, the Canyon Rim Visitor Center landscape design largely serves parking and access needs while missing the opportunity to interpret, engage, or serve a broader purpose within the site and region. While there was consideration of regional needs in the project's location, what were not considered in the design program goals were sustainable potentials and development of identity of the site itself. The site landscape feels underutilized and barren and is inconsequential to the reason people visit.

Figure 4.25 Neighborhood Transect.

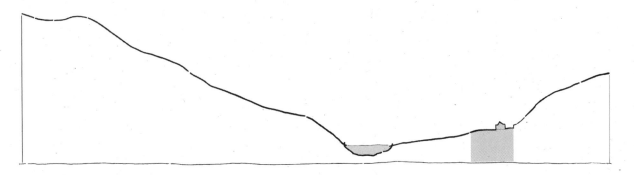

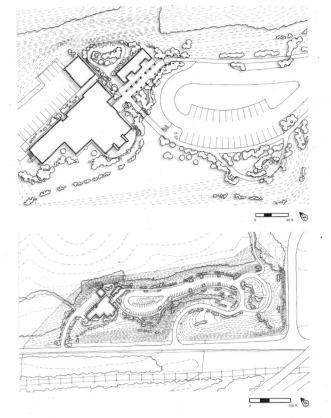

Figure 4.26 The Site Plan.

Figure 4.27 Site Plan Enlargement.

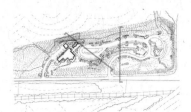

Figure 4.28 Site Sections.

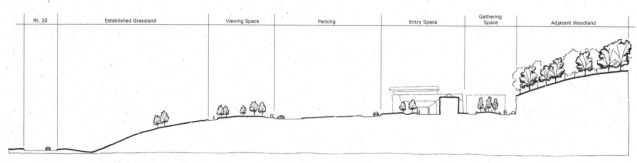

| Rt. 20 | Established Grassland | Viewing Space | Parking | Entry Space | Gathering Space | Adjacent Woodland |

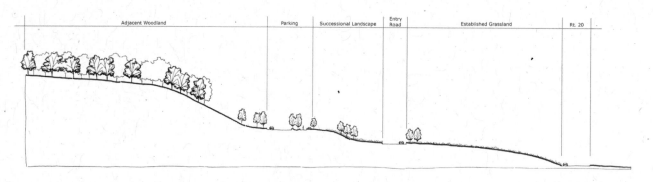

| Adjacent Woodland | Parking | Successional Landscape | Entry Road | Established Grassland | Rt. 20 |

Figure 4.29 Site Detail.

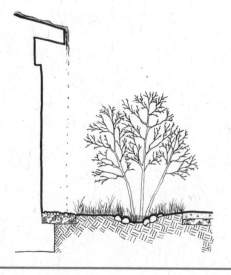

Regional and Site Assessment

Site Design Form

Patterns

The Sandstone Visitor Center design outcome—beginning with the site plan, plan enlargements, sections, and a site detail—are shown in Figures 4.25 through 4.29. The project is analyzed with respect to two central dimensions of sustainable site design process and outcomes: landscape form and landscape function.

A virtual clean slate for development, the predesign site provided open views and no spatial definition. To create spatial drama and interest, the site layout is organized so that the site and context reveal themselves as one moves from the entry, through the landscape, to the visitor center, as can be seen in Figure 4.30. Arriving by car, the entry road follows the topography—first curving away and then back again to arrive at the building. Likewise, the pedestrian path, from car to building, curves and passes through various conditions—meadows, copses, and tree groves. Figure 4.31 shows views of the surrounding hills that are seen upon looking back after passing through areas of dense vegetation. These plantings are placed to define the plateau edge and focus views inward. Curved vehicular circulation, set into the grade, is designed to be invisible from across the valley.

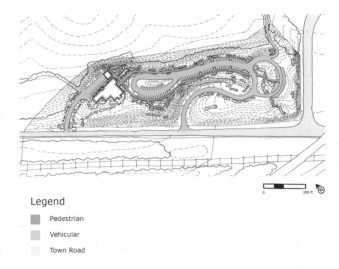

Legend

- Pedestrian
- Vehicular
- Town Road

Figure 4.30 Circulation.

Movement through the site follows a horizontal, open, sweeping vista of rolling meadow punctuated with areas of dense woodland growth. Over time, visual access along the open plateau will continue to decrease in certain areas where the copse thickets and hedgerows succeed to dense woodland patches and edges. This spatial framework can be seen in Figure 4.32. After several more years of growth,

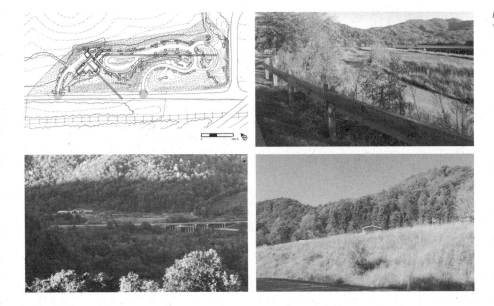

Figure 4.31 Site Organization.
Views across the river valley.

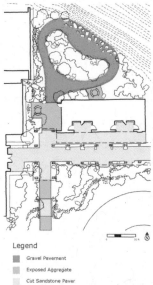

Figure 4.32 Spatial Framework. Tightly planted tree groves form a copse of successional planting that define the plateau edge on this previously wide-open site.

Legend

- ▇ Gravel Pavement
- ▇ Exposed Aggregate
- ▇ Cut Sandstone Paver

this formerly barren site's most prominent space-forming feature will be a mix of vegetation types that dominate the hardscape elements.

Materials

The site's former use as a quarry is expressed with sandstone in the architecture and in numerous ways in site pavements, as can be seen in the images of Figure 4.33. Locally quarried sandstone is used as cut stone for terraces and walks, monolithic slabs for a bridge, boulders for seating, river jacks in swales, and crushed stone for use in exposed aggregate concrete. These site materials provide smooth transitions and convey a common vocabulary between very different modes of construction lending multiple textures of golden yellow sandstone to nearly all hardscape surfaces.

Site Design Function

Natural Systems

The site hydrology, depicted in Figure 4.34, is designed to function as green infrastructure—to manage site stormwater and to irrigate new vegetation. The hydrologic sequence begins at the highest site elevation where roof

Figure 4.33 Materials. Site materials derived from local stone.

runoff is captured in a gravel swale alongside the building façade, which allows for an otherwise unattainable rich foundation planting. The shallow swale shown in Figure 4.35 collects runoff from the roofs and expands to collect parking and entry pavement runoff. The moist and shaded microclimate created here is abundantly planted and is a focal point crossed on a stone bridge to the visitor center

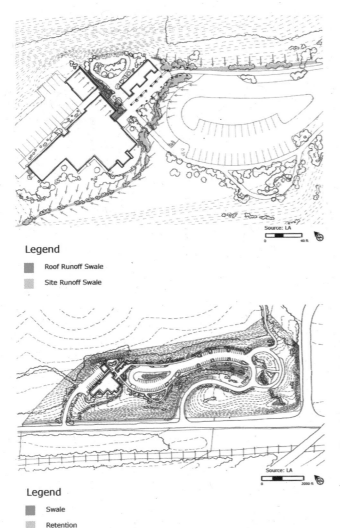

Legend

■ Roof Runoff Swale

▨ Site Runoff Swale

Legend

■ Swale

▨ Planting

Figure 4.35 Stormwater Management Swale. The vegetated gravel swale is designed to capture roof runoff, which makes foundation plantings possible in this otherwise non-irrigated landscape.

Legend

■ Swale

▨ Retention

Figure 4.34 Stormwater Management Plan. Diagram of the site stormwater strategy—from swales that capture runoff along entry roads to wet basins in meadows. Stormwater flow and interpretation is focused around the building entrance in the form of swales, rain gardens, hedgerows, copses. A diverse, cultivated swale garden is found at building entry.

Figure 4.36 Stormwater Techniques. Reinforced turf parking pavement and vegetated swale through lawn area are two stormwater management techniques that impact site form.

building entry. The wildflower garden seen in Figure 4.35 is the most intensely planted area on the site in terms of density and maintenance requirements. Rainwater, captured and conveyed, none of which is piped, supports trees, shrubs, and wildflower groundcover otherwise impossible to maintain without irrigation. During periods of little rainfall, much of this area is a dry stone swale. The stormwater strategies employed on the site, which yield near zero site runoff, include minimized hardscape footprints, groundwater recharge, a reinforced turf paving area, vegetated swales, and a stormwater infiltration basin and are shown in Figure 4.36.

Figure 4.37 Meadow, Grove, Copse, and Old Field.

Prior to design, in some areas of the abandoned site native grasslands emerged while in others the slopes were covered with invasive vegetation such as crown vetch (*Coronilla varia*) and Japanese honeysuckle (*Lonicera japonica*), likely planted or blown in from slope-stabilizing strategies within the hilly region. Given the minimal half-inch soil layer atop fast-draining highway fill, the new vegetation approach of the site design is experimental and mimics a variety of natural conditions, from native grasslands to old fields and copses to successional forest, as can be seen in the images of Figure 4.37.

The visual objective to blend this formerly disturbed site (Figure 4.38) with the surrounding intact-forested hills serves to define space. In addition to acres of natural grasslands on sloped areas with little soil volume, over 680 canopy and understory trees, 600 shrubs, and 3,200 plugs were planted. The proposed vegetation strategy provides a diversity of over 85 woody species in varying conditions and sizes to mimic natural growth. For example, the project planting schedule specified *Acer rubrum*, or Red Maple, in five forms: (1) multistemmed 3- to 3.5-inch caliper B&B, (2) single-stemmed 3- to 3.5-inch caliper B&B, (3) 8- to 10-foot bare root/container, (4) 4- to 5-foot bare root/container, and (5) 24- to 36-inch bare root/container. Utilizing a variety of plant sizes and conditions saves on cost. It also provides visual diversity in the plant palette and a feeling that the installation was not completed all in one day but has evolved over time. Figure 4.39 shows an example of the small planting material used in the design to allow for rapid succession.

The site planting design is largely a **low-maintenance** one with a transition from less to more cultivated as one approaches the visitor center building entrance where the intermittent swale is cultivated as a wildflower garden. The cultivated landscape area makes up approximately 2 percent of the entire site while the mown area is 10 percent of the site. The remaining area is in meadow and succeeding woodlands that require annual inputs such as monitoring for invasives and an annual mowing to suppress succession and weed growth. This comparison of natural versus cultivated vegetation is shown in Figure 4.40. Unlike landscapes that are held in a rigid maintenance regime, such as lawn, the woodland landscape is designed to evolve into a mature native landscape.

Figure 4.38 A Disturbed Site.
(Credit: Viridian Landscape Studio LLC)

Figure 4.39 Planting Material. Designing with small planting material allowed for quantity and accelerated growth. Because plenty of water was available in swales, the material grew in quickly. (Credit: Viridian Landscape Studio LLC)

Legend

▪ Cultural Vegetation Zone

▫ Natural Vegetation Zone

Figure 4.40 Natural vs. Cultural Vegetation Zones. The vegetation zones that are ornamental and require higher maintenance are minimal, while natural vegetation zones cover the majority of the site and are mowed and maintained once annually.

Human Systems

In addition to fulfilling basic park orientation and comfort needs, the site is designed to provide areas for gathering for watershed interpretation and for contemplation of the changing landscape. Although not located in the most dramatic setting within the park, the site's height above the valley floor and open views across the New River Valley are compelling. Several overlooks provide views of the sur-

rounding hills and the bridge crossing over the New River. Gathering spaces such those shown in Figure 4.41 dot the site; one is a long pergola structure that integrates the two buildings and provides seating and information on the surrounding watershed. Since education was a primary program element, a group gathering space for park interpreter lectures is tucked between the two buildings engaging the

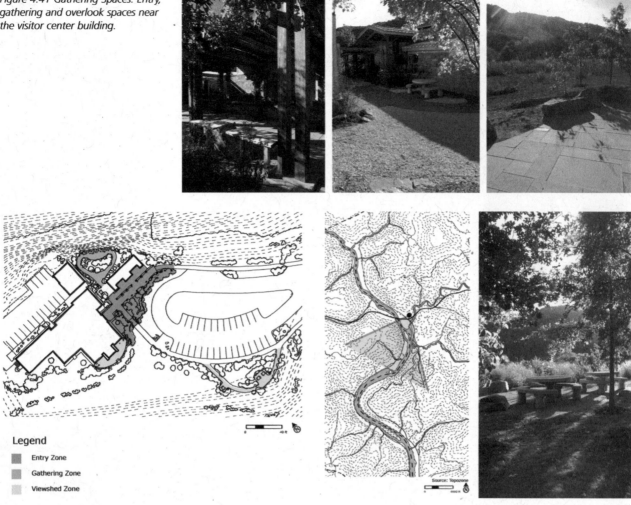

Figure 4.41 Gathering Spaces. Entry, gathering and overlook spaces near the visitor center building.

Legend

▮ Entry Zone

▮ Gathering Zone

▮ Viewshed Zone

Figure 4.42 Landscape Zones.

Figure 4.43 Views. Views across the river valley from the site picnic groves.

former quarry rock face as a backdrop (see Figure 4.42). Native trees, shrubs, and groundcover are labeled and serve to define the gathering space. Stone boulders throughout the site are used as seating in areas where contemplation is conducive at scenic overlooks and building terraces, as seen in Figure 4.43. Picnic areas are densely planted with tree groves to provide shade in this hot climate.

Maintenance

The nature of the landscape architecture profession is that typically the designer is involved until the moment the design is installed—and not thereafter. In this project, however, Viridian Landscape Studio recognized that awareness of the maintenance regime required for this landscape was essential to realizing the original design intent. One misunderstanding and the meadows would be lawn, the copse succession would be destroyed, and the plant diversity and design would be lost. Working with the National Park Service and the USDA, the landscape architects developed a document for long-term maintenance of site vegetation (see Figure 4.44). Because natural succession takes place, this maintenance approach helps keep the ongoing costs to a minimum of annual labor inputs.

Sandstone Visitor Center Maintenance Plan

While the full management plan contained photos, plant lists, a plan, and specific instructions for each vegetative zone, the following is an excerpt of the basic general requirements outlined by the landscape architects and the USDA for the site.

General Requirements of Maintenance Plan

1. Maintain the natural form of all trees and shrubs. DO NOT top trees.

2. Hire a qualified arborist to prune dead or diseased branches from trees adjacent to pedestrian areas.

3. Train staff to recognize invasive plants at the seedling and adult stages, including, but not limited to, *Coronilla varia* (Crown vetch), *Lonicera japonica* (Japanese honeysuckle), *Rosa multiflora* (Multiflora rose).

4. Monitor and remove invasive species within all management zones. Use either mechanical or chemical methods as defined below:

a. Carefully hand pull or dig out invasives taking care not to damage surrounding plants.

b. Spot spray weed outbreaks as recommended within the Landscape Management Section of this report.

5. Consult with the Resource Management Staff at Great Smoky Mountains National Park for invasive plant control.

6. DO NOT mow or use weed-whackers near trees.

7. DO NOT mow to less than recommended mowing height. This will kill the grasslands.

8. Monitor for deer damage during establishment years. Use repellant as necessary.

9. Additional planting shall consist only of locally native species.

10. Keep photo records and written logs as a record of the successes and failures of all planting and management techniques.

11. Watering Requirements during Year One and Two—Establish an Emergency Drought Watering Plan. Other national parks use a water truck, fire-fighting equipment, or backpack tanks. Backpack tanks are used for small areas (e.g., visible spots near the visitor center entrance and walkways to the center).

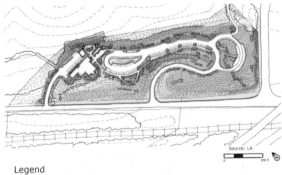

Legend

- Entry Landscape & Mowstrip
- Old Field, Early Woodland & Copse
- Open Grassland

Figure 4.44 Ongoing Site Maintenance Plan. Viridian Landscape Studio provided a plan, photos, and narrative describing maintenance requirements and needs for each planting zone proposed.

Site Design Engagements

The Sandstone Visitor Center landscape was designed not as a backdrop for architectural uses but as the subject of ecological and cultural engagement. Ecological engagement of the landscape occurs primarily in the form of *restoration,* where much of the formerly barren site is becoming restored through **successional landscape change** to its original native woodland ecosystem. Ecological engagement also occurs, though with a more minor emphasis, in the form of *regeneration*, through the use of building and parking lot runoff to water site landscape zones.

The project's planning and design—from siting the building, parking lots, and entry drive to the detailing of pedestrian gathering spaces and paths to the vegetation and stormwater infrastructure—captures the character of the region, its topography, curving roadways, views, and material qualities. As seen in Figure 4.45, the visitor center building entrance was purposely oriented to one side of the building to emphasize the richly planted and swaled landscape rather than focus on the building as the sole destination. Sequencing throughout the site begins with a single walkway through naturalized planting to a successively more furnished, signed, and visually stimulating planting sequence near the building.

Figure 4.45 Landscape Focus. The visitor center entrance is off axis, allowing the landscape to be the primary focus upon entry.

Following is a list of specific site design elements that take advantage of natural phenomenon, site activities, and amenities that engage the user with the site and its regional, environmental, and cultural systems. These cultural engagements, as depicted in Figure 4.46, are categorized as elements, views, or nodes.

Element: Signage. In the early 20th century, the property was donated for educational uses and was the site of a regional school. Education remains a key program element with the new use. Selective signage, such as that shown in Figure 4.47, is used "actively" to interpret the site's location, history, and connection to the watershed. A series of sandstone plaques poetically reference the New River watershed. Subtle signs describe natural process such as stormwater, call out **native plants**, and describe water conservation techniques. Passive interpretation such as reading the changing landscape can be noticed only over time with subsequent visits.

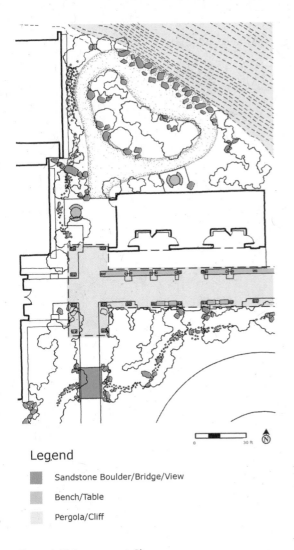

Legend

■ Sandstone Boulder/Bridge/View

■ Bench/Table

■ Pergola/Cliff

Figure 4.46 Engagement: Plan.

Views: Regional Connection. The primary view across the New River Valley is celebrated by several overlooks that make a connection between the site and its regional context. Dotted boulders for seating, picnic areas in the landscape, and a curved stone terrace adjacent to the building provide indoor and outdoor venues, shown in Figure 4.48, for this visual connection.

Node: Stone Bridge. At the visitor center entry, a stone bridge crosses a swale that collects water from the parking area and building roof. The building entrance

Figure 4.47 Engagement: Signage.

Figure 4.48 Engagement: Regional Connection.

is turned at a right angle to this entry path making the building secondary to the landscape features; a trellis, swale, and garden.

Element: Vegetative Succession. Vegetation is spaced and managed to create a foreground in this otherwise wide open space, establish biodiversity, and develop an ongoing site narrative of vegetative succession, such as the copse shown in Figure 4.49.

Node: Quarry History. The outdoor gathering space shown in Figure 4.50 is used for educational programs and is defined by the 50-foot-high quarried sandstone rock face. Sandstone boulders, used for seating at the base of the rock face, feel as though they spalled off the face of the cliff. Its natural wall is used as a point of discussion about the area geology and the former site uses.

Figure 4.49 Engagement: Vegetative Succession.

Figure 4.50 Engagement: Quarry History. A gathering space for park interpretation of cultural and natural site and regional history.

Outcomes

The Program/Site/Context Comparison

Predesign Site/Context Conditions

The sustainable outcome of a project is determined largely by the design team's approach toward three tasks: (1) the development of program goals, (2) the choices made in the assessment of site character, and (3) choices made in the assessment of the context. In the accompanying chart, the key features of these three tasks are listed in relation to four important sustainable factors: (1) environmental factors, (2) economic factors, (3) cultural factors, and (4) educational factors. The chart shows the connection between qualities inherent in the context and the ensuing program development mandates. It also shows that the initial program goals drafted by the client developed largely from *regional* needs. The predesign conditions of the site are shown in Figure 4.51.

Postdesign Site/Context Impacts

The Sandstone Visitor Center design outcome, shown in Figure 4.52, affected the region at all scales—from statewide scale to site scale. Through its educational and orientation elements, this project, identified as a *sustainable integrator,* meets the needs of a growing tourist industry and provides jobs in the community. The site program makes connections to the greater watershed functions by providing educational cues that enable local schoolchildren and tourists to become stewards of the natural environment. Mirroring the strengths of the region, the site's regenerative vegetation and green infrastructure improve this former brownfield site.

The scales of sustainable planning and design that influenced the Sandstone Visitor Center design were **regional planning** and **site planning**. This means that the economic and environmental needs of the region as well as the degraded site conditions were the driving forces behind program decision-making. It is at these two scales where inspiration was derived and where the site design had its most critical impacts.

Figure 4.51 Predesign conditions.
(Credit: Viridian Landscape Studio LLC)

As mentioned, several statewide regional planning initiatives in West Virginia initiated this project, namely the National Coal Heritage Area, the Coalfields Expressway, and The New River Gorge National River. The broad needs of the region were manifold and largely dictated the project location, site amenities, and educational focus of the site design. The site's location in a sparsely populated area with few park service amenities was in need of economic incentives to boost the tourist industry and improve opportunities not just in the town of Sandstone but also within the larger region.

Figure 4.52 Postdesign Impacts.

Case Study—Sandstone Visitor Center

Program, Site, and Context Relationship

	INITIAL PROGRAM GOALS	SITE CHARACTER	CONTEXT CHARACTER
ENVIRONMENTAL FACTORS	Inflict minimal environmental impact	Shallow, rubble gravel fill with a thin cap of soil	Intact, healthy, and contiguous hydrologic and vegetative ecosystems
	Obtain LEED certification	Steep 3:1 man-made slopes	
	Mend derelict site	Old field regrowth and invasive plants	
ECONOMIC FACTORS	Provide a southern gateway for the New River Gorge National River	13-acre abandoned site	Regional need for economic stimulation to provides job opportunities by growing the tourist industry
	Provide a tourist rest stop off Interstate Highway 64	An existing site access road used for the school and later for access for gravel dumping	
		Site donated by the Richmond family	
CULTURAL FACTORS	Maintain access to historic Richmond Cemetery	An exposed historic sandstone quarry face	Rich regional cultural history that built upon environmental beauty, cultural heritage, and natural resources
	Make use of local expertise and resources	A public access road to historic Richmond Cemetery	
EDUCATIONAL FACTORS	Provide an interpretive center for the New River Watershed education for local schoolchildren and tourists	The site was disturbed, which created opportunities for sustainable education.	Environmental education deemed important to the preservation of area natural resources

Meanwhile, site-planning opportunities were dictated largely by previous development of the property. With few intact resources for protection, the site's natural systems—its soils, slopes, vegetation, and hydrologic systems—needed restoration or improvement. New site damage could be minimized by developing previously used portions of the site.

Improving Site Efficiency & Sustainability

The specific details and techniques of this site design are critical to site function, spatial quality, and experience of the site user. The following design techniques were used to improve the site, mitigate the impact of development and create a compelling, functional site design regardless of the conditions of the context.

Vegetated swales

Reinforced-turf parking area

Biodiverse meadows

Environmental education

Minimized hardscape footprints to improve groundwater recharge

Improving Regional Efficiency & Sustainability

This design did more than improve the 13-acre site. It restored an otherwise abandoned site to usefulness within the larger Sandstone community and contributed to restoring environmental health within the region. Meanwhile the rest stop, exhibits, and insight into West Virginian cultural history help feed the tourist industry. A low-maintenance, naturalized approach as well as restoration of ecosystem function describes the greater New River Watershed and helps to blend the site with its surroundings. The following planning and design techniques aided in integrating the site with its context.

Site reuse

Public open space

Reduced and prescribed maintenance regime

Use of local materials/resources

Cultural and historic elements

Plant community restoration

Sustainability Criteria Met?

Five landscape sustainability criteria were presented in Chapter 1 as a means for evaluating landscape sustainability—*Connectivity, Meaning, Purpose, Efficiency,* and *Stewardship.* Our discussion now turns to the design outcome of the Sandstone Visitor Center as we evaluate it in relation to these criteria.

Connectivity

The Sandstone Visitor Center site design:

- restores an otherwise abandoned site to usefulness within the Sandstone, West Virginia community, providing access to the historical cemetery.

- attracts visitors to this economically struggling area.

- restores site health and function that integrates with the regional intact ecological system.

- connects north and south reaches of the New River Gorge National River area through park interpretation, facilities, and amenities.

Meaning

The Sandstone Visitor Center site design:

- fosters visitor understanding of site ecological processes by employing specific points of intersection along the main paths of access, such as the swale-crossing bridge at the front entry.

- expands the meaning and explains the purpose of natural processes through selective signage placement explaining the breadth of the park service's regional goals down to detailed site maintenance strategies.

- engages the visitor with scenic overlooks to bring the site into relationship with its context.

- provides a materials palette that describes regional visual vocabulary.

Purpose

The Sandstone Visitor Center site design:

- creates a site specific landscape identity that goes far beyond the conventional design approaches that just provide for basic program needs such as parking, picnicking, and access.

- presents a decentralized site whose purpose is multi-fold. Building orientation and circulation sequence is laid out to provide the visitor with a varied landscape experience in keeping with the National Park Service mission to bring tourists closer to the Sandstone landscape.

- allows the landscape its own future with or without its designed purpose as a visitor center site. This is achieved by regenerating ecological function.

Efficiency

The Sandstone Visitor Center site design:

- employs green infrastructure. Allows natural processes, such as stormwater cleansing swales and vegetative succession areas, to function naturally without excessive manipulation. This saves on cost, maintenance, and improves function.

- uses local stone, planting, and soil materials reducing long-distance shipping.

- improves the future impact of site development through the planning for future ecological needs such as planting thick tree groves in parking lot planting islands to take up stormwater and to provide shade.

- reuses a former invasive filled, incongruous site rather than use a pristine intact site elsewhere.

Stewardship

The Sandstone Visitor Center site design:

- provides systematic instructions and plan for informing park staff on site maintenance.

- allows for changes and assumes a work-in-progress status as the landscape changes over time.

Parallel Projects

The Cusano Environmental Education Center at John Heinz National Wildlife Refuge, Philadelphia, PA, USA

Located just one mile from the Philadelphia International Airport, this 1,200-acre freshwater tidal marsh, the last of its kind in Pennsylvania, was established as a refuge in 1972 and is managed by the U.S. Fish and Wildlife Service. The landscape architecture firm of Andropogon Associates Ltd. was retained for a site design that would integrate parking, paths, and information with outdoor exhibits. The mission of the Cusano Environmental Education Center is to demonstrate, within an urban setting, the importance of the natural world to the human quality of life and inspire visitors to become responsible stewards of the environment (U.S. Fish and Wildlife Service). The visitor center is located on a formerly disturbed site with the building raised above ground level upon piles to allow for natural site water flows. This v-shaped building surrounds and

Figure 4.53 View across wet meadows at the Cusano Environmental Education Center.
(Credit: Andropogon)

protects a wetland habitat that provides intimate bird-side viewing, shown in Figure 4.53. Strict stormwater management was critical to this project and these systems are designed to mimic natural water systems that once existed on the site. Like at Sandstone Visitor Center, education was an important component to the program and techniques such as **rainwater harvesting**, porous pavement, and graywater recycling are exposed and described to visitors while functioning to reduce site water usage.

Government Canyon Visitor Center, Helotes, Texas, USA

Unlike the Sandstone Visitor Center, the Government Canyon Visitor Center, shown in Figure 4.54, is located in an area of intense growth along the recharge zone for the single source of drinking water for the city of San Antonio, Texas. Like our case study, it serves as a gateway to the 8,600-acre Government Canyon State Natural Area. The design preserves a critical aquifer while restoring a landscape of native vegetation. William McDonald, a landscape architect with the Texas Parks and Wildlife Department, and Lake Flato Architects worked together to minimize development impact in terms of building footprint, materials, water usage, and maintenance needs. Because of the need for air conditioning in this hot climate and the desire to reduce the building footprint, the building and landscape share functions as a shaded and breezy exhibit space. The landscape collects rainwater that is filtered

Figure 4.54 Government Canyon Visitor Center, Helotes, Texas. (Credit: Chris Cooper)

and used for irrigation. Historic reference to this former ranch is made in the local and regional material used in the structure and landscape materials.

5 FORM-MAKING

How is sustainable design articulated through cohesive, imageable and artful form and space?

Paradise Valley Residence

Can we achieve high design and be environmentally responsible at the same time? I think we can. I don't think that what I call the "green badge of courage" should necessarily result in a landscape that's ugly or crude. That's the challenge for designers: How do we create landscapes that are imbued with a sense of beauty while rethinking every aspect of our work as part of this larger environmental agenda?

—Nicholas Dines

BACKGROUND

Careful attention to form-making is an important aspect of the sustainable design process. The meaning and function of the landscape, planned and conceptualized in the analysis and programming phases of design, are communicated and realized through its physical form. The discipline of landscape architecture is, by definition, an integration of art and science. This sets it apart from the more purely scientific disciplines of engineering and ecology, and the purely creative pursuit of fine art. While the technical aspects of form-making are clearly critical to the utilitarian or scientific function of the sustainable landscape, the visual and spatial aspects of form-making create its social and cultural meaning and function. Both aspects must be present and integrated in successful design, but sustainability in its earlier applications often focused on the scientific and utilitarian.

Lewis Mumford was a keen observer of the relationship between art and "technics." He used the term *technics*, as distinct from technology, to mean the "wishes, habits, ideas, goals" of a society as well as its "industrial processes." In making this distinction, he observes that earlier civilizations reached a high degree of technical proficiency without becoming so obsessed with the methods and aims of technology. In his 1952 book *Art & Technics,* Mumford observes that "man was perhaps an image maker and a language maker, a dreamer and an artist, even before he was a tool maker." Yet Mumford contends that modern man's emphasis on technology and coinciding devaluation of the esthetic symbol has contributed to the depersonalization and emptiness of much of contemporary life:

> Precisely in those areas where modern man has seemed most prosperous and secure, most efficient in action, most adept in thought, we begin to realize that something has been left out of his regimen, something essential to his organic balance and development. What is that missing element? That missing element, I suggest, is the human person. . . The great problem of our time is to bring back, into the very heart of our culture, that respect for the essential attributes of personality, its creativity and autonomy, which Western man lost at the moment he displaced his own life in order to concentrate on the improvement of the machine *(Mumford 1952).*

In a time when art is often dismissed as a luxury or mere ornamentation, Mumford's ideas run completely to the contrary: that turning more purposely and deliberately toward art can reverse the soullessness and single-minded march of our technological world. His call for development to take the "human as its measure" through integration of artistic impulses and achievement is more relevant today than ever, given the exponentially greater role technology has come to play in our lives.

In his examination of the real contributions of art, Mumford emphasizes the need for abstraction in expression. "At some very early stage in his development as artist, man discovers the fact that works of art must have attributes of form and proportion and organization similar to—though surely not identical with—those that attract him in natural forms. To gain more than passing attention, the work of art must take on such organic character." Yet he observed that the mere substitution or replication of such inspirations is both boring and lacking the human urge to express, interpret, and create new meaning. The organic character of which he spoke was not meant to copy nature altogether, but rather to abstract the formal and spatial characteristics of nature (Mumford 1952). Garrett Eckbo, a pioneer of modern design in landscape architecture, strove for rigorous spatial development in his landscapes inspired by modern art, itself highly abstract. He believed that "the more abstract is form, the more clear and direct its appeal" (Treib 1997).

The profession of landscape architecture is rooted in traditions of form-making that are based on the inspiration of natural form. Jens Jensen believed deeply in the artistry and spiritual inspiration to be found in the prairie landscape, developing his technical knowledge of vegetative communities and landforms that made his interpretations sustainable and authentic. Ian McHarg, in exploring the ideal expression of landscape form, proposed the standard of *fitness*, as opposed to standards of art, as the way to unite the natural and the cultural worlds:

> In turning to nature to find the basis for form, the Naturalists have concluded in favor of fitness. Unlike art, the term we use, fitness is an appropriate criterion both for natural objects and creatures and for artifices, whereas art is only applied to the last. The Naturalists have decided that the earth is fit and can be made

more fitting. Of all roles that man can play, those of apperception and communication are thought to be dominant as the basis for creative expression. The manner of expression is of paramount importance to the objective of making the earth more fitting. What is the expression of fitness?

(McHarg 1969)

Exploration of the aesthetics of ecological design was the subject of Joan Nassauer's 1995 essay "Messy Ecosystems, Orderly Frames." In it she seeks to answer: What makes ecological form existing within a human landscape—which, when patterned after nature, is perceived of as messy—acceptable and accessible to people? Her conclusion to this question is: providing landscape form that exhibits human "cues to care" creates the orderly frames that appeal to people and create comfort for them in ecological landscapes. "Landscapes that we describe as attractive tend to conform to aesthetic conventions for the display of care, which can be exhibited in virtually any landscape." This could take the form of mowed strips of grass that buffer a walkway from a meadow planting used in the Sandstone Visitor Center, or the transformation from upland natural wetland (the messy ecosystem) to structurally edged open water (the orderly frame) in Tanner Springs Park, for instance.

We can reason that peoples' affinity for and acceptance of a landscape is a necessary aspect of its sustainability. Alternatively, we can also reason that people's health and well-being is an important sustainability contribution to be made by designed landscapes. Research on the restorative aspects of everyday landscapes—their role in the well-being of everyday people—conducted by Rachel and Stephen Kaplan found that four spatial characteristics contribute to restorative experiences of landscape: complexity, mystery, coherence, and legibility. Coherence and legibility provide information that can help with making sense of the environment through clear organization and distinctiveness. Complexity and mystery, on the other hand, provide information that suggests the potential for exploration and open-ended interest (Kaplan 1998). These findings have important implications for spatial organization and form-making.

STRATEGIES FOR SUSTAINABLE FORM-MAKING

Many of the following ideas about form-making are familiar basic landscape architectural design strategies that, when integrated with sustainable design strategies, give compelling human form to the sustainable landscape. They remind us to maximize the original tools of our craft, many of which are rooted in traditions of "design with nature," while we pursue new ideas about green design.

1. *Create space.* Define distinct spaces using biological or sustainable inert materials. The Paradise Valley Residence project uses both plant material and architectural walls to create edge and massing that contributes to user understanding and affinity.

2. *Develop a natural landscape matrix.* Wherever possible, create smaller patches of cultural landscape spaces within larger matrices of natural landscape spaces to minimize inputs and maximize ecological function.

3. *Organize space.* Form relationships among the spaces you create with clear and strong organizational structure. This structure may be articulated with subtlety or boldness, but should act to make the site cohesive while providing appropriate connection and separation of spaces. Make use of diagramming in the design process to develop and strengthen site organization.

4. *Remember and apply the basic design principles of* unity, balance, *and* emphasis. These qualities are the things that make many of the most visually distinctive and moving intact natural landscapes memorable to us. Often these formal qualities are part and parcel of the ecological integrity of a system but get left out of the equation when modeling natural ecosystem function in cultural landscapes. The dense planting of copses set in the meadow landscape of the Sandstone Visitor Center, for instance, is mimicking a natural pattern of density that creates visual emphasis and unity inspired by nature. It also serves the goal of stimulating a successional landscape that will eventually transition back to its native woodland.

5. *Maximize the unique qualities of the landscape medium.* Use the basic tools of landscape architecture—planting and landform— to create beautiful and innovative form in the landscape. Rely less heavily on inert materials that require more energy to create and construct, and which provide less ecological service.

6. *Make functional form.* Maximize the formal potential of functional elements and areas such as parking and stormwater management. Instead of relegating parking to an uninspired patch of paving, transform it into a parking court that integrates vegetation and structure to link it to architecture and landscape.

7. *Create connections to regional form.* Use materials and forms that reflect the contextual cultural and ecological vernacular. The use of stucco walls, ceramic urns, and water troughs in the Paradise Valley Residence case study that follows is an example of this strategy.

8. *Anticipate change in form.* Accommodate and embrace the seasonal and lifetime weathering, growth, and regeneration of the landscape. Make conscious decisions about elements that will be maintained in a more static state versus elements that will be allowed to change and succeed through their natural lifecycle, such as the Sandstone Visitor Center's use of a meadow landscape versus restored woodland.

9. *Frame landscape views and spaces with architecture.* The Paradise Valley Residence is a great example of extending architectural elements into the landscape and landscape elements through the building to frame landscape views and integrate interior and exterior spaces.

10. *Use natural forms and spatial models for inspiration.* Use natural forms and functions to inspire design organization and form. In the Whitney Water Purification Facility, the entire landscape abstracted a watershed, with a progression of hill, stream, and pond landscapes.

METHODS FOR SUSTAINABLE FORM-MAKING

Paul Laseau, in his book *Graphic Thinking for Designers*, illustrates the use of drawing as a way of developing ideas through more abstract diagrammatic methods in the beginning of the design process to less abstract and more concrete methods as design resolution is reached. As a language for graphic thinking, diagrams are an essential part of the design process, helping to refine and test ideas about form as it continues to develop through schematic and even construction documentation stages. Taking time and graphic care to refine key diagrams can also be a critical communication tool to make complex design decisions understood by clients and stakeholders.

While landscape architects certainly use diagramming to develop their design ideas, the terminology and distinction between different types and purposes of diagramming is relatively loose and undefined. Developing a rigorous language of diagrams that recognizes the need to think about designs holistically, as well as pulling them apart into existing and proposed system components such as site uses, circulation, hydrology, and vegetation, is critical to a thoughtful analysis and integration of design intention. The use of line diagrams facilitates thinking about primarily plan view (horizontal) spatial organization and pattern, while the use of figure-ground diagrams is especially useful in exploring and creating ideas for three-dimensional (3D) form and its spatial characteristics with regard to massing versus openness in a landscape.

Line Diagramming: Organizational Patterns

Architects use the term *parti* to describe the most basic organizational principle that expresses a structure's design. It is the scheme, main concept, or idea that explains better than anything else the character and appearance of a design. A French term meaning *choice* or *decision*, a parti represents the reasoned, creative direction a design proposes. "It provides a horizontal thrust that connects program, site experience, form and tectonics together in such a way that, if very well done, it also points to a vertical dimension. The parti may start from a particular architectural concept interpreting a specific dimension of architecture (context, precedent, composition, materiality, etc.). However, in order to become a parti, it needs to become comprehensive, cross-dimensional, bringing all aspects of a design within its domain" (Bermudez 2006).

Applied to the sustainable design of landscape, a medium of continuous landform and diverse natural and cultural systems, the organization of a site must be more concerned with existing conditions than even the most site-based work of architecture. The contextual emphasis of the sustainability framework presented here suggests that site pattern might well be derived from neighborhood or regional patterns. Making use of contextual pattern analysis to create site patterns of environmental fitness provides spatial organization that holds regional meaning and identity. The use of simple line diagramming to distill and make sense of the complexities of regional patterns helps us to make connections from larger scales of form to site form. The linear forces of arroyo, house, outdoor path, and nodes are synthesized through the site organization diagram for the Paradise Valley Residence, for example.

The integration of human structure in landscape design must be sensitive and responsive. Yet sensitivity and responsiveness should not be confused with lack of deliberate design intention or direction; it is precisely because of the complexity of landscape that a clear and creative organizing synthesis is needed. The Paradise Valley Residence project uses two contrasting systems of site organization to create interesting tension and integration of form: the linear force of the arroyo, a regional ecological form that passes through the site, and the gridded arrangement of the house that is based on the neighborhood street system and the *hacienda* form of architecture.

Figure-Ground Diagramming: Spatial Patterns

The articulation of space through massing of structure, landform, and vegetation is another aspect of form-making that is benefited from a diagrammatic approach. Figure-ground diagramming, which is based on patterns of solids and voids, is a method that is usefully adapted to a variety of spatial thinking about landscape. In this type of diagramming solid tone is contrasted against white space. Originally conceived as a way of analyzing urban patterns of buildings and public civic space, the figure-ground diagram has an association with "positive" and "negative" space, where the buildings can be seen to form positive outdoor spaces like plazas and streets.

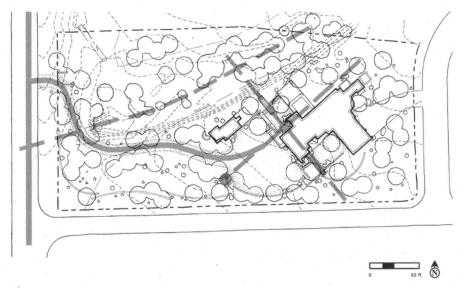

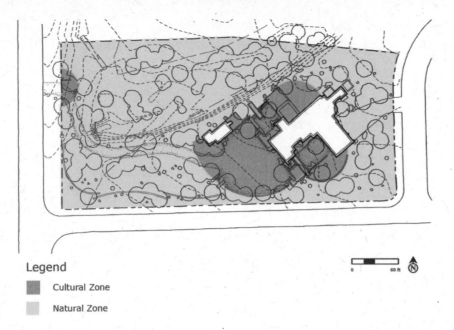

Legend

■ Cultural Zone

■ Natural Zone

The development of positive site-level landscape space and spatial hierarchy, shape, and balance can effectively be explored through figure-ground drawing. The distinction between sloped areas and flat areas; low, medium, and high vegetation; impermeable thickets versus open canopy forest can all be tested through the figure-ground relationship, which can be examined using subtleties of gray-scale tones to convey a variety of dense to open conditions or vertical dimensions.

Figure-ground diagramming is also a good way to develop the balance of programmatic types of spaces in the landscape, which may have more subtle physical spatial differences but other visual or functional distinctions. For instance, if a sustainable form strategy, as suggested above, is to create a matrix, or dominant body, of natural landscape types such as woodland, wetland, or meadow, with smaller spaces of cultural landscapes, this concept can be furthered through the use of figure-ground diagramming. In the Paradise Valley Residence, the site was returned to desert matrix, with small patches of cultural courtyards placed as interface between house and desert.

Materials and Detail Design

Conception of sustainable design form in the more holistic, spatial sense can be accomplished through the type of diagramming described above. The mood and feel of a design form, however, is often dictated by the selection of materials and detail inspiration used to create form. Sustainability considerations typically dictate that materials are selected on the basis of their embodied energy and recycled or renewable resource use, decisions that can be made at the end of the design process. Yet sometimes form-making can begin with the idea for a detail or a certain material. Elements such as Tanner Springs Park's wellspring stonework, Paradise Valley's architectural window walls, and Sandstone Visitor Center's quarry wall can provide inspiration that drives form-making. Rigorous exploration and attention to scale, proportion, color, texture, and joinery can create detail elements that are critical to the physical realization of the design concept.

Applying inspiration from a project's ecological or cultural context to detail design deepens the meaning and fit of a site detail element. Whether through the choice of materials such as locally produced stone or industrial metals, or through the adaptation of form such as a "stream" inspired drainage swale or a dry-laid fieldstone wall, adapting contextual form and function to new site elements can provide the sense of regional distinctiveness that so many conventional landscapes lack.

CASE STUDY— PARADISE VALLEY RESIDENCE

LOCATION: Paradise Valley, Arizona, USA
SITE SIZE: 1.5 acres
CLIENT: Private residents
DESIGNERS: Landscape Architect—Steve Martino, Phoenix, Arizona
  Architect—Phoenix Design Group, Phoenix, Arizona
  Interior Designer—Elizabeth Kidwell, Phoenix, Arizona
FORMER SITE USE: Previously undeveloped
LANDSCAPE BUDGET: $200,000
DATE OF COMPLETION: 1999

(Credit: historicaerials.com)

Overview

This residential design project offers an especially compelling example of the sustainability benefits of fine form-making. In a region where the sustainable landscape is often reduced to the concept of xeriscaping, the spatial and formal qualities of this landscape demonstrate the increased value of integrating creative, architectural form with ecological systems of vegetation, landform, and hydrology to create human landscapes of visual delight, bioregional identity, and cues to care.

Project Inception

The project came about through the clients' desire to restore a desert landscape as a setting for their new home in the Phoenix **suburb** of Paradise Valley. The home was envisioned as a contrast to many of the newer surrounding homes in the neighborhood that have developed imported landscapes. With backgrounds in interior design and real estate, the clients also wanted the landscape to engage with the structural forms of the architecture, linking interior spaces of the house with exterior spaces of the site.

Design Concept

The Southwestern United States has one of the most distinctive and compelling forms of **regional vernacular**

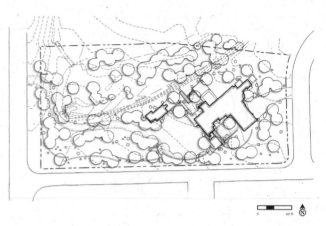

Figure 5.2 Paradise Valley Residence Site Plan.

Figure 5.1 Native Sonoran Desert. Landform, vegetation, geology, and climate combine to create a dramatic and distinctive natural landscape. This location near Sedona is in the high desert, while the lower elevations of the Phoenix region support a slightly different type of plant community.

architecture and landscape. Appreciation for the native desert landscape as a model for developed landscapes has recently grown, aided by both the necessity to limit water consumption as well as the growing popularity of Southwestern culture with its unique blend of Native American, Mexican, and historic American "old West" influences. Where once this landscape was largely viewed as uninhabitable and drab, the forms, pattern, textures, and colors of desert plants and soil are increasingly embraced by the public (see Figure 5.1). This project expresses and interprets the Southwestern vernacular on several levels.

The site plan for the project is shown in Figure 5.2. The main concept behind the design is to create a native desert landscape within which a modern homestead is placed. The home is laid out in the style of a historic hacienda, with walled enclosures that separate and protect the domestic spaces from the wild spaces. While the domestic spaces are more refined and articulated through architectural features, they reflect the external desert landscape in their plant palette, materials selection, and use of color and offer near and distant views into the wild "external" landscape. Access to the site is intended to provide a journey through the wild desert to the domestic spaces and structures within.

The character and form of these spaces and structures is related to a second major emphasis in this design concept: the development of strong architectural form that extends from the house itself into the landscape, engaging and highlighting key elements and views.

Project Philosophies and Approach

The clients are a couple who desired an outdoor living environment for themselves along with a native plant habitat landscape that would invite wildlife to be a part of their garden. One of the pair is a native of the Phoenix area and has a lifelong affinity for the desert. As seasonal residents who split their time between the Southwest and the Northeast, they desired a low-maintenance environment that would afford the convenience of living within the Metro Phoenix

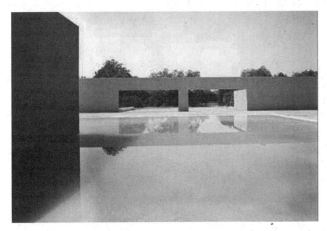

Figure 5.3 San Cristobal. A residential property designed by Luis Barragan.
(Credit: Barragan Foundation)

area but a sense of seclusion and wilderness as well. Admirers of Mexican architect Luis Barragan, they requested that the landscape be inspired by his work, which is known for its marrying of a minimalist modern architectural vocabulary with Latin American natural and cultural influences. An example of his work is shown in Figure 5.3.

The couple's other home in New Preston, Connecticut, has been developed with very similar values for the indigenous northeastern landscape and careful attention to architectural quality.

In Steve Martino the clients found not only fellow-admirers of Barragan, but also a veteran designer skilled in bringing together concern for distinctive architecture and the native desert landscape. They were familiar with Martino's work at the Desert Botanical Gardens in Phoenix's Papago Park. Martino's philosophy is very simply one of authentism and efficiency: When in the desert, embrace the desert. Whether the site has been cleared of its native landscape, or retains intact or damaged habitat, Martino's approach is always built around the notion of a native desert landscape as the basic underpinning of the site.

With a small practice that has focused on southwestern landscapes since the 1980s, Martino has well-developed expertise in native plants and uses them not only because they are drought-tolerant, but primarily because they are beautiful and expressive of place. He has been a pioneer in the region's development of an appreciation of the desert aesthetic, having encouraged the establishment of one of the early native desert plant nurseries to provide dependable commercial supplies of plant stock. Although he works in other project types, a majority of the firm's project portfolio is residential, a large and critical sector of the site development business. With his regional and residential focus Martino has established a seasoned relationship with several architects who understand and appreciate his approach. He has won several national ASLA design awards for his work. The practice is small with only one or two other associates in his office (after a brief period in the 1980s when his office grew to over a dozen employees), allowing Martino to maintain his philosophy through selectivity of projects and retaining close involvement with each project through construction.

Martino considers this project one of his most successful in striking the right balance between landscape and architecture to achieve a classic southwestern home environment.

Program Type and Development Trend

Program Type: High-End Residential

Spectacular views, unique landscapes, lakesides, shorelines, mountains, and cliffs often characterize high-end residential neighborhoods. Areas such as the coastal communities of Carmel, California, or East Hampton, New York, partially due to their sensitive natural environments, have building codes that help shape the character of the community as well as preserve the natural environment. Carmel's Coastal Land Use Plan states: "The combination of the City's natural setting and the subdivision patterns is responsible for much of the City's character. The keys to making this marriage of a grid subdivision and a constrained environment work were to avoid over-building and to recognize the natural constraints at each location. For example, most roads were not paved to their full, dedicated width. Instead, the minimum width necessary for access and safety was the standard. This allowed roads to follow the best topography

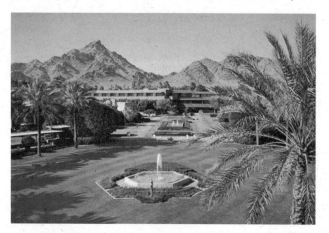

Figure 5.4 The Arizona Biltmore. Located near the case study subject, this site typifies the type of sweeping views and settings desired by high-end residential and resort properties.
(Credit: Arizona Biltmore Resort and Spa)

Figure 5.5 A Desert Lawn. This residential landscape located adjacent to the case study subject demonstrates the persistence of the lawn ideal.

within the rights-of-way and to avoid significant trees" (City of Carmel-By-The-Sea, California).

While many high-end Paradise Valley properties are located within golf course developments or walled-off estates, the community itself is noted for the open views its many resorts offer, as can be seen at the Arizona Biltmore pictured in Figure 5.4. Yet in the Phoenix area there has been relatively little comprehensive planning-level regulation to avoid over-building and to encourage subdivision patterns to recognize natural constraints and sensitive environments.

The most consistent American residential program element is the ubiquitous swath of green lawn, an example of such can be seen in Figure 5.5. While nearly every project case study discussed in this book has minimized high-maintenance lawn areas in favor of increasing low-maintenance habitats, this project's desert Southwest context makes clear the allure of lawn in our society's collective identity.

Trends that favor indigenous vegetation on residential properties have developed through a variety of forces. In the Southwest, the growing reality of limited water supply for a burgeoning population has encouraged the use of xeriscaping. In Milford, Connecticut, the "freedom lawn" is promoted by the town as a native, multispecies mix of nitrogen-fixing plants and grasses that forms a low-maintenance lawn-like matrix and provides stormwater biofiltration benefits. One oft-cited precedent-setting example of high-end residential property that celebrates native landscapes is

the 150-acre former estate, Bloedel Reserve, on Bainbridge Island in Washington State. This property was designed to balance the partly cultivated landscape with fostering of the native plant community of old-growth forest.

Development Trend: Suburban Infill

The phenomenon of **suburban infill,** like urban infill, promotes development in areas of existing infrastructure and redevelopment of existing properties, especially where building sites are scarce. Although primarily known for its uncontrolled sprawl, this trend is also occurring throughout the Phoenix metro area. Paradise Valley consists of low-density one-acre lots and discourages high-density housing which is not a sustainable practice for this region. Suburban infill typically means intensified development that focuses on transit options, mixed uses, walkable communities, and the improvement of open spaces, the town of Paradise Valley and the greater Phoenix region recognize the need to balance these aims with community well-being and economic development while also honoring the unique qualities of the place (Calthorpe, 1991). The focus of this high-end residential property case study is an example of a suburban infill development in an established residential community.

Figure 5.6 Paradise Valley Residence—National context.

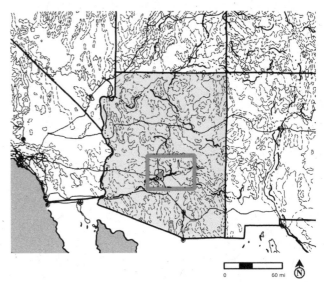

Figure 5.7 Paradise Valley Residence—State context.

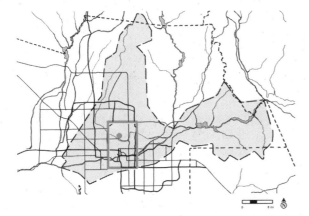

Figure 5.8 Paradise Valley Residence—Watershed context.

Context

The Paradise Valley Residence site-to-regional context is shown through a progression of scales in Figures 5.6 through 5.11. Through regional analysis, the site design process is infused with an understanding of potentials and challenges. It situates the site relative to area history, regional attitudes, and ecological health. Descriptions of landscape form, function, and philosophies of this area of Arizona explore a combination of factors to which the project design uniquely responds.

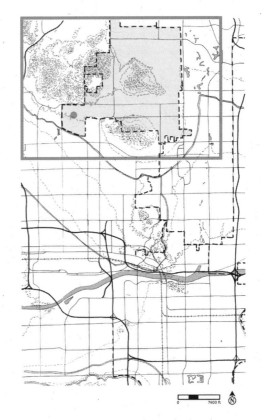

Figure 5.9 Paradise Valley Residence—Metropolitan regional context.

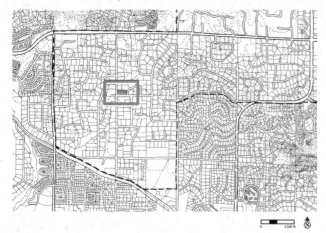

Figure 5.10 Paradise Valley Residence—Neighborhood context.

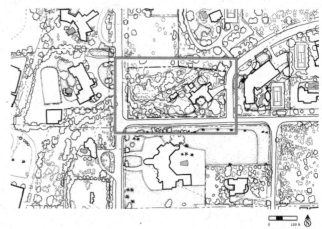

Figure 5.11 Paradise Valley Residence—Site adjacencies context.

Regional Form

Natural Patterns

Arizona has two primary geological formations, the Colorado Plateau in the north and the Basin and Range area in the south. The town of Paradise Valley lies in the Basin and Range area, which consists of dramatic elevational contrasts—parallel mountain ranges with near flat valleys between (see Figure 5.12). The Phoenix Mountains run roughly northwest to southwest in this area. Included in this range is Mummy Mountain (2,260-foot elevation) to

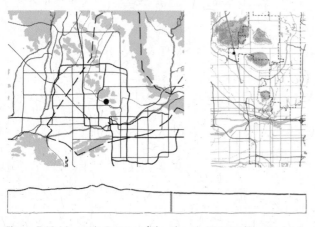

Figure 5.12 Mountain Ranges of the Phoenix Metropolitan Region in relation to site location.

the northeast of the site and Phoenix's primary skyline view—Camelback Mountain (2,704-foot elevation) to the southeast. From the site, the walls and vegetation frame views northwestward to these mountains.

Located in the northern Sonoran Desert, the soil is classified as Cavelt Gravelly Loam, which is excessively drained and has a less than 1 percent organic matter content. Desert landscapes are defined as receiving less than 10 inches of rainfall a year and evaporating more than 10 inches of rainfall a year (Center for Sonoran Desert Studies). Despite the desert conditions, extensive underground aquifers formed in this area during the last glacial age and during intermittent wet cycles thereafter.

Development Patterns

The metro Phoenix area has been inhabited for thousands of years, first by the Hohokam Native Americans as early as 3,000 years ago. These earliest known dwellers of the Sonoran Desert employed sophisticated irrigation channels; some channel locations are still used today (National Park Service). While the Hohokam culture disappeared long ago, today's Arizona still has 23 Native American reservations—more than any other state in the country. Native Americans in Arizona total near 300,000 and nearly 28 percent of state land is owned by Native American cultures such as the Maricopa Indians (U.S. Census Bureau 1999), known for their red clay jars and bowls, an example

Form-Making

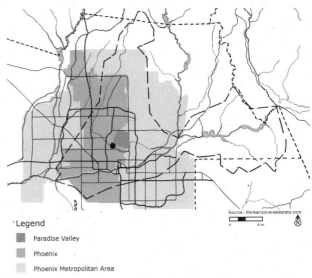

Legend

■ Paradise Valley

■ Phoenix

□ Phoenix Metropolitan Area

Figure 5.14 Metropolitan Phoenix Area. Paradise Valley is located in the heart of the metro region.

Figure 5.13 Maricopa Pottery and Its Material Source. (Lower Photo Credit: Old Territorial Indian Arts)

of which is shown in Figure 5.13. In nearby Scottsdale, six miles from Paradise Valley, a 50,000-acre Native American Reservation was established in 1879. A portion of the reservation is maintained as a natural preserve while an equal portion is cultivated with cotton and vegetables. Much of the Arizona aesthetic is derived from these native communities.

Intensive agricultural development occurred in the first half of the 20th century. Today, 36 percent of the state is farmed—roughly 5 percent in irrigated crops such as lettuce, cotton, and hay and the remainder are cattle and sheep ranches. Much of the agriculture occurs in alluvial basins adjacent to rivers such as the Colorado, Salt, Verde, and Agua Fria rivers.

Today, the greater Phoenix area, often referred to as the Valley of the Sun, is a densely populated area covering three counties, as seen in the shaded area of Figure 5.14. What has determined the development pattern is very rapid growth; the population more than doubled between 1960 and 1990. In this time, urbanized land area grew by 199 percent; 40 percent of new development replaced former agricultural land, and 32 percent took the place of undeveloped desert (Morrison Institute for Public Policy). The progression of this growth can be seen in the comparison of maps in Figure 5.15. While there is indisputable evidence of sprawl, unlike many urban centers in the United States where city centers deteriorate while sprawl continues outward (as in Milwaukee, Wisconsin), has also been growing increasingly dense with over 4,000 infill housing units added between 1995 and 2005 (Davis 2008). Factors such as air conditioning, beautiful scenery, economic incentives, climate, flat areas suitable for building, state and federal efforts to secure water supply, and delayed

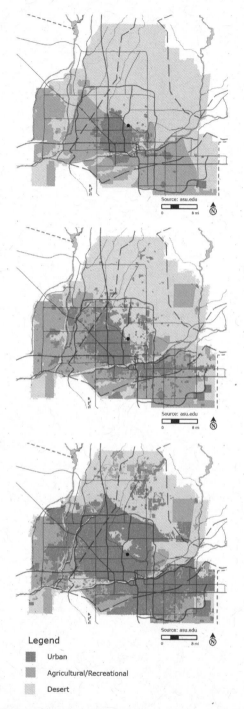

Figure 5.16 Sprawl Against Landform.
(Photo Credit: Richard M. Allen/Gemland.com)

freeways all contributed to simultaneous increased development density as well as sprawl (Morrison Institute for Public Policy).

Still, during the 1990s, most new homes concentrated on the fringe, which expanded from 11 miles from downtown Phoenix in 1970 to 21 miles in the late 1990s. This has produced a pattern where the concentrated grid meets and surrounds pristine protected mountain ranges, illustrated in Figure 5.16.

Legend

■ Urban

■ Agricultural/Recreational

□ Desert

Figure 5.15 Rapid Growth. This land cover sequence shows the urban expansion of the Phoenix metropolitan region from 1955 to 1975 to 1995.

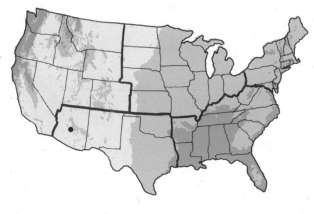

Legend

◼ 0 - 20 Inches/Year

◼ 20 - 50 Inches/Year

◼ 50 - 180 Inches/Year

Figure 5.17 Southwestern U.S. Rainfall Patterns.

Regional Function

Natural Systems

Water availability is the single largest issue in the desert landscape of the Phoenix metropolitan area. Water use and

reuse are critical for this growing area, which gets very little rainfall (shown in Figure 5.17)—4 to 9 inches per year (U.S. Geological Survey). Despite monsoons in the late summer that deliver most of the annual rainfall, much is lost during long periods of drought and a high evaporation rate.

Far from turning on the tap without giving thought to where water is coming from, the Phoenix area has a very measured, regulated, and complex water supply system. Three sources supply the greater Phoenix area: (1) the Colorado River via a canal called the Central Arizona Project, or CAP; (2) the Salt River via a series of canals called the Salt River Project, or SRP; and (3) underground aquifers.

The Phoenix metro area, which includes our site in the town of Paradise Valley, lies within the greater Colorado River watershed. Cities with the highest rates of urban growth in the United States: Phoenix, Tucson, and Las Vegas, all use the Colorado River, without which their rapid growth in this arid area would not have occurred. The Colorado River watershed, shown in Figure 5.18, drains an area of 246,000 square miles, including parts of seven western U.S. states and Mexico. Beginning in Colorado, it flows into the Gulf of California and finally to the Pacific Ocean. Along its way, the river has carved several canyons,

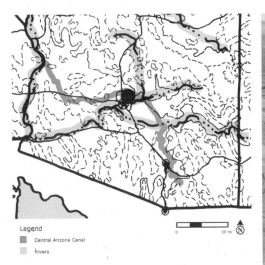

Legend

◼ Central Arizona Canal

◼ Rivers

0   30 mi   Ⓝ

Figure 5.18 Colorado River Watershed.
(Photo Credit: Bureau of Reclamation)

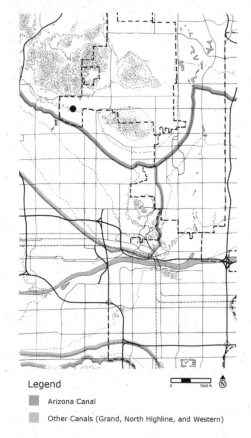

Legend

█ Arizona Canal

█ Other Canals (Grand, North Highline, and Western)

Figure 5.19 Phoenix's Salt River Project Canals.

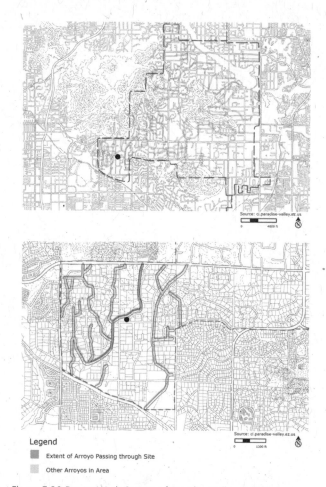

Legend

█ Extent of Arroyo Passing through Site

█ Other Arroyos in Area

Figure 5.20 Desert Wash System of Paradise Valley and Site.

one of which is the Grand Canyon. It is difficult to fathom this large river being depleted, yet starting in 1855, every drop of river water of the Colorado has been apportioned. Complex legal water rights covering many federal and state municipalities divide, pump, and pipe the river into storage reservoirs in many directions. Due to usage and drought, over the course of the 20th century the water reaching the Colorado Delta has diminished by over 75 percent.

The Central Arizona Project (CAP) is a 336-mile open-air aqueduct (or canal) that diverts Colorado River water to the Phoenix area. One of the largest and most expensive aqueducts in the United States, it took 20 years to complete, at a cost of $3.6 billion. Simplified concrete-lined canals divert the river for irrigation. Not resembling an ecosystem at all, many canals are lined with chain link

fence and are excluded in community open space planning (Keane 1998). Slowly changes are being sought to incorporate parks and vegetation with the canals and make them a destination. Roughly 25 percent of this captured water is used for drinking while 75 percent is used for irrigating agriculture and hydroelectric power.

The CAP project was approved to supply water needed for the growing region in part in exchange for stopping the practice of pumping aquifers (CAP 1997). For many years, underground aquifers were pumped as a primary water source. Aquifers are now viewed as nonrenewable resources since they recharge at a geologic timescale. These resources were overdrawn, dropping the groundwater hundreds of feet (City of Phoenix). In 1980, the practice was outlawed in Arizona. Recently, however, recharging the underground aquifers with excess water from the Colorado River is being used as a safety measure, should the Colorado source run dry as predicted sometime in the future. Because of the political stipulations of the apportioning of the Colorado River, Arizona has a lower priority than other states regarding supply. To safeguard against lost access to the Colorado source as droughts and growth take their toll, Arizona has created large lakes to replenish the underground aquifers (Jenkins 2006).

A smaller watershed, the Salt River is almost exclusively used by Phoenix and the city's beginnings are credited to this water supply. The Salt River Project, the canals of which are depicted in Figure 5.19, began in 1903 with the Roosevelt Dam, which regulated this seasonal river prone to drought and flooding. The river drains an area of approximately 5,980 square miles and consists of a vast network of reservoirs, dams, and channels, which control a steady flow of water.

Paradise Valley in particular contains dozens of what are called "washes," or **arroyos**, which are small intermittent streams that capture rainwater from the surrounding Phoenix Mountain Preserve, Mummy Mountain, and Camelback Mountain. The desert wash system is shown in Figure 5.20. One of these washes is found in the case study site. The washes are protected and enhanced according to the ordinance of the Paradise Valley Planning Commission.

Salt River Project Guidelines to Watering Your Property

"Irrigation is one of the reasons why desert residents enjoy year-round recreation, beautiful landscaping, and agricultural success."

Salt River Project

From the Reservoirs to Your Yard

So how does the water get from the reservoirs to your yard? After you place your water order, we combine it with all the other water orders from the Valley, and release the requested amount of water from the storage dam. The water then flows into the seven main canals crossing the Valley.

An SRP employee, known as a "zanjero" (pronounced sahn-hair'-oh) opens a gate to release the water from the canal into a system of smaller waterways called laterals. The lateral brings the water to a specific delivery point where a zanjero opens SRP's gate, releasing the water into your neighborhood.

The neighborhood delivery point is the end of the SRP system. From here, the system bringing water to your property is made up of open ditches, underground pipelines, control gates, and valves. This system is owned, operated, and maintained by the people who use the system in your neighborhood and is referred to as the "private system."

You and your neighbors are responsible for seeing that the water gets from the SRP delivery point to your property.

(www.sedona.biz)

Paradise Valley is located within the Southern Basin and Range bioregion where the dominant ecological community is the Sonoran Desert Scrub, depicted in Figures 5.21 and 5.22. The prevalent vegetation tends to consist of small leaved succulents. The area is comprised of two primary plant communities, the creosote bush community and the palo verde-saguaro community.

The austere Sonoran Desert with its cactus and pastel palette is the signature landscape for which the Phoenix area is known. However, residential aesthetics generally tend toward water-loving plants such as palm trees, and lawns that require high water inputs and do not provide much-needed shade. The town of Paradise Valley requires homeowners to submit a Native Plant Preservation Plan for

Figure 5.21 U.S. Natural Regions: The Southern Basin and Range (Harker 1999).

approval of new construction. This ordinance ensures that mature native plants are not unnecessarily destroyed or removed (Town of Paradise Valley). Many people moving to the area have come from less arid areas of the country and while admiring the desert landscapes, they prefer lawns that offer some reprieve from the desert climate. Since most soils contain less than 1 percent organic matter and topsoil is typically only one-half inch thick, these lush green landscapes can only be sustained with large water inputs. **Xeriscaping** has become an increasing trend in recent years in part because of rising water costs and in part because of new suburban community-mandated maintenance requirements.

Human Systems

The lure of the Phoenix area and the reason it attracts many for retirement, vacation, second homes, and relocation is the beauty of the natural environment, the snow-free climate, the growing economy, and the affordable cost of living comparative to nearby states. Roadway grids first laid out as a meridian base line in 1863 established the basis for neighborhoods, urban centers, and open space systems that dominate the Phoenix area. While they avoided the large mountain landforms, they eradicated much of the more subtle landform along with most of its natural washes and desert landscape. A comparison of the aerial photos shown in Figure 5.23 shows the changes in the landform since the mid-1950s.

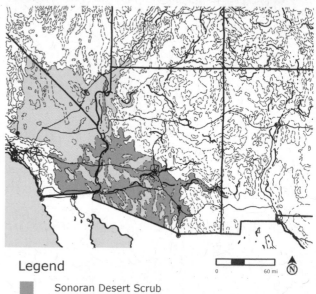

Legend

■ Sonoran Desert Scrub

■ Others Habitats in Bioregion

Figure 5.22 Southwestern United States' Desert Zones.

Paradise Valley, largely a built-out residential community, is comprised primarily of single-family residential land use, dominated by 1-acre lots—larger than the typical Phoenix lot size. Preservation of open space is therefore addressed not through new acquisitions but through careful protection of existing preservation areas (Paradise Valley General Plan). The absence of major commercial or civic arterial

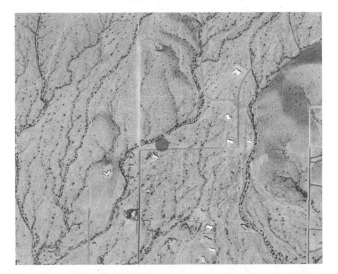

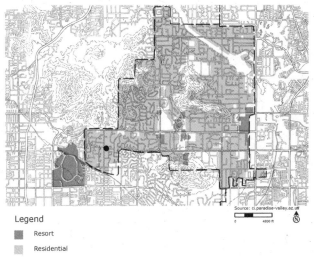

Legend

▪ Resort

▪ Residential

Source: ci.paradise-valley.az.us

0   4000 ft

Figure 5.24 Land Use in Paradise Valley.

Figure 5.23 Paradise Valley Then and Now. The subtle landforms of the low desert are legible in the 1957 image above, while they have mostly disappeared in the 2004 image below.
(Credit: historicaerials.com)

roads and land uses creates a quiet, low-density feel to the area. The high concentration of vacation resorts in the area, shown in the dark shaded region of Figure 5.24, such as the Arizona Biltmore, lends added emphasis on the quiet residential, scenic open space qualities of the community.

Regional Philosophies

Conservation versus Development

The "new frontier" attitude persists when it comes to regulating for environmental protections in this part of the United States. While the Arizona State Parks, The Game and Fish Commission, and Department of Fish and Wildlife have begun to encourage watershed and habitat protection areas, they have not mandated it and much of the Arizona environment continues to be converted from native landscape to sprawling new development. Seventy percent of the state's wet marshes have been destroyed, as have nearly 90 percent of riparian ecosystems (Center for Wildlife Law at the University of New Mexico). Despite this early loss of biodiversity and somewhat lax state regulations, roughly two-thirds of Maricopa County land is publicly owned or owned by Native American reservations that are protecting natural resources (Morrison Institute for Public Policy). Phoenix has acquired and nearly doubled its open space by 17,000 acres since the 1960s—more than any city in the United States, except for San Diego (Morrison Institute for Public Policy). These open spaces are concentrated in mountainous areas—such as the 6,000-acre Phoenix Mountains Preserve—where the rugged topography severely restricts development. Open space in the form of regionally significant green belt areas to limit urban growth along the northern edges of Phoenix and Scottsdale are discussed, but there are no immediate plans for implementation.

More critical than open space acquisition, regional water conservation has been in place since 1986. While sustainability has been part of the agenda for many years, there is much debate in Arizona about what constitutes sustainable growth in relation to water resources. Recent regulation, for example, requires subdivision developers in the Phoenix area to demonstrate a one hundred year "assured supply" of water per parcel prior to building (Jenkins 2006). In some cases, this also means that new homeowners agree to pay pumping costs should aquifers be needed to supplement their home water use. The reality of the growth rate—one acre every three hours—and the exorbitant cost of pumping have many concerned about whether this "promise to pay" is realistic. Multiple dubious strategies for justifying new growth have many area inhabitants concerned with issues of rapid growth and depleting resources (Morrison Institute for Public Policy).

One initiative that takes advantage of the region's harsh climatic conditions is a partnering between Arizona State University and the City of Phoenix to use the city as a laboratory for a program called the Global Institute of Sustainability. Research conducted to counter the heat island effect (days hotter than 110 degrees increased from 6 days per year in the 1950s to 22 days per year in the 2000s), includes examination of the effects of taller buildings to increase density and shade, installation of shade structures along streets, and the replacement of palm trees with shade trees to make the downtown more inhabitable. This and many other initiatives by nonprofit and government organizations promise improvement of the built environment to address climatic challenges in the Sonoran Desert.

Development in the Southwest has been spurred through a series of economic activities. In 1867, prospectors found copper ore in the mountains of central and southern Arizona. This and other findings began a "rush" on excavation of gold, silver, and zinc extraction mining in the area that spurred development in Arizona until 1936. Agriculture was improved through the employment of an advanced irrigation system. At that time, agricultural efforts, however, were still limited by summer droughts and only expanded after dams were built to control water year round. In 1947,

Figure 5.25 Public Art: City Boundary. *This project created a terraced water-harvesting device that interprets ancient Native American irrigation technology to help this prominent corner of Papago Park revegetate with native species. (Photo Credit: Steve Martino.)*

the Motorola Company established itself in Phoenix, bringing the first of a string of high-tech businesses to Arizona, which persist and grow today. Some of the more recent economic stimulus packages include sustainable technologies such as harnessing the sunny days into solar panel–producing electricity. New homes and a growing high-tech industry have spurred a competitive job market.

Cultural Resources

While today Arizona has a dynamically mixed culture like many others in the United States, the local aesthetic borrows heavily from the desert landscape and indigenous cultures. The distinct Southwestern architecture of the area mimics the Spanish and Mexican cultures that once inhabited Arizona, while ancient Native Americans like the Hohokam and Anasazi, who created an aesthetic in their crafts and petroglyphs, still define the Arizona identity today.

More modern cultural resources include architectural works that interpret and respond to the desert environment. Frank Lloyd Wright celebrated the desert environment with his design and establishment of Taliesin West in the 1920s. This studio and school is located in what was once the desert outskirts of Phoenix, where it now has been encroached upon by the suburban community of Scottsdale. Architect Paolo Soleri developed experimental architectural form that responds to desert ecology with his

Arcosanti project begun in the 1960s. Located in the high desert northeast of Phoenix the development embodies Soleri's concept of arcology—ecological human habitats—as an alternative urban development in the age of environmental crisis and sprawl. While these works have provided models for regional architectural form, they have not influenced land use planning to reflect their values.

A strong value for regional cultural identity is reflected in the City of Phoenix's Public Art Program, which has become a national exemplar since its inception in the 1980s. The incorporation of art into infrastructure such as highways, parks, and utilities has become a hallmark of this program. Landscape architect Steve Martino collaborated with environmental artist Jody Pinto on an award-winning, landscape-based public art project located in Papago Park, shown in Figure 5.25.

Regional Setting for Pioneer Site

In summary, the surrounding context of the featured residential landscape is shown to be in a cycle of rapid growth that is proving difficult to sustain given its location in the Sonoran Desert. Arid conditions, limited water allocations, and unchecked sprawl plague the larger region of Phoenix, while the town of Paradise Valley, despite build-out, tries to maintain its natural resources and sense of character even as its extensive tourist industry grows. Thus the juxtaposition of this sustainable residential site within a context out of environmental balance defines it as a "sustainable pioneer."

Site

Design Considerations

Existing Site

The 1.5-acre home site is bounded on three sides by roads. All three are residential in nature: one a major north–south corridor with lots of open desert character and the other two, more suburban in character. Although the parcel was developed as part of a newer, small cul-de-sac subdivision, overall the neighborhood is one that has some interesting cultural and natural character and a sense of openness,

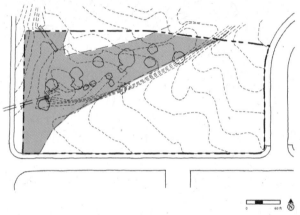

Figure 5.26 Pre-Design Site Conditions. The vegetated desert wash that passes through the site is contrasted against the cleared area of the site in this 1996 aerial image. As the site photo illustrates, wash contains a regionally characteristic mix of native desert species and gravelly soil.

which is more common in Paradise Valley but unusual for the sprawling Phoenix region. The presence of a natural arroyo passing through the site, which might have been viewed as a constraint for more conventional home-site development, presented deepened opportunities for creating habitat in this case. As can be seen in Figure 5.26, the site had not previously been developed and retained some native landform and vegetation, but much of the site had been disturbed by dumping associated with adjacent road and home-site construction.

PARADISE VALLEY RESIDENCE SCALES OF LANDSCAPE INFLUENCE	ECO-REGION	COMMUNITY	NEIGHBORHOOD	SITE

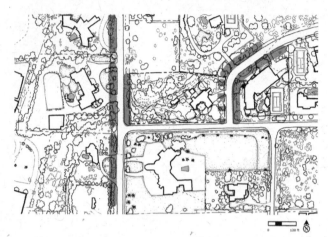

Figure 5.27 Neighborhood Road Frontages.

Program Development

The primary scale of landscape influence for this project is the neighborhood. The neighborhood's relatively large parcel size, in contrast with the greater Phoenix pattern of small residential lot sizes, provides an opportunity for each site to have patch function and integrity of its own. The presence of several parcels and corridors that have retained some natural form and function through the use or conservation of native plantings creates a patchwork with opportunities for connectivity. The neighborhood's diverse and

distinctive architectural character offers a break from the standardized sprawl that covers much of the region.

In a larger sense, the Sonoran Desert regional scale, whose character is so absent in the main fabric of the metropolitan region, provides the basic landscape inspiration for the site.

The primary scales of *design program* focus for this project are site planning, site design, and detail design. In the absence of neighborhood and local frameworks for an integrated approach to sustainable planning and design, the particular site and adjacency conditions of this project presented key site planning opportunities for maximizing sustainability. Martino encouraged the clients to obtain approval to deviate from the subdivision's requirements of street-side walls and to reverse the frontage of the home in order to showcase the preservation and restoration of a desert environment along a major north–south road corridor. The existing neighborhood frontages can be seen in Figure 5.27. While several of the neighboring home sites have recently been developed or redeveloped with more conventional, less sustainable approaches, the project site's orientation toward this desert road aids in retaining and emphasizing the open desert character.

In siting the house and developing its outdoor spaces, protection of intact areas and restoration of disturbed areas was a prime objective. The drainage easement protects the arroyo from being developed and this area did have some

PARADISE VALLEY RESIDENCE SCALES OF PROGRAM FOCUS	REGIONAL PLANNING	DISTRICT PLANNING	SITE PLANNING	SITE DESIGN	DETAIL DESIGN

Form-Making

existing vegetation that was preserved. But additional vegetation was introduced with the site design to enhance the habitat quality and integrate it with the rest of the site.

The finer scales of site design and detail design are where the architectural interest was developed with subtlety and sophistication.

The detailed program that was tailored out of the basic program goals and specific site conditions can be summarized as follows:

Environmental

- Desert landscape restoration and enhancement
- Site grading to flow to arroyo

Cultural

- Water features that express scarcity
- Barragan architectural/sculptural influences
- Southwestern vernacular spatial influences
- Entry sequence of natural to cultural spaces
- Views to near and distant desert features
- Strong delineation of private and public spaces

The Paradise Valley Residence design outcome is illustrated in the site plan, sections, and detail views shown in Figures 5.29, 5.30, 5.31, and 5.32. The project is analyzed with respect to two central dimensions of sustainable site design process and outcomes: landscape form and landscape function.

Conventional High-End Residence Design

Two Paradise Valley Neighbors

One needn't look far from the project site to find an example of more conventional residential site design. On two sides of the site there are homes that rely on irrigated exotic plantings, elaborate fountains, and swimming pools for the majority of their site coverage. Although the neighborhood has a relatively intact natural desert landscape matrix, these sites have developed a whole new identity for themselves that has very little to do with the desert landscape that surrounds them. While the early urbanization of the Southwest was typically treated in this oasis-type manner, the concept of xeriscaping, encouraged by the exponential growth of an area that receives very little rainfall, has begun to take hold. Yet these neighboring landscapes demonstrate the lingering urge for the pastoral and the exotic.

These sites, shown in Figure 5.28, treat the landscape as a sort of island on which the house is set as centerpiece and is easily viewed from the street across an open front yard expanse of lawn. The backyard is the private domain and is walled off from its surroundings. While there are some native plants in evidence, they are minor elements and are not used in plant community groupings but as specimen plantings in an overall exotic cultivated landscape.

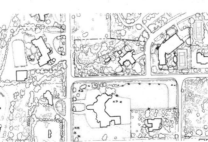

Figure 5.28 Site Neighbors.

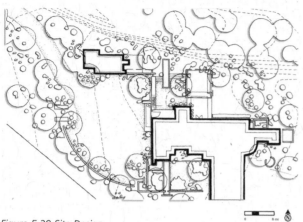

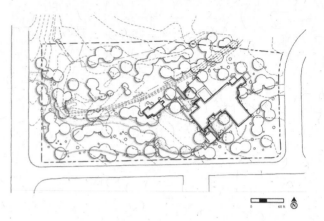

Figure 5.29 Site Design.

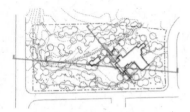

Figure 5.30 Site Sections.

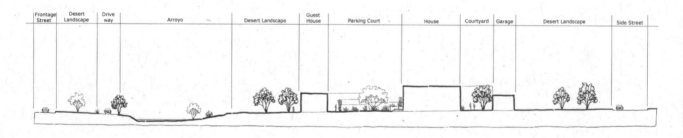

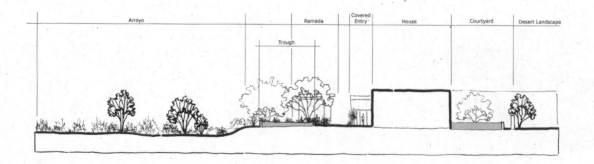

Form-Making

Figure 5.31 Courtyard Section.

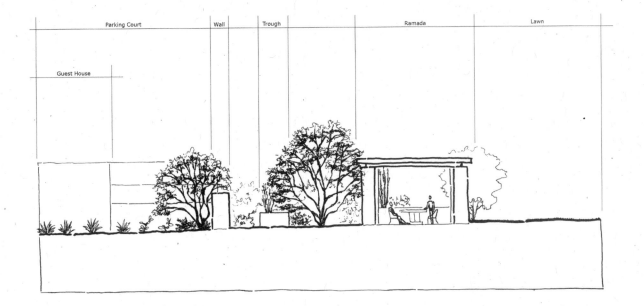

| Parking Court | Wall | Trough | Ramada | Lawn |

Guest House

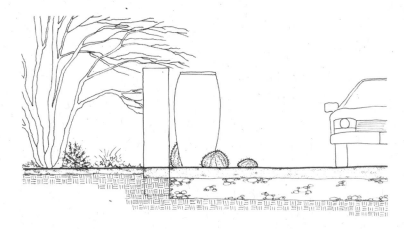

Figure 5.32 Parking Court Detail.

Site Design Form

Patterns

The arroyo gives the site its strongest natural pattern, with its linear landform trajectory through the site creating the basis for natural and cultural zones and access. The organization of the site, shown in Figure 5.33, shows how the **architectonic** site elements connect through the house in two axial directions creating unification of the site and integration of interior and exterior spaces. Although the native desert landscape is the underpinning of the site, extension of architectural elements into this landscape is strategically employed to integrate structure and site and to intensify the perception of nature. This site engagement is shown in Figure 5.34.

Figure 5.35 A Historic Hacienda. (Credit: Haciendas Del Sol)

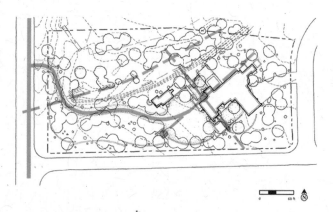

Figure 5.33 Site Organization.

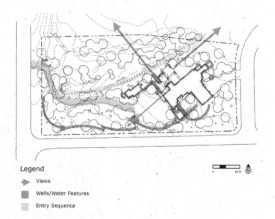

Legend
- ➤ Views
- ▇ Walls/Water Features
- ▦ Entry Sequence

Figure 5.34 Organizing Site Elements.

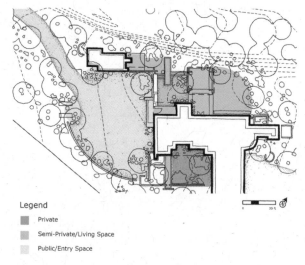

Legend
- ▇ Private
- ▇ Semi-Private/Living Space
- ▢ Public/Entry Space

Figure 5.36 Courtyard Spaces.

As mentioned earlier, layout and articulation of the house is based on that of historic haciendas, in which the buildings form courtyards, such as the one shown in Figure 5.35, where elements of water, shade, and enclosure create a respite from the harsher characteristics of the desert. These sites were typically the homesteads or estates of

Figure 5.37 Shade and Protection.

Materials

Materials used in the constructed landscape are also selected to reflect the regional architectural vernacular. Stucco is a historic material often employed in arid climates and was first used in this region in the pueblo architecture of Native Americans. Masonry walls covered with various coatings that began simply with mud and evolved to contemporary stucco (sand, lime, cement, and water) reflect the natural resource base and architectural history of the Southwest. Though stucco structures have been fairly ubiquitous to the region until recently, the homogenization/globalization of the building industry has begun to produce structures that use wood and other nonregional materials more freely. Martino uses stucco walls throughout the site, giving them artful distinctiveness with bold colors that pick up on the flashes of color found in desert flora, geology, and skies, forming both architectural and sculptural lines in the landscape

The use of mulch in planting beds has become about as ubiquitous as lawn in the American landscape, regardless of geographic location. The mulch material is typically shredded wood or stone of some sort and is used in ways that separate planting areas from lawn and paved areas meant for circulation. This has become even more pronounced as the practice of irrigation has become more standard and specialized. Wood mulch models the way plants exist in a natural wooded landscape, with twigs,

ranches or other productive or open space landscapes upon which the owner derived sustenance. As can be seen in Figures 5.36 and 5.37, this project offers a modern interpretation of the hacienda, with walled enclosures of varying proportions that define courtyards related to the house and guest house, elements that suggest or provide the cool and calm qualities of water, and overhead structures that create open-air shady spots for outdoor living. Away from the house, the repeated use of stucco walls in a variety of sculptural alignments that introduce curvilinear forms and gradually descending heights plays off the placement of plant materials and creates permeable edges that subtly define zones of the site and views to the landscape beyond.

The development in which this home is situated originally required homes to have 6-foot-tall walls around the properties. On this site, surrounded by street on three sides, this would have required such walls on two of the intended back- and side-yard walls. Whereas these types of walls and other structures placed in the landscape typically provide primarily utilitarian functions such as physical enclosure or grade retention, the walls designed by Martino play a more visual, perceptual role of contrasting the native landscape features against cultural form. This contrast acknowledges human presence without eliminating natural form and function, demonstrating a harmonious relationship between nature and culture.

Figure 5.38 Sterile and Segregated.

leaves, and other organic material, or **biomass**, littering the ground and continually breaking down and enriching the soil and keeping it moist. When this biomass is particularly heavy and the canopy is dense and lets little sunlight in, other plants are inhibited from growing. In a desert landscape the plants produce much less biomass, corresponding with the lower precipitation available. There is therefore very little canopy vegetation and the rocky, gravelly soil is much more exposed. The practice of mulching with processed stone is better adapted to a desert landscape, but often translates to a sterile landscape, as can be seen in Figure 5.38.

Figure 5.39 Integrated Desert Paving.

Mulch *per se* is not a part of Martino's landscape materials vocabulary. Instead he refers to the surfacing of his landscapes, shown in Figure 5.39, as *desert paving,* where planting areas and circulation areas are more subtly distinguished. He does not have defined planting beds that are separate from permeable circulation areas. The driveway and auto court, for instance, is surfaced in decomposed granite, a material that blends with the natural desert soil and provides a dust-controlled smooth surface. The auto court is shaped in a graceful and generous circular space (approximately 55 feet in diameter), that is functional but flexible in use and identity. The placement of plants in natural, dispersed groupings across the gravelly, sandy landscape is interrupted by the driveway; a lifting of a few layers of the desert—not disruption of the whole system—to make way for a path. Impermeable surfaces are limited to just a few concrete areas directly adjacent to the buildings where concrete is transitioned to the decomposed granite through the use of exposed aggregate paving.

The use of water in this landscape is particularly pointed at expressing its preciousness and limits in an arid environment. At a basic level, the natural desert ecosystem form that blankets the majority of the site, equipped with a drip irrigation system, is tailored to low water inputs. But beyond this, Martino has centered his design on a set of contemplative elements that represent human uses and need for water.

A pair of low, concrete water troughs are placed on an axis that pierces the house and points to the arroyo on the northern edge of the site, toward which the site's grade is pitched. This feature is reminiscent of one used in Barragan's *Los Arboledas* project. It also evokes the horse troughs prevalent in landscapes of the Old West.

A reference to water that does not involve the actual use of water is the placement of large pottery urns and water vessels in terminus locations of other axial lines of the design. They are reflective of southwestern culture in their material use and finish and are a universal spiritual symbol of sacredness and offering. The placement of the vessels is framed in various ways, with wall segments or alcoves.

Site Design Function

Natural Systems

As depicted in the drainage maps of Figure 5.40, this project makes functional connections to the larger watershed by its hydrological and habitat linkage to the arroyo that passes through the site. The arroyo, as discussed in the context section of the case study, is an important natural corridor in this highly developed metropolitan area where such natural systems have all but disappeared. Impermeable surfaces on the site are kept to a minimum with the use of decomposed granite surfacing and those areas that do not drain toward the arroyo shed water into large areas of desert landscape prior to reaching the street on the southern side of the site.

Plant communities, landform, and soils of the Sonoran Desert are combined on the site to create functioning habitat. Martino's plant palette gleans the richness of color, texture, and form from desert species, with the drama of succulent, herbaceous, and woody flowering species playing against the backdrop of sage green, fine textures of the canopy and lower shrub species.

While the planting areas close to the house within the courtyard areas are subtly refined with more deliberate placement and interaction with architectonic elements, they still use native species. As can be seen in the landscape zone outline in Figure 5.41, there is not a strict dividing line between natural and cultural areas but rather a smooth and seamless transition. Within the courtyard, one small panel of lawn is provided (about 900 square feet). The remainder of the landscape is treated with the native plant palette and drip irrigation, rendering it a very low-maintenance and low-input landscape.

The canopy layer is comprised of only three tree species—mesquite, ironwood, and palo verde—two of which several existed on the site prior to development and are preserved. The pattern of the planting, shown in Figure 5.42, is based on the scattered groupings spread across gently rolling rocky desert soils found in nature. There are not distinct ground cover, shrub, and canopy layers, but blended groups that reach overall heights of approximately 25 to 30 feet.

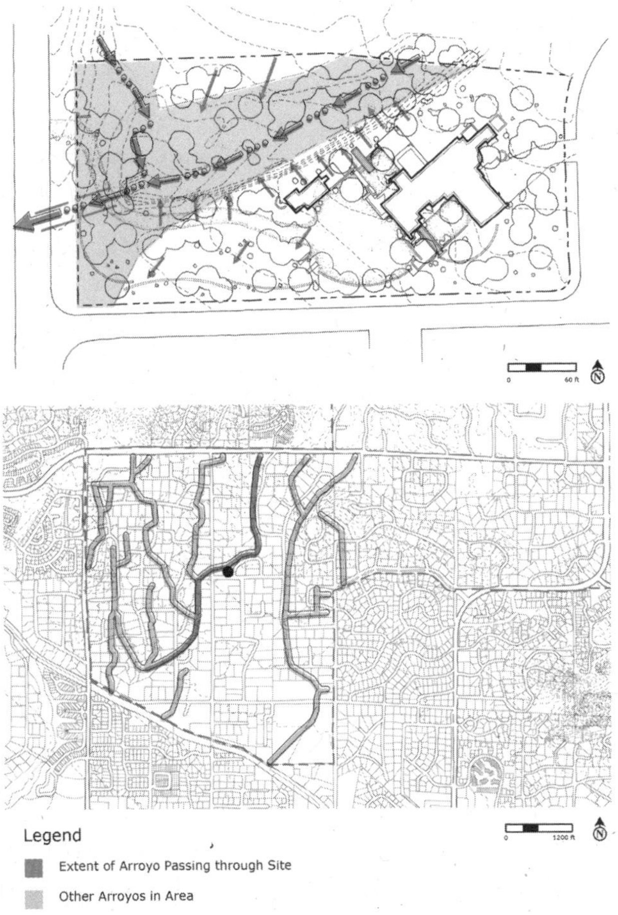

Figure 5.40 Hydrological Linkage.

Legend

■ Extent of Arroyo Passing through Site

▨ Other Arroyos in Area

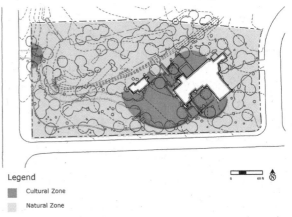

Legend

■ Cultural Zone

▨ Natural Zone

Figure 5.41 Landscape Zones.

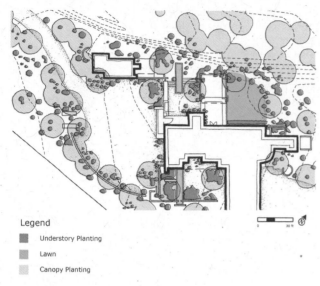

Legend

■ Understory Planting

■ Lawn

■ Canopy Planting

Figure 5.42 Planting Pattern.

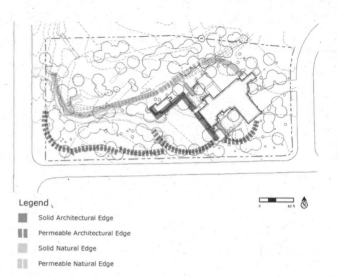

Legend

■ Solid Architectural Edge

▮▮ Permeable Architectural Edge

▮ Solid Natural Edge

▮▮ Permeable Natural Edge

Figure 5.44 Site Edges.

Human Systems

In terms of human uses, the layout of the house in relation to new and preexisting site spaces and features, seen in Figure 5.43, promotes many distinct opportunities for exchange between indoor and outdoor living. Each indoor living space

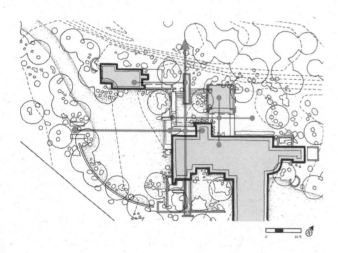

Figure 5.43 Indoor-Outdoor Linkages.

has well-defined outdoor spaces that share common functions. For instance, the bedroom has an isolated courtyard and garden on the south side of the house, while the kitchen is aligned with the outdoor dining area. The living room, kitchen, and detached guesthouse have linked, but distinct spaces on the north side of the house that have a permeable edge at the arroyo and views to the mountains that pop out at the city edge. Figure 5.44 shows the edges of the site. While the home's desert surrounds and linkage provide valued privacy, more importantly they afford varied opportunities for contemplation of nature.

The experience of this landscape unfolds in a well-choreographed sequence. As shown in Figure 5.45, there are two entry points for the house: The entry where visitors are welcomed is via a long winding drive off of the neighborhood's main road, and the owner's more utilitarian entry, which includes the garage, is located off the less traveled back street. The main road has other houses along which it fronts, but has retained desert character and arroyo and mountain views, while other streets in the neighborhood have taken on a more suburban, highly developed feel. The original intent with the subdivision was to have the entry off of the back street and therefore the building envelope, with its typical arrangement of a large backyard and smaller front yard, worked well for creating a drive through a

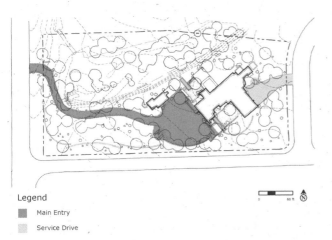

Legend
- Main Entry
- Service Drive

Figure 5.45 Site Access.

desert landscape and over the arroyo as a first dramatic step in the landscape sequence.

The site sequence, shown in Figure 5.46, continues with arrival to the parking and entry court where a large-scale space opens up, the desert landscape gains refinement, and the entry to the house and outdoor living space is defined. Once inside the thick walled and gated entry point, a covered porch directs one either to the front door of the house or to the corridor of outdoor living spaces aligned along the arroyo. The water trough and arroyo edge are within view of this point. The corridor is terminated at either end by the guest house and the lawn panel with its framed mountain views.

A beneficial consequence of the site's extensive native desert habitat coverage is the long-term simplification of its management. While drip irrigation is available and was critical during the establishment period, the vegetation is drought resistant. Compared to other natural habitat types such as meadow or woodland, desert restoration has a less transformational establishment period, since the vegetation is naturally slow-growing and low in biomass. This makes it a little less daunting for clients, who have generally been conditioned to expect instant landscapes. The shade and protection provided by overhead structures, permeable paving, and lack of features such as a swimming pool add to the site's long-term regenerative and energy-efficient characteristics.

Figure 5.46 Site Sequence. The top view shows the front visitor entrance, the middle view shows the arrival court, and the bottom view shows the interior courtyard looking out to the small lawn area.

Site Design Integration

Engagements

Engagement of the Paradise Valley residence landscape with ecological form and function occurs primarily through *restoration*. Intact remnants of native plant communities and landforms existed on the site and repair of the disturbed portions of the site allowed for reconnecting a significant patch of native landscape to the arroyo corridor.

Following is a list of specific site design elements that take advantage of natural phenomenon, site activities, and amenities that engage the user with the site and its regional, environmental, and cultural systems. These cultural engagements, as depicted in Figure 5.47, are categorized as elements, views, or nodes.

Element: Sustainable Water Features. The trough and vessels used in the design, rather than flaunt a wasteful or frivolous use of water for this environment, communicate a sense of knowledge and respect for its wise use. An example of this is the reflective pool shown in Figure 5.48.

Element: Garden Walls. Structures that are both freestanding and connected to the house, an example of

Figure 5.48 Engagement Element: Reflective Water.

Figure 5.49 Engagement Element: Urns in Arid Landscape.

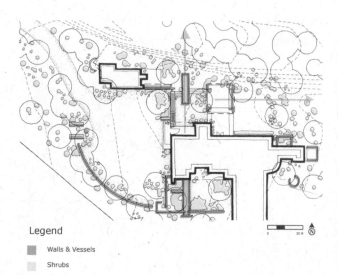

Legend

■ Walls & Vessels

░ Shrubs

Figure 5.47 Site Engagements.

Figure 5.50 Engagement View: Framed Through Wall.

Figure 5.51 Engagement View: Framed Through Ramada.

which is shown in Figure 5.49, are proportioned and toned to highlight plant materials and provide subtle distinction between cultural and natural landscape spaces.

Views: Desert Mountains. The wall that connects the guesthouse to the main house has a "window" that frames a view from the parking court to the desert skyline, giving a hint of what lies beyond. The wall is brightly colored to call attention to both the view and the foreground plant material. Other views of the contextual landscape are framed from various points within the corridor of living space described previously, as can be seen in Figures 5.50 and 5.51.

Path: Desert Driveway. The front entry drive is an important interface with the desert landscape and

sets the tone for the remainder of the site experience. Removing the more private and utilitarian features such as the garage to the reverse side of the home allows for a graceful and efficient circulation plan.

Outcomes

The Program/Site/Context Comparison

Predesign Site/Context Conditions

The sustainable outcome of a project is determined largely by the design team's approach at the project outset toward

	INITIAL PROGRAM GOALS	SITE CHARACTER	CONTEXT CHARACTER
ENVIRONMENTAL	Native desert landscape habitat	Previously undeveloped site	Majority of riparian corridors have been destroyed
		Natural arroyo/drainage easement covering part of site	Water supplied from outside sources via industrial canals
		Other natural areas disturbed by nearby construction fill	Landscape matrix is highly developed with small patches of unlinked open space, primarily associated with mountains
CULTURAL	Southwestern vernacular architectural and landscape design influences	Views of surrounding mountains	Imported landscape and architecture influences
	Contemporary design influence of Barragan	Vernacular feel to one of road frontages; generic and imported feel to other two	Strong regional vernacular architectural and landscape forms
SOCIAL	Contemplative use of landscape Use of landscape to create privacy	Relatively large site in comparison with regional pattern	Contrast of resort versus workaday populations, land use
		Road frontage on three sides creates exposure and privacy challenge	Use of walls, walled subdivisions to create privacy where small parcels limit extent of landscape

three areas of design decision-making: (1) the selection of program goals, (2) the judgments made in the assessment of site character, and (3) the judgments made in the assessment of the context. The relationship of these decisions can be demonstrated via three groups of predesign factors: environmental, cultural, and social. The view of the predesign relationship between site, context, and program for the Paradise Valley Residence project is summarized in this way in the table above. This analysis shows that the initial program goals drafted by the client developed largely from regional conditions. Later, the landscape architect refined the program to develop specific site responses to these larger contextual issues.

Postdesign Site/Context Impact

The outcome of this particular site design project has its greatest sustainability impact at the site level itself. While the arroyo is addressed on site, it really doesn't link to a larger neighborhood function. The creation of a well-functioning and substantially sized ecological patch allows for integrity without dependence on adjacent land. While the

landscape does link to a corridor of natural character along the frontage road, the site creates a discreet and individualized cultural identity that is not necessarily intended to link to neighboring architectural character.

Jumping out to the regional scale, the project also contributes to a valuable growing cumulative effect, produced by similar project patches dotted throughout the metropolitan area, of linkage to the larger natural desert bioregion. Figure 5.52 shows various Martino-designed sites.

Improving Site Efficiency & Sustainability

The Paradise Valley Residence project demonstrates the use of the following techniques to integrate sustainable form and function, improve the site, mitigate the impact of development, and create a compelling, functional site design on its own terms, independent of the context.

- Architectonic forms integrated with natural environment

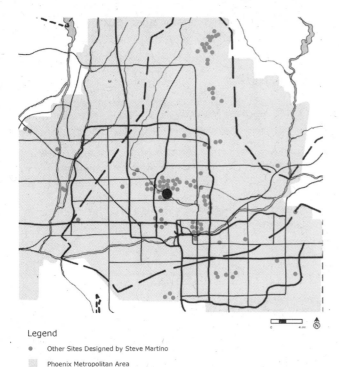

Legend

● Other Sites Designed by Steve Martino

Phoenix Metropolitan Area

Figure 5.52 Sites Designed by Steve Martino in Metro Phoenix.

- Meaningful site organization, artful edges
- Sequence/narrative of native landscape

Improving Regional Efficiency & Sustainability

As a "sustainable pioneer" in relation to its surroundings, the following techniques integrate context concerns with the site design solution, creating a positive connection and larger impact.

- Natural landscape site matrix
- Focused views to contextual native landscape focal points
- Linkage to larger street identity/pattern
- Functional and visual linkage to local hydrological system

Sustainability Criteria Met?

The site design outcomes of the Paradise Valley Residence are outlined in relation to the five *landscape sustainability criteria* presented in Chapter 1 as follows:

Connectivity

The Paradise Valley Residence site design:

- links conceptually to its cultural context through the use of vernacular forms of architecture.
- links conceptually to its ecological context through the preservation and restoration of native desert habitat.
- connects physically to its hydrological context with ecological stormwater management.
- provides a sense of neighborhood native landscape continuity with its entry orientation.

Meaning

The Paradise Valley Residence site design:

- interprets scarcity and importance of water in the arid southwestern region.
- provides contemplative opportunities for the experience and understanding of the desert landscape through circulation, views, and focal points.
- integrates modern architectural expression with vernacular architectural form.
- integrates color, texture, and form dimensions of the native landscape with architectural expression.

Purpose .

The Paradise Valley Residence site design:

- creates patches of desert habitat that are viable with or without the residential land use.
- creates a site landscape sequence that satisfies utilitarian needs such as parking without sacrificing spatial quality and landscape identity.

- establishes clear and well-transitioned zones for public versus private use, and both natural and cultural function.

Efficiency

The Paradise Valley Residence site design:

- allows natural processes of stormwater and vegetative growth to function naturally without excessive manipulation and inputs.

- uses "desert paving" interchangeably in vegetated and circulation areas as a native surfacing material that encourages stormwater infiltration.

- uses a suburban infill site rather than a more secluded site out in the larger desert wilderness.

Stewardship

The Paradise Valley Residence site design:

- visibly demonstrates sustainable site development techniques in clear contrast to neighboring properties where irrigation and imported landscapes prevail.

- has been managed as intended to allow natural processes to establish and develop the habitat.

Parallel Projects

Turtle Creek Pump House, Highland Park, Texas

This 2007 ASLA Residential Design Honor Award winner takes a defunct historic municipal water pump house and reuses it as a place for art exhibition, play, education, and guest housing. Located adjacent to Turtle Creek, water was pumped out of the creek and distributed throughout the area via the pump house. The deteriorating facility was purchased by the adjacent resident who wished to preserve the site and its structures and sustainably transform their use from industrial to artistic.

Designed by MESA in collaboration with D.I.R.T. Studio, the concept of deconstruction was applied as the original mechanical equipment, tanks, pipes, and structures were catalogued, reassembled, and repurposed to create outdoor interpretive spaces that explore the element of water. The wet garden, for instance, is surfaced with 70-year-old broken concrete slabs interspersed with native grasses and ground-level misters and outfitted with benches and tables fashioned from electrical panels and steel well heads. The tanks have become outdoor rooms with the roofs removed but trusses left in place, windows cut from the walls, plantings cut into the floor, and splash basins built into other portions of the floor. Pools, spillways, runnels, and other features convey water from one

Figure 5.53 Parallel Project: Turtle Creek Residence. (Credit: MESA)

space to another and eventually release it back into Turtle Creek.

In addition to the inventive reuse of the site itself as well as the recycling of various construction materials, the site applies sustainable stormwater management principles in the form of a paver and grass system used for the parking court and a buffalo grass roof placed over new bathroom facilities, which serves as a viewing platform for the tanks. The site, impermeable and sterile in its former industrial use, is now being reclaimed by native Texas vegetation designed to respond to a variety of light and moisture conditions present in the garden spaces.

Not strictly residential in use, the client invites the public to use and explore the site. As such it is a hybrid typology that supports residential, institutional, and civic types of uses, which is common to several of the case studies presented. As another example of a sustainable pioneer, one of the designers has this to say of the project in relation to its context:

> Turtle Creek carves a deep ravine through a Dallas neighborhood where the mosquitoes are as big as horses, and the houses are larger than life. Amidst the elaborate manicured landscapes sits a vacuous abandoned pumphouse with reservoirs that once supplied the neighborhood's water. These asphalt and concrete volumes transform with a new flow of arts events and everyday play. Wild and wooly edges of native Texas tangles creep into thick edges, framing the luminous voids.
> *D.I.R.T. Studio*

Malibu Beach House; Malibu, California

Designed by Pamela Burton and Company, this 2008 ASLA Residential Design Award of Honor project also derives much of its sustainable influence and character from its context, as can be seen in Figure 5.54. The site occurs within a compact transect that spans ocean, beach, cliff, residential strip, Pacific Coast Highway, commercial strip, and scrub-vegetated coastal mountain range. The goal of the landscape design was to create an exuberant yet sustainable garden to complement a newly constructed modern home and to tie together three oceanfront lots, while blocking views of the highway and commercial strip.

The typical response in planning residential sites along the Pacific Coast Highway is to completely block the highway and strip with the building backed all the way up to the road and the majority of the outdoor space completely oriented to the ocean. However, in this case the Japanese concept of *borrowed landscapes* was employed in the site planning and design to create a central garden space framed by the main house and guesthouse that affords views to both the ocean and the mountains, while still affording a private and protected outdoor living area. In this way the dunes, grasses, and sand are invited into the site from the beach beyond to frame ocean views, and chaparral plantings screen the highway and commercial strip, framing views of the chaparral-covered coastal mountains. A hillside arroyo across the highway is directed toward the property, bringing intense rainwater. The reconstructed arroyo is a feature of the design, providing a functioning physical connection with the adjacent native landscape.

The landscape architect steered the client away from using water-intensive green lawn and persuaded them to use dry beach sand planted with drought-tolerant, ornamental grasses as ground cover as well as permeable paving and scented ground cover in the parking areas. Over time the owner became convinced of the value of planting in a sustainable manner and is very pleased with the opportunity for the varied views and enhanced feeling of open space the innovative site plan creates. The project also demonstrates to other property owners, with its open, more visually accessible design, that viable, usable, beautiful gardens can be created and maintained with minimal water. As written by the landscape architect in their award submission:

> This project proves that by paying attention to the surrounding environment and the different requirements of surrounding landscapes and private gardens, designers can, in their daily practice, balance clients' needs with sustainability.

6 DESIGN EFFICIENCY

How does design efficiency serve multiple goals in sustainable landscape design?

Gannett/USA Today Headquarters

BACKGROUND

Design efficiency is important for sustainable sites that strive to create compelling places while remaining cost-effective and resource-conscious. To maximize the outcomes of design efforts, several stages of the landscape design process require critical evaluation as to their efficiency. The term *efficiency* is used here to describe copious and rigorous planning that (1) makes use of existing ecologies and structures rather than incurring the costs of demolishing and recreating new ones, (2) devises details and constructions that fulfill multiple purposes rather than just a single function, and (3) insures low-input rather than intensive site maintenance requirements. This chapter provides examples of approaches that are inherently efficient in achieving sustainable landscapes because they broaden the spectrum of uses for site protection, construction, and maintenance.

Existing site features, whether immediately recognized as amenities or not, should not be destroyed but rather noted during initial site assessment, protected and incorporated into the new design. Where possible, one of the first principles taught in medical school is *Primum non nocere,* or *First, do no harm* to your subject. A site approached with the same principle must be sensitively developed to retain its healthy ecosystems without which its character would be lost. Preserving the essence of a site—its healthiest, intact, and mature systems—is the simplest way to "add" inherent value to the site. Limiting construction footprints also saves on cost and on time waiting for the landscape to grow in. Strategic sustainable site planning comes down to weighing options between planning needs and ecological integrity. Questions arise such as, "Does this roadway need to cross a wetland or should the site planning be revisioned to avoid it?" or "What is the cost of retaining and regrading a steep slope for an access drive versus rethinking the parking lot and building locations?" While *Primum non nocere* is feasible where natural systems are intact, it is not always possible on previously developed sites. However, the very fact that ecosystems are always in flux and tend to regenerate themselves means that new life can be breathed into brownfield sites. In the case of brownfields, the opposite of *Primum non nocere* occurs where instead of existing features being protected from development, responsive development can actually add to and improve a site's ecological viability. The 25-acre predesign site of the Gannett/USA Today Headquarters included a mix of previous land uses that challenged the site planning process. Portions of the site included a dumpsite, a neighborhood detention basin to remain, and a natural wooded knoll. The resolution to build upon the damaged portions of the site and keep the ecological ones intact maximized the landscape program, ensured the site's sense of place within the surrounding suburban sprawl, and more than fulfilled the client's goals for an excellent headquarters facility. Although not always immediately evident, with a basic understanding of healthy ecosystems, site planning can accommodate efficient use of existing opportunities in the landscape.

The second aspect of sustainable design efficiency is devising open-ended and integrated uses for landscape constructions. The most popular sustainable techniques in practice today are construction applications such as best management practices (BMPs) and low-impact development (LIDs). A vast improvement over conventional structural stormwater systems, LIDs such as filter strips and vegetated buffers cost less, improve infiltration, and require little maintenance. While these kinds of sustainable techniques work well to define and manage site systems, often their awkward placement within the landscape makes them aesthetically undesirable. Moreover, because these elements are used to fulfill regulatory requirements rather than integrate with the total design, they are placed in the farthest corners of the landscape or fenced off from the rest of the landscape, which testifies to the dichotomies at play between landscape form and function. Both needs can be fulfilled by site elements such as planting and pavements that move beyond single-purpose sustainability objectives to play formal and spatial roles. The stormwater basins at the Menomonee Valley Industrial Center, for example, command attention in the parkland of this industrial development. Rather than looked upon as unsightly or dangerous, the basins were designed to sweep through the site in sinuous curves following the site's former rail lines. An interactive pathway delineated by the basins connects the neighborhood to the river in this floodplain topography. Specialized site sustainability techniques such as LIDs should be integrated into the larger site-planning goals to play a more prominent role in form-making and conceptual development.

Finally, high-maintenance landscapes are costly and detrimental to the environment and clients are becoming less inclined to incur these costs. Additionally, unfulfilled maintenance regimes can wreak havoc on a beautiful design if the client cannot comply. Low-maintenance naturalized landscapes are efficient because they require little inputs and evolve largely on their own with minimal human input. To balance maintenance inputs after construction, small areas of higher-maintenance landscapes can be designated near high use areas while larger areas of naturalized landscapes can occupy the fringes of use. Naturalized landscapes do still require monitoring and maintenance, however, landscapes designed for change over time are more efficient than landscapes that remain static. This consideration during the design phase translates to a more sustainable site during long-range management.

STRATEGIES FOR DESIGN EFFICIENCY

Efficient use of site resources as well as appropriate new applications are critical to sustainability. Following is a list of strategies that help protect or mend existing resources or that generate new sustainable ones.

Vegetation

- *Do not disturb existing established vegetation in the first place.*

- *Avoid removal of existing trees.* Extensive tree root systems absorb stormwater and allow infiltration, which replenishes stream base flows and recharges groundwater, meanwhile reducing downstream flooding.

- *Maximize tree canopy cover.* Tree canopies help reduce negative impacts of development and create environments that are more comfortable. Tree leaves reduce the impact of rainfall, which reduces soil erosion.

- *Revegetate.* Areas disturbed by construction should be stabilized as soon as possible to retain the soil in place. Grass is usually the simplest and fastest approach.

Follow this with a revegetation of a mix of plants—a ground layer, shrub, and tree matrix will hold the soil best in the short and long terms.

- *Improve biodiversity.* Introduce a variety of native plants—not just one or two—to the site that mimics the bioregion to improve the viability and resilience of site vegetation for the long term.

- *Use plants as more than objects.* Plants can be used to accent, shade, buffer, or create space. Look beyond plants as objects and use them in mass for creating meaningful and rich landscapes.

- *Fill in gaps.* Assess gaps in otherwise healthy ecosystems and mend them. Connect to mature, stable ecologies outside the site.

Soils

- *Do not disturb intact landforms in the first place.*

- *Minimize soil disturbance.* Regrade only where necessary.

- *Localize site disturbance.* Keep site disturbance within tight limits. During construction, strictly designate and ensure observance of construction limit lines, tree dripline protections, and stream setbacks.

- *Rebuild disturbed soils.* Use expert input to evaluate, reconstruct, or build new soils that will sustain long-term life on the site.

Hydrology

- *Do not disturb intact hydrological systems in the first place.*

- *Protect existing waterways.* Be aware of and devise setbacks that keep construction away from lakes, rivers, ponds, intermittent and ephemeral streams, underground water tables, lenses, and aquifers.

- *Increase site stormwater infiltration.* Use filter strips, grassed swales, infiltration trenches, and vegetated buffers to capture and allow stormwater to infiltrate.

- *Use permeable pavements*. These can be in the form of unit pavers or porous pavements such as asphalt and concrete. Use them for paths, plazas, and parking lots.

- *Decentralize site stormwater management*. Stormwater collected from large areas into one system causes site damage. Address small areas of stormwater catchment as close as possible to where the water meets soil—in a swale, filter strip, etc.

- *Use cisterns and rain barrels*. Capture and reuse rainwater in clean, enclosed containers either above or underground for reuse in irrigation, recreation, or display.

- *Utilize drip irrigation to minimize water waste*.

- *Reduce pavement dimensions and reduce building footprints*. Regulations often require development that accommodates the worst-case scenario. Demonstrate and convince municipalities of the benefits of reducing pavements.

- Use not just one strategy, but the above strategies in combination.

Energy

- *Minimize the need for high-energy inputs in the landscape.* Use solar-powered lighting or low-voltage lighting, minimize planting areas that require weekly maintenance, reduce areas of mowing and irrigation. Use organic soil amendments.

- *Do not clear-cut the site*. Reconstructing or turning the ground layer into lawn increases the heat-island effect, raising the temperature and contributing to global warming.

- *Use local materials*. Local materials are recognized as extensions of the local landscape and have cultural connotations such as the agricultural stone walls of New England. Local materials require less embodied energy for shipment. Repurpose discarded materials.

- *Use local nurseries*. Local nurseries provide climate-appropriate plants grown in local conditions. Because locally grown native plants are not always commercially available, shipping across the country is often required.

For high-profile and high-volume planting projects, contract-grown plants arranged with a local nursery helps guarantee quality and reduces travel cost and energy outputs.

- *Use local experts/resources*. Sustainable design requires input from experts in various fields. When faced with unknown consequences of site systems, tap local experts. This is especially critical when designing outside of your range of expertise such as within another biome.

- *Use brownfield rather than greenfield sites*. Building on a predeveloped site makes use of existing infrastructure and utilities, and through site repair can regenerate damaged landscape systems and reconnect cultural ones.

Cultural Connectivity

- *Provide access*. Bike paths and pedestrian ways should be provided where possible to connect between shared uses such as neighborhoods, open spaces, schools, work, and shopping.

- *Incorporate green open space infrastructure*. At the site level, devise green infrastructure that ties in a framework of ecological and cultural elements. Connect to a larger regional system where possible.

METHODS FOR DESIGN EFFICIENCY

The structures, tools, and techniques discussed as follows, gleaned from the projects in this book, are mindful of site efficiency and typically play multiple roles within the landscape design. As suggested by the context-informed framework presented here, these elements can function on a site level or reach outward in some form into the site's local or regional context. Therefore, the site design methods are divided into two groups—those that contribute to site efficiency and those that contribute to regional efficiency.

Improving Site Efficiency

Pavements

Permeable Surfaces

Permeable surfaces can be used for many applications in place of impermeably paved areas. Select materials and construction methods that allow infiltration to reduce runoff. This technique is limited to where subsurface soil and hydrology conditions allow for infiltration. It reduces the need for stormwater catchment and management mechanisms because the pavement itself is the management system.

Reinforced-Turf Parking Areas

Reinforced turf is useful in areas that receive infrequent use such as event parking. This technique reduces overall paving footprints, reduces the heat island effect, saves on paving and drainage costs, and improves stormwater infiltration. It also visually reduces the extent of site paving.

Minimized Hardscape Footprints to Improve Groundwater Recharge

Many techniques are used to minimize hardscape footprints to increase groundwater recharge. In addition to the ones mentioned above, these techniques include minimizing building and parking lot footprints, providing public transportation and bike racks to reduce parking lots, demonstrating alternative options to towns that require overbuilt parking lots, providing significant shade planting in parking lots, and green roofs. With less pavement, stormwater makes more contact with the soil and has the potential to infiltrate—relieving flooding and water quality problems.

Stormwater

Vegetated Swales

Vegetated swales are surface stormwater conveyance systems that support vegetation. Trees, shrubs, and grasses contribute to the management of stormwater by moving water from one part of the site to another while allowing for cleansing, infiltration, and groundwater replenishment. When integrated into the landscape as buffers adjacent to parking lots, they serve multiple purposes.

Hardscape Swales

Hardscape swales provide desirable surface stormwater conveyance while allowing for interaction, aeration, and process awareness, which may not be possible with vegetated swales.

Bioretention Ponds and Treatments

A bioretention pond is a system that manages and treats stormwater by using a specially designed planting soil bed and planting materials to filter runoff (Connecticut Department of Environmental Protection 2004). The rainwater is processed as it flows through a site via open-air swales and basins planted with vegetation. This type of stormwater management slows, absorbs, and filters contaminants and sediment from the water, in contrast with conventional closed drainage systems where water is conveyed in pipes, increasing its destructive potential and eliminating positive interaction with the environment. This system, when sited appropriately, can look very natural or, alternatively, be designed as an architectural feature in a courtyard.

Stormwater Basin Enhancement

Retrofitting existing stormwater basins and ponds can slow down water and increase infiltration while improving habitat and providing an aesthetic feature in the landscape. Often, retrofitting an existing basin means adding berms to slow water runoff and provide vegetation in the bottom of the basin for water uptake. Adding a sediment forebay to a stormwater pond, for example, allows incoming pollutants to settle out before reaching the main pond and cleanses water moving into outlet areas beyond. Dense planting along banks further helps pollutant uptake and integration within naturalized planting schemes. Daylighting pipes into treatment swales prior to entry into a pond can also enhance treatment.

Plantings

Plant Community Restoration

Quantity, quality, variety, and location of plantings dictate the impact of a planting design. While large quantities of any type of vegetation may provide some benefits, the types and arrangements of vegetation selected for landscape architectural projects are often sterile, exotic, and do not constitute ecological place-making. Although recreating a vegetation palette to mimic the true complexity of a local biome is very difficult, complex and varied plant combinations can approximate local biodiversity, provide shade, and add spatial interest and habitat for ecosystem function. Woodland restoration can also improve surrounding areas by creating privacy buffers and sound attenuation. It also benefits a site by providing spatial interest and a sense of place by using native, indigenous species and plant communities.

Biodiverse Meadows

Meadows, versus labor-intensive monocultures such as lawn, are nearly self-sustaining, requiring low initial inputs until established and annual mowing and periodic invasive plant control. Thereafter they contribute to habitat value, biodiversity, and stormwater infiltration. Plants chosen for meadows that provide stormwater filtering are resilient and can withstand dry spells as well as inundation by water during rainy seasons.

Structures

Intensive Roof Gardens

Roof gardens (as distinct from green roofs) are designed primarily to allow access to the outdoors from otherwise confined indoor areas above ground level. Environmental benefits of roof gardens are reduction of the heat island effect and provision of habitat, as well as the repurposing and reduction of roof runoff.

Extensive Roof Gardens/Green Roofs

Vegetated building roofs insulate buildings and decrease energy costs, absorb rainwater and reduce runoff, improve aesthetic character, and provide habitat. Typically the vegetation is primarily perennial, drought-tolerant plant types, planted in a relatively continuous and thin (6 to 12 inches) medium of sand and soil, underlain by an overflow drainage system and waterproofing.

Cultural Connections

Sequence and Narrative of Native Landscapes

Exposing site users to a meaningful and rich sequence of landscapes and regionally distinctive outdoor spaces reinforces the value of the native landscape and the many functions/pleasures it provides.

Preservation of Historic Site Artifacts

The patina of age and layers of cultural occupation of a site are made visible through the integration and preservation of obsolete elements that have endured. The juxtaposition of such human relics with new site form and function can create stimulating visual contrast and intellectual or emotional stirrings. While we have long valued certain types of historic buildings and other artifacts, we have only recently begun to consider the value of more utilitarian forms that reflect our industrial heritage, and which often have some negative connotations with regard to sustainability. The preservation of such forms provides honest confrontation with the past, rather than erasure—not as punishment or to induce guilt, but as a thread of continuity and identity.

Site History Reflection

Successful form-making and functional design recognizes, interprets, or commemorates past site uses and character. Through the use of cultural design narratives and vernacular materials or program elements, the historic identity and use of the site can be put to efficient purpose in creating meaningful and memorable space.

Environmental Education

The core of learning is not in the information being predigested from the outside but in the interaction between a person and an experience (Louv 2006). Informing the public about sustainability engages users with the site and brings the ideas of sustainable site design into the public sphere, where it can influence attitudes and public policy.

Integrating Processes/Systems

Model Ecosystems

Develop awareness of large-scale ecosystems and landscape units, such as watersheds, while working at the site scale. The workings and characteristics of large ecosystems are difficult to perceive as a whole, due to their scale and complexity. The creation of smaller-scale, functional iterations of such systems provides opportunities for learning through clearer perception and interaction.

Integrate Architectonic Forms with the Natural Environment

The strict separation of natural phenomenon and cultural phenomenon perpetuates the misplaced notion that humans are not natural and that nature is necessarily destroyed by development. The use of architectonic forms in naturalized landscapes can serve to create a visually stimulating synergy that works on many different levels: ecological, spatial, intellectual, and cultural; and demonstrates the possibility of a sustainable human ecology.

Meaningful Site Organization, Artful Edges

The establishment of a strong site organization rationale is critical in highly naturalized landscapes where complexity can be perceived as chaos. Ideally, the site organization can be related to a sustainable pattern or system alignment in the landscape. Related to this spatial organization, finesse in the alignment and expression of spatial edges in the landscape is critical to the aesthetic success and legibility of the design. Deciding where hard, solid edges are needed and desired, versus where more permeable, soft edges are preferable to separate spaces and functions can be challenging in the outdoor environment.

Create Multi-Use Sites

When developed sites perform multiple functions, such as stormwater management, industrial development, and recreation, they are more efficient, productive, flexible, and satisfying. Just as we are shifting toward mixed-use architectural zoning, where residential units might be built above commercial storefronts, for instance, so too are we realizing the benefits of mixed-use landscapes. Programming and site planning for flexible and varied use creates land use efficiencies and improved character of potential "nuisance" land uses, while displacing possible development of other intact natural sites for these uses.

Site Mending and Care

Brownfield Remediation

Brownfields that require capping to isolate soil contaminants present special challenges to sustainable landscape design. Because the planting medium has limited depth and because the drainage is inhibited, plantings and subgrade conditions must be carefully designed to function together, while still allowing for the integrity of the cap to remain. Other more temporary landscape-driven remediation techniques, such as phytoremediation, may also be employed to harness the biological processes of plants to remove contaminants from the soil.

Reduced Maintenance Regimes

Sustainable plantings often require a departure from the conventional maintenance regime where mulched plant beds, mown lawn, and isolated trees are the norm. Sustainable plantings are often paired with stormwater management and require an understanding of the larger site system design. Maintenance guidelines and descriptions with photos provide the client and maintenance crew a baseline of what to expect over time and what the inputs will be to achieve a stable yet evolving planting. Involving maintenance crews during the design process incorporates their experience and affords the project increased support.

Improving Regional Efficiency

Stormwater

Improvement of Regional Hydrological Systems

The site's place within its local watershed offers opportunities to preserve, enhance, or restore natural land cover in drainage corridors that flow to and from off-site areas. As design elements, these features add visual interest and meaning, as well as a basis for site organization.

Linking Site Hydrology to Adjacent Development/Open Space

Open space can be used to treat stormwater runoff from off-site development areas. Development of biofiltrating natural wetlands for surface stormwater treatment improves water quality, provides flood control, and creates wildlife habitat benefits that conventional subsurface treatment cannot equal. This practice reduces infrastructure costs for site developers and public infrastructure providers, and can increase the functional and aesthetic value of open space areas both on and off site.

Plantings

Plant Community Restoration

Plant community restoration is a means of achieving biodiversity, a low-maintenance landscape, increasing wildlife habitat, and improving stormwater quality and quantity. It benefits the design by providing spatial interest and a sense of place. Connecting to existing contiguous vegetated areas or systems extends wildlife corridors across site boundaries.

Cultural Connections

Focused Views to Regional Landscapes

Siting gathering spaces and nodes to provide well-framed and distinctive views to distant natural landform provides a sense of connection to and awareness of the larger environment.

Local Cultural and Historic Elements

Providing cultural and historic elements such as historic remnants or reused, recycled, or local materials provides depth and a local perspective to a site—linking cultural memory of a place and people. This cycle of using what is locally available, or reused in new ways, reduces project costs, environmental costs, and improves local economies. Use of local materials and resources rather than shipping materials, expertise, and resources from afar provides regional connection and recognition to the project. While this strategy may feel limiting, often it provides a starting point for envisioning a project concept that includes the essence of the site and region.

Trail/Pathway System Linkages

Context analysis develops awareness of pathway systems and other major pedestrian circulation routes, nodes, and destinations. Site planning and design link outside pedestrian circulation to the site and extend and connect circulation through the site. Ease and connectivity of pedestrian and other nonmotorized movement across neighborhoods, local areas, and regions can add up to decreased dependence on autos. The benefits of trails are multiplied when they connect with other trail systems to create longer segments. Increased access to larger populations, increased recreational flexibility, increased safety due to reduced isolation, shared stewardship opportunities, and increased community connectivity are just a few of these benefits.

Integrating Processes/Systems

Program the Site to Complement and Support Adjacent Land Uses

Develop awareness of adjacent land use types, scale, and patterns. Site planning and design can link or complement contextual land uses with suitable site uses. Being a good neighbor is sustainable; this need not require sacrificing optimal site utilization or actual physical linking with neighboring uses, but a sensibility that sees the site as part of a larger nested environment from which it can benefit and to which it can contribute.

Linkages to Larger Street Identities and Patterns

The street is the civic corridor that links sites and has the potential to create larger sustainable community identity and function. Consider the character and pattern of the existing streets around which the site is located and reinforce sustainable patterns such as native vegetation and open drainage systems with site planning and design decisions.

Site/Context Landscape Matrix

Use the native landscape as a basis for coverage of the entire site, with patches of cultural landscape or structure carved out. This increases opportunities for linkage to off-site corridors, nearby natural patches, or a larger natural matrix. Likewise, linking the site's cultural landscape themes, features, or qualities to off-site landscape can strengthen the local cultural open space system.

Site Use and Care

Public Open Spaces

Well-designed public open space is a sought-after commodity in urban, suburban, and rural areas. Oftentimes sustainable projects, even if on private property, attempt to designate areas or resources for shared or public use: for example, an area of community gardens, a public park on the property of a utility, a shared stormwater system that doubles as connector to area bike and walking trails. These considerations require extensive public process and understanding of the surrounding area potentials and needs.

Community Involvement with Maintenance

Community involvement should serve to achieve consensus among constituents whether vocal or underrepresented. The process should be inclusive, representative, and interactive (Franklin 1997). With the atypical maintenance regimes required of natural landscapes, constituent awareness and commitment are key to ensuring success. Community involvement in site maintenance brings people together around the common goals of land stewardship.

Site Reuse

Reuse of a brownfield site rather than a pristine site saves cost and provides opportunities to integrate site restoration into the program. Site reuse often fills a vacant gap in the greater regional landscape matrix, making the site valid and useful again within the community and spurring other positive changes beyond the site.

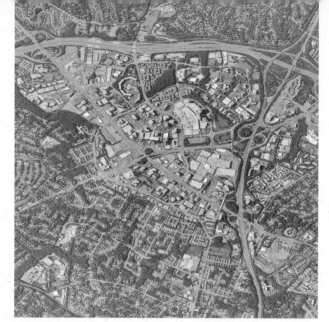

(Credit: historicaerials.com)

CASE STUDY— GANNETT/USA TODAY HEADQUARTERS

LOCATION: McLean, Virginia, USA
SITE SIZE: 25 acres
CLIENT: Gannett Company Inc.
DESIGNERS: Landscape Architect—Michael Vergason Landscape
    Architects, Ltd. Alexandria, Virginia
    Architect—Kohn Pedersen Fox Associates, New York, New York
    Civil Engineer—Huntley, Nyce and Associates, Chantilly, Virginia
    Water Feature Engineering—Aqua Engineering Inc.,
    Fort Collins, Colorado
FORMER SITE USES: Undeveloped property, disturbed by construction
    fill, containing a regional stormwater pond and intact woodland
LANDSCAPE BUDGET: $6.5 million
DATE OF COMPLETION: 2002

Overview

The Gannett/USA Today Headquarters is a project that maximized design efficiency by taking advantage of existing site qualities and improving their function.

The site planning addressed the program requirements *vis-à-vis* the value of existing site amenities and opportunities. Despite the client's initial desire to build on the site's wooded knoll, the program challenges were met with an alternative site planning proposal that preserved this intact and healthiest portion of the site, which provides a backdrop for the campus landscape and a place of active and passive recreation. Likewise, an existing stormwater basin was retrofitted with the construction of a narrow runnel that aerates water. This runnel is part of the primary landscape feature integrated into the grade change and features small waterfalls, narrow paths, and bridges. The stormwater basin function and aesthetic were improved with native riparian plants and the addition of a forebay that slows down water. It also serves as a focal point of the landscape. The highest maintenance areas are found closest to the building and the farther areas such as the woodland, pond edge, and highway buffers require minimal intervention.

If the wooded knoll area had become the building site as originally planned, the site would have been leveled, leaving little sense of place. Instead, the Gannett/USA Today Headquarters site planning used layers of resources, meaning, and function to contribute to the sustainability of the site and region. Several construction techniques that contributed to site and context efficiency are the stormwater basin retrofit, a reduced maintenance regime, use of local materials, and plant community restoration. These elements all play several important roles and are integrated within the landscape.

Project Inception

The Gannett Company, with over 46,000 employees, 85 daily newspapers, and hundreds of other publications, is the largest newspaper publisher in the United States. Following a history of growth and diversification begun in 1905, the creation of its most circulated newspaper, *USA Today*, established the Gannett Company as a news innovator. In 1986, the company moved from New York to Arlington, Virginia, to combine the two entities into one facility. Then in 2001, the new Gannett/USA Today Headquarters was built in nearby McLean, Virginia.

McLean lies adjacent to Tysons Corner and across the Potomac River from Washington, D.C., and is part of the rapidly developing area of commercial and office uses located at a strategic intersection formed by the Dulles Airport Access Road and the I-495 Capital Beltway. It also is home to upscale residential neighborhoods that serve diplomats, members of Congress, and government officials in Washington, D.C. Nearby Capitol Hill is pictured in Figure 6.1. The Gannett Company considered over 50 sites for their new headquarters before choosing this 25-acre parcel. The site itself was a patchwork collection of undeveloped, disturbed, and regulated land.

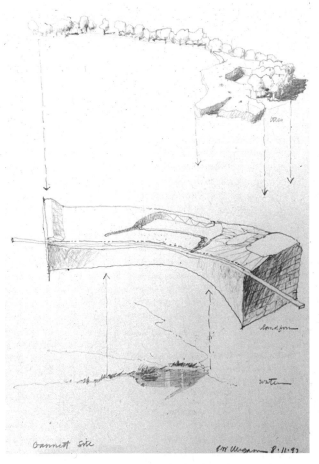

Figure 6.2 Site Systems Analysis. The design used the concept of site repair beginning with analyses of site systems, vegetation, landform, and hydrology.
(Credit: Michael Vergason Landscape Architects)

Figure 6.1 U.S. Capitol Building in Washington DC.
(Credit: wikipedia.org)

Design Concept

In a region legendary for its uninspired development patterns and function, the site planning and design of Gannett/USA Today Headquarters stands apart. The design team employed *site repair* as the primary site planning technique. The concept of site repair as described in Christopher Alexander's 1997 book, *A Pattern Language*, suggests that site planning take into account the time, costs, and effort needed to restore intact ecological systems. It advises to avoid intact areas and focus new development in already damaged areas. A sketch in this analysis approach is shown in Figure 6.2. This approach reversed the initial intentions of building on the pristine portions of the site and served to protect a stand of mature trees.

The American Society of Landscape Architects recognized the site solution developed by Michael Vergason Landscape Architects with its 2008 General Design Award of Honor. In this sprawling metropolitan region with little intact ecological or cultural integrity, the concept of site repair offers an improved relationship between development and the environment for corporate landscapes.

Site Repair by Christopher Alexander

"Buildings must always be built on those parts of the land which are in the worst conditions, not the best. This idea is indeed very simple. However, it is the exact opposite of what usually happens; and it takes enormous will power to follow it through.

What usually happens when someone thinks of building on a piece of land? He looks for the best site—where the grass is most beautiful, the trees most healthy, the slope of the land most even, the view most level, the soil most fertile—and that is just where he decides to put his house.... It's only human nature; and, for a person who lacks a total view of the ecology of the land, it seems the most obvious and sensible thing to do. If you are going to build a building, 'build it in the best possible place.'... When we build on the best parts of the land, those beauties which are there already—the crocuses that break through the lawn each spring, the sunny pile of stone where lizards sun themselves, the favorite gravel path, which we love walking on—it's always these things that get lost in the shuffle. When the construction starts on the parts of the land which are already healthy, innumerable beauties are wiped out with every act of building.

People always say to themselves, well, of course, we can always start another garden, build another trellis, put in another gravel path, put in new crocuses in the new lawn, and the lizards will find some other pile of stones. But it just is not so. These simple things take years to grow—it isn't all that easy to create them, just by wanting to. And every time we disturb one of these precious details, it may take 20 years, a lifetime even, before some comparable details grow again from our small daily acts.

If we always build on that part of the land which is most healthy, we can be virtually certain that a great deal of the land will always be less than healthy.

If we want the land to be healthy all over—all of it—then we must do the opposite. We must treat every new act of building as an opportunity to mend some rent in the existing cloth; each act of building gives us the chance to make one of the ugliest and least healthy parts of the environment healthier. As for those parts, which are already healthy and beautiful, they of course need no attention. And in fact, we must discipline ourselves most strictly to leave them alone, so that our energy actually goes to the places which need it. This is the principle of site repair."

(Alexander 1977)

Project Philosophies and Approach

The Gannett/USA Today Headquarters' initial design program set out to create a state-of-the-art work environment for their 1,750 employees relocating into McLean/Tysons Corner, an **edge city** in Fairfax County, Virginia. World-class architecture and innovative site design would provide amenities to serve this new population with restaurants, a bank, health club, basketball and tennis courts, jogging trail, and softball diamond.

The philosophies of the client and designer are critical in forming a site design's sustainable outcomes. On this project, the client did not initially share the landscape architect's vision for sustainable site planning. The initial philosophy of the client and design team was to provide a highly visible state-of-the-art headquarters that would attract and retain the best employees. At the time, their philosophy did not consider sustainable goals. As the project design unfolded, however, new awareness broadened the client's understanding of sustainability issues and interest in pursuing LEED certification.

Michael Vergason Landscape Architect's work takes cues from natural and cultural processes. They believe that landscape architecture should respond to the fundamental human need for connection to the surrounding world. Despite the site's location in a densely developed suburban landscape with little cultural or ecological features to draw from, the landscape architects performed regional analyses of the stormwater management system and borrowed from natural phenomenon to create form and meaning.

The result is a project that borrowed from a variety of influences but focused on improving—and not damaging—the immediate site while maximizing opportunities for employee engagement with landscape phenomenon. The various zones of the site are depicted in Figure 6.3.

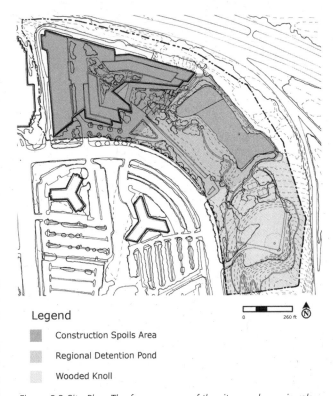

Legend

- Construction Spoils Area
- Regional Detention Pond
- Wooded Knoll

Figure 6.3 Site Plan. The former zones of the site are shown in relation to the new site features.

Program Type and Development Trend

Program Type: Corporate Campus

The corporate headquarters landscape became a staple of the landscape architecture profession in the mid-20th century when suburbanization that created changes in residential land use patterns carried over into the business world. The location of businesses, and especially their elite headquarters, into spacious park-like settings created appealing environments for executives and employees and aesthetic statements that represented the stature of the company, much like turn-of-the-century private estates.

With globalization of business and commerce, corporations became ever-larger and broader in scope, and the corporate headquarters as a self-contained campus emerged. Greater emphasis was put on design that contributed toward brand recognition. In 1964, for example, the president of The Deere & Company in Moline, Illinois, was interested in portraying a "modern but down to earth and rugged philosophy" through the design of its new world headquarters (The Deere & Company). Designed by architect Eero Saarinen and landscape architect Hideo Sasaki, the 1,400-acre complex is one of the early examples of the form. In 1970, PepsiCo moved from New York City to new world headquarters in Purchase, New York, which featured architecture designed by Edward Durrell Stone set on a campus of 144 acres designed by the landscape architecture firm of Stone's son, Edward D. Stone, Jr. The integration of site, architecture, and outdoor sculpture stands as an enduring corporate campus classic.

Today's corporations identify branding, attention to employee needs and desires, employee health and wellness, emerging interest in sustainability and social responsibility, and flexibility in expanding and downsizing as incentives to building corporate campuses.

Development Trend: Edge-City Infill

Corporate headquarters have created outstanding examples of positive landscape identity in such campuses, but they can also be seen as contributing to the trends of sprawl, greenfield development, and the edge-city phenomenon. The vast scale, monotony, and segregation of highly developed corporate and commercial land uses in edge-city places like California's Silicon Valley and here in Tysons Corner creates places that are lifeless and disconnected—the ultimate "geography of nowhere" (Kunstler 1993). The dominance of corporate culture has been blamed, in large part, for these patterns. And so as corporations come under increasing scrutiny for their social and environmental impacts, they are searching for ways to convey and conduct themselves in more community-minded and ecologically driven ways, including their own physical office environments (Wohlsen 2005). While several principles of sustainability can readily be applied to any site, regardless of context, the selection of an edge-city infill site for a corporate campus is a sustainable land pattern decision. Designing sites to apply sustainable principles in these environments not only displaces potential greenfield or sprawl development and provides responsible leadership from corporate entities, but can lead to a shift in surrounding patterns by example.

Context

The regional context of the Gannett/USA Today Headquarters is shown in a sequence of scales in Figures 6.4 through 6.9. Through regional analysis, the site design process is infused with an understanding of potentials and challenges. It situates the site relative to area history, regional attitudes, and ecological health. Descriptions of landscape form, function, and philosophies of this area of Virginia explore a combination of factors to which the project design uniquely responds.

Figure 6.4 Gannett/USA Today—National Context.

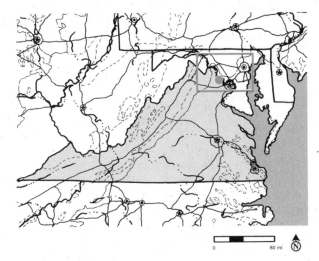

Figure 6.5 Gannett/USA Today—State Context.

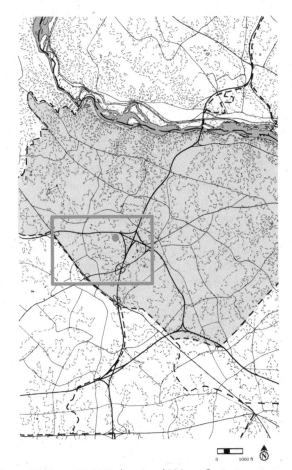

Figure 6.8 Gannett/USA Today—Local McLean Context.

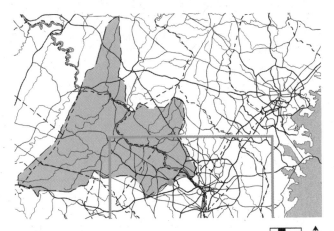

Figure 6.6 Gannett/USA Today—Potomac Watershed Context.

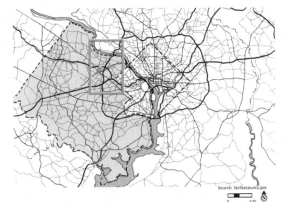

Figure 6.7 Gannett/USA Today—Metro Washington DC Context.

Figure 6.9 Gannett/USA Today—Neighborhood Context.

Regional Form

Natural Patterns

The Gannett/USA Today site is located in the Middle Potomac Watershed, which empties into the Chesapeake Bay, the largest **estuary** in the United States. The Middle Potomac area, outlined in Figure 6.10, is among the most heavily developed watersheds that contributes to the Bay, which has experienced many years of declining health. Landmark conservation and restoration efforts for the Chesapeake Bay have developed because of a 1983 EPA-mandated report, which highlighted four critical problems: the overabundance of nitrogen and phosphorus in the water, dwindling underwater bay grasses, toxic pollution, and the over-harvesting of living resources. This resulted in the Chesapeake Bay Agreement and Program, which created an unprecedented partnership between three states, (Virginia, Maryland, and Pennsylvania) and the District of Columbia, to improve the conditions of the Bay. The Program coordinates assessment, improvement, and monitoring efforts in concert with local jurisdictions (Chesapeake Bay Program).

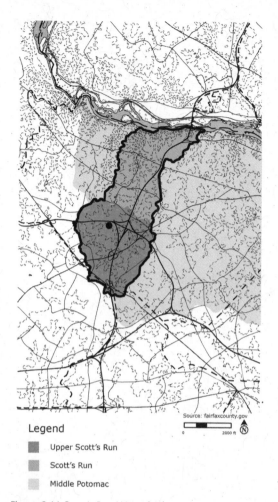

Legend

■ Upper Scott's Run

■ Scott's Run

□ Middle Potomac

Figure 6.11 Scott's Run Watershed.

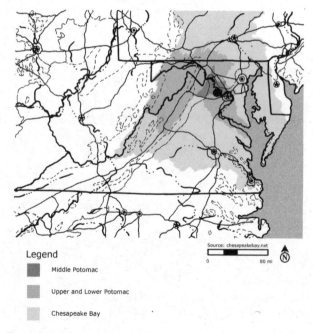

Legend

■ Middle Potomac

■ Upper and Lower Potomac

□ Chesapeake Bay

Figure 6.10 Potomac Watershed.

The Scotts Run subwatershed, shown in Figure 6.11, within which the Gannett/USA Today Headquarters site is located, flows from its headwaters in the highly developed Tysons Corner area, through moderate and low-density residential communities, and into parkland along the Potomac River, seen in Figure 6.12. The Gannett/USA Today site is within a smaller subwatershed area known as Jones Branch and houses a local **stormwater detention pond** addressed as a part of the new headquarters site design.

The project area lies in the Southern Coastal Plains natural region in an area on the edge of what is known as the Piedmont. This is depicted in Figures 6.13 and 6.14. These two regions, separated by a "fall line," are named for

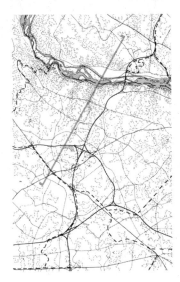

Figure 6.12 Regional Transect. The site
is in the transition area between the
Piedmont and Coastal Plains, draining
to the middle Potomac River.

where an uplands region meets a coastal plain, often indicated by waterfalls. The term *Piedmont* signifies land at the foot of the mountains, characterized by rolling hills. At the fall line the geology changes from crystalline bedrock to unconsolidated sediments of the Coastal Plain. This physiography is shown in Figure 6.15. The Oak-Hickory Pine Forest vegetation in this area has been dramatically altered by a long history of clearing, logging, agriculture, and development. Some evidence by early explorers' accounts indicate that parts of this area were occupied by open savannah-like woodlands and grasslands, which would have been maintained by fire by Native Americans. Outside the increasing urban and suburban areas, the region is a patchwork of secondary forests, pastures, and fields used for tobacco and grain production.

Development Patterns

With its singular distinction as the metropolitan region surrounding the nation's capitol, contradictory influences contributed to its sprawl pattern. Over the years, federal government–related development pressures and the transience and mobility of political populations collided with a value for history and natural resources, creating a patchwork of development that, unlike the urban core of Washington, D.C., has little coherence. An early plan of the City of Washington by l'Enfant is shown in Figure 6.16.

The post–World War II expansion of the U.S. federal government spurred rapid growth in these once rural outskirts of Washington (see Figure 6.17). Along with government entities, large businesses settled in nearby Fairfax County, Virginia, attracted by its close proximity to the capitol. The technology revolution also contributed to this rapid population growth and development. This boom, concentrated in a relatively short period of time, has resulted in a wide array of community types, many of them planned, but not in relation to one another.

The Bureau of Labor Statistics has divided the Washington metropolitan area into three geographic categories, shown

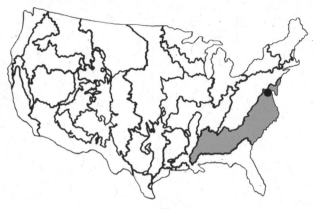

Figure 6.13 U.S. Natural Regions: Southern Coastal Plains. (Harker 1999)

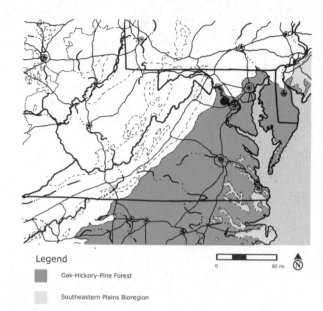

Oak-Hickory-Pine Forest

Southeastern Plains Bioregion

Figure 6.14 Oak-Hickory-Pine Forest Locations.

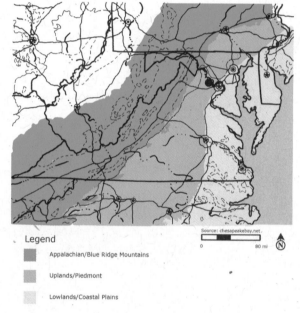

Legend

Appalachian/Blue Ridge Mountains

Uplands/Piedmont

Lowlands/Coastal Plains

Figure 6.15 Physiography.

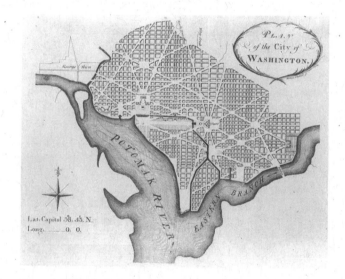

Figure 6.16 l'Enfant's Washington D.C Plan. (Credit: Library of Congress)

in Figure 6.18—core, suburbs, and exurban areas—based on population, employment, and commuting patterns. Due to Fairfax County's rapid growth, the designation of *core* has expanded far beyond its former Washington, D.C., limits to encompass the entire area of Fairfax County. Although Fairfax County is heavily developed, its development pattern is less like an urban core and more typical of

Design Efficiency

Figure 6.17 Historic Agriculture. The outskirts of Washington DC, prior to WWII, were rural and experienced rapid growth thereafter. (Credit: Moutox Orchard)

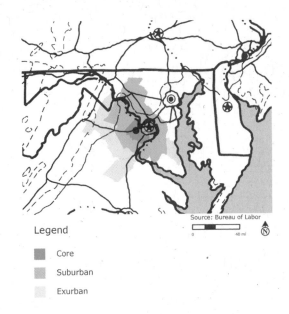

Legend

■ Core

▨ Suburban

▨ Exurban

Figure 6.18 Metropolitan Washington Development Densities. These areas are defined by population, employment, and commuting patterns.

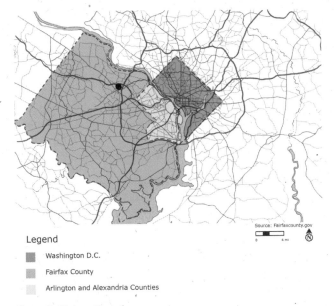

Legend

■ Washington D.C.

▨ Fairfax County

▨ Arlington and Alexandria Counties

Figure 6.19 Area Counties.

sprawl with wide, dominating roads, buildings surrounded by parking lots, and highly separated land uses. More than any other case study included in this book, the Gannett project context is defined by *county* boundaries, as outlined in Figure 6.19. Despite a handful of incorporated towns, independent cities, and well-defined communities, Fairfax County, largely one continuous urbanized region, consists of unincorporated areas—not towns—called **census-designated places** (CDPs). These areas are under jurisdiction of the 400-square-mile county.

Reston, Virginia: A Planned CDP

One of the largest and most well-known unincorporated communities in the United States is the new town, or planned community, of Reston, Virginia, located just a few miles west of the Gannett site. Conceived by Robert E. Simon in 1964, the planned community of Reston forged a concept in which a guiding development principle was to improve quality of life. Beyond the influence of the new town movement, which grew out of the Industrial Revolution's impact on urban living conditions, Reston was part of a reaction to the new suburban communities of the post-war era such as Levittown, New York. Among the problems in these communities to which Reston attempted to respond were income and land use segregation, a lack of natural preservation, and a lack of civic space and community ties.

(Reston Historic Trust)

A predecessor of new urbanism, this community shares some of its principles, but differs in a few key ways. Almost all buildings are oriented away from main streets, and few major arteries have complete sidewalk networks, although pedestrian and bike travel is easily accomplished on the extensive but isolated nature paths. This inward orientation of buildings was a preference of the early developers of Reston, who wished to avoid the commercial strip effect in favor of a more park-like look. However, this pattern simply produced a modified, more aesthetically pleasing suburban form while perpetuating segregated functions. This was bolstered by Fairfax County's development regulations and transportation planning, which encouraged auto-centric circulation and de-emphasized pedestrian connectivity in developed areas.

The Gannett/USA Today Headquarters site itself is within the unincorporated community of McLean within the area known as Tysons Corner. The opening of Tysons Corner Center in 1968, one of the earliest and largest super-malls in the United States, spurred the growth of the larger Tysons Corner area, which now includes a host of commercial shopping centers and business parks. The sequence of this growth can be seen in the aerial photos of Figure 6.20. With its reputation for large and relatively inexpensive commercial facilities, Tysons Corner is the opposite of what is termed a **bedroom community**, with its daytime population nearly four times that of its resident population of about 20,000. Movement is afoot to improve what many see as an undesirable suburban pattern and identity. According to a spokesperson for the Fairfax County Chamber of Commerce, "Right now Tysons Corner is the most successful office park in the world. What we want is a downtown" (Fairfax County Chamber of Commerce). To answer this call, **transit-oriented development** is planned for a portion of Tysons Corner that creates a mix of residential and commercial development. The proposed transit plan is shown in Figure 6.21. The development would replace existing structures with taller, more dense buildings with a closer relationship to new roads, to create

a traditional downtown pattern. It is hoped that this transformation will extend into other areas of Tysons Corner, as the county proceeds with a master plan effort that will produce zoning and land use regulation changes to support the new pattern. Key to this development is a planned metro-rail line to connect Washington, D.C., to Dulles Airport with four stops in the Tysons Corner area.

As suggested by the previous discussion, Fairfax County has a low percentage (approximately 9 percent) of open space, as seen in Figure 6.22. Although there is a system of parkland within Fairfax County associated primarily with recreational parks and limited riparian buffers (as opposed to larger tracts of natural open space), connectivity is low. While there is no dedicated public open space near or adjacent to the site, downstream areas of the Scotts Run watershed do have substantial open space along the Potomac River. Urban open space that provides critical public realm identity and activity is largely lacking in past development.

The Chesapeake and Ohio Canal National Historic Park is a significant cultural and recreational open space that spans over 180 miles along the Potomac River from Georgetown northward past Scotts Run confluence, providing a widely used regional hiking and biking trail. There are several on-

Figure 6.20 Tysons Corner Development. Growth of Tysons Corner between 1949, 1962, and 2003. (Credit: historicaerials.com)

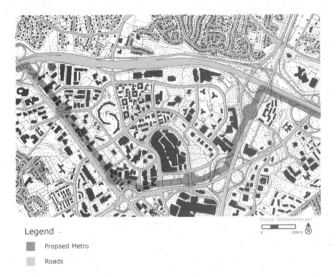

Legend

■ Propsed Metro

Roads

Figure 6.21 Proposed Transit. This new extension of the transit line between Dulles and Washington DC is planned to accommodate a planned shift in emphasis for Tyson's Corner from auto-centric commercial to multi-modal mixed use.

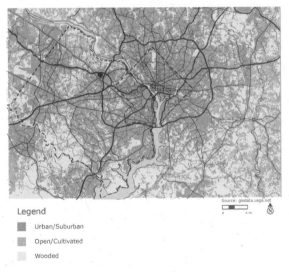

Legend

■ Urban/Suburban

Open/Cultivated

Wooded

Figure 6.22 Land Cover. Fairfax County has a low percentage (approximately 9%) of open space.

and off-road local trail segments in Fairfax County and increased interest and effort in providing some trail connectivity such as the north–south Cross County Trail to the west of Tysons Corner. However, overall open space connectivity is hindered by the magnitude of development and traffic congestion in the area.

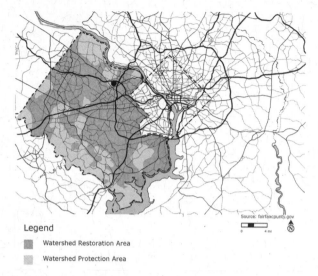

Legend

■ Watershed Restoration Area

■ Watershed Protection Area

Figure 6.23 Watershed Management Initiatives. Restoration is proposed for much of the area's impaired watersheds.

Regional Function

Natural Systems

There is little vestige of ecological function in the vicinity of the project site. What linkage there is to the larger watershed and bioregion revolves around the Scotts Run Creek that drains the Tysons Corner area. A 2005 report found that 70 percent of streams in the Scotts Run watershed are in fair to very poor condition, shown in Figure 6.23, with extensive erosion and inadequate vegetative buffers. While relatively forested in its downstream areas, the county's Stormwater Management Plan calls for restoration in its upper reaches where it is impacted by development. The management plan for Scotts Run calls for improving stormwater management through a reduction in impervious land cover and replacement of aging infrastructure that will slow water movement and allow for pollutant filtration (Fairfax County Stormwater Planning Division).

The Gannett project site is located on the Jones Branch tributary of Scotts Run, which is a 270-acre sub-basin. The site is a central collection point for the majority of the Tysons Corner development area, prior to its controlled release to Scotts Run under the Dulles Toll Road via a cul-

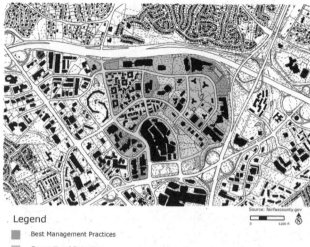

Legend

■ Best Management Practices

■ Conventional Detention

■ Surface Flow from Jones Branch Watershed/No Treatment

Legend

■ Surface Hydrology

■ Jones Branch Sub-Watershed

Figure 6.24 Jones Branch Water Treatment.

vert. The diagram in Figure 6.24 shows the analysis of the stormwater control types in this area, from quality- and quantity-controlled to no control. Within the immediate site area as well as the larger regional watershed system this highly developed area has contributed to the overall degradation of natural hydrologic systems.

Human Systems

As of January 2007, the estimated population of Fairfax County topped the one million mark, making it by far the most populous jurisdiction in the Commonwealth of Virginia and the Greater Washington, D.C., area, with one of the highest median household incomes of any county in the United States. The county has a strong service economy and many residents work for the federal government or its contractors. It also is home to several large national corporations such as Capital One, General Dynamics, and Freddie Mac. With the tremendous population concentration, land use relationships and circulation systems are of paramount concern.

The McLean Hamlet across the Dulles Toll Highway just north of the site, the transect of which is shown in Figure 6.25, is a residential enclave within this sprawling region. A neighborhood of over 500 homes built between 1965 and 1995, it has been a vocal neighbor to Tysons Corner, often resisting the increased scale and massing of development and visual and traffic impacts.

This area has become infamous for ever-increasing congestion brought about by auto-dominated development. The problems associated with traffic are magnified by the presence of two major airports, Dulles and Reagan National. The future Dulles Corridor Metrorail Project, the plan for which is shown in Figure 6.26, will provide needed transportation relief and a shift to a more sustainable diversity of transit options.

Other alternative modes of circulation such as trails are becoming more desired in the area. Yet such trails, where they exist at all, are fragmented and disconnected. Fairfax Trails and Streams (FTAS), a grassroots trail and environmental advocacy group, aims to create this network and help protect the watershed. Their primary projects are the Pimmit Run Trail in McLean to the east of Tysons Corner, and the Cross County Trail, which runs north–south at the western edge of the county.

Figure 6.25 Neighborhood Transect. Neighboring McLean Hamlet is the adjacent residential neighborhood that initially resisted the development due to prominence of the proposed structure.

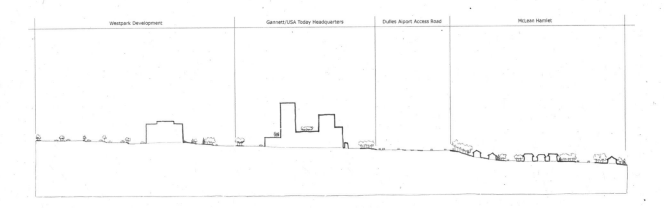

Legend

■ Existing Mass Transit

■ Roads

● Project Location

✳ Dulles International Airport / Washington D.C

Source: fairfaxcounty.gov

Figure 6.26 Transit and Roads. Future mass transit is planned to supplement the existing overtaxed transportation system.

Regional Philosophies

There is ambiguity in regard to conservation versus development in this region. Regional initiatives such as the Chesapeake Bay conservation and the regional transit planning efforts are being implemented on a broad scale. Moreover, urban areas such as Washington, D.C., and Alexandria are steeped in history and culture, and value open space planning. Meanwhile, Fairfax County, as outlined in its Comprehensive Plan, focuses attention largely on new development with few strategies for conservation, creation, and linkage of open space.

Whereas many regions have difficulty with regional planning because of strong town-level autonomy, here the integration of the county's communities could be used to greater advantage. While the planned community of Reston was an early attempt to create stronger community coherence within the county, neighboring Arlington County has recently become a national model for comprehensive smart growth and transit-oriented development strategies, winning the Environmental Protection Agency's 2002 National Overall Excellence in Smart Growth Award.

For over 30 years, Arlington's government has had a policy of concentrating much of its new development near transit facilities, such as Metrorail stations and the high-volume bus lines. Within the transit areas, planning policy encourages mixed-use, pedestrian-oriented, highly dense development, which tapers down to residential neighborhoods. In contrast to Tysons Corner, Arlington adopted a General Land Use Plan to create a coordinated vision for the whole community.

Despite the apparent lack of an overall planning approach that would provide integrated thinking about conservation and development outside of Arlington, projects such as the Gannett/USA Today Headquarters and the proposed Tysons Corner/Metro transit–oriented development are at the forefront of more sustainable development in Fairfax County.

Regional Setting for Pioneer Site

The region surrounding the Gannett/USA Today Headquarters, with its few sustainable qualities creates the setting for a *sustainable pioneer* project. Its lack of regional planning coordination and the absence of local jurisdictions have resulted in piecemeal and rapid development to accommodate the pressures of the region's prominent national role. While Chesapeake Bay conservation planning efforts have developed awareness of water quality and habitat issues, they have not had major effects on development regulation and land use planning in this part of the watershed. The region's general wealth of and value for historic sites and districts has been overwhelmed by the wholesale change and rapid growth experienced in Fairfax County. With a lack of strong transit options, auto-dominant patterns of sprawl facilitate segregated land uses.

These piecemeal land use patterns present challenges to connectivity, but provide fertile ground for pioneering sustainable land-based development that can improve the watershed and provide an example for a region just beginning to realize a need for better land use planning and integrated site design.

Site

Design Considerations

Existing Site

The predesign site, shown in Figure 6.27, was a leftover 25-acre parcel—partially developed and partially disturbed—within the built-out Westpark Office Development. Roughly 5 acres were developed to serve as the office park's stormwater basin (which the new design needed to retain and incorporate) and 20 acres were used as a dumping area. The remaining area was a relatively intact wooded knoll. Located adjacent to the Dulles Airport Access Road and Beltway intersection, the site provided convenient access to the city, airport, and visibility at this busy crossroads.

Program Development

Site environmental/ecological program elements encompassed both the building placement and landscape features. Multiple site layout alternatives were tested for creating the least ecological damage to the site as well as the least visual impact for the surrounding neighborhoods. Other considerations were optimal building orientation and profile for light penetration, highway sound attenuation, and to lower operational building costs in relation to heating and cooling. After these initial decisions were made, the program expanded to include vegetated roofs, views, grading, and rooftop terracing.

With site repair as a central landscape program goal, the woodland knoll was enhanced and modified to include areas of open space for a variety of recreational uses. Outdoor spaces with trails, a pavilion, and an active recreation area are tucked into existing mature woodland. This rich woodland was improved by the removal of invasives, and the addition of native trees to comprise woodland communities such as Pioneer Sapling Mixed Forest, Pioneer Hardwood Forest, Virginia Pine Pioneer Forest, and Hardwood Sapling Mixed Forest. Additionally, the stormwater basin was conceived as a site asset to be enlarged—improving both the ecological function and its visibility as a feature from the building.

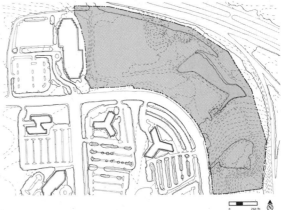

Figure 6.27 Predesign Site Plan. Wooded knoll on eastern portion of site prior to design. This is where the original building was sited. Later this area was set aside for open space and recreation. (Photo Credit: Michael Vergason Landscape Architects)

In order to make the building as comfortable as possible, the design team changed the program from the original plan for one tall tower to two high-rises—one for Gannett and one for USA Today—mitigating their scale and potential detachment from the landscape. Further program refinement of landscape spaces created primary circulation and gathering for active recreation and secondary paths and seating for more contemplative exploration of the site's natural areas along the pond and woodland.

Although some coordination on district stormwater goals was incorporated, the primary focus for program development was on site-related landscape sustainability.

A Conventional Corporate Campus Design

Capital One Financial, McLean, Virginia, USA

Many corporations in recent years have embraced the phenomenon of the corporate campus, purchasing rather than leasing real estate as a safety net from market fluctuation. Minimizing commuting time between departments in the same company, defining employee culture, and controlling the ability for growth without being at the mercy of the real estate market are cited as attractions of the corporate campus concept (Frej 2002). The corporate environment in the Westpark Office Development, where Gannett/USA Today Headquarters is located, is a conventional office park with parking lot–encircled buildings and no open space components. In recent years, corporate campus developments have begun to move into Tysons Corner. One such project, the 28-acre Capital One Financial, has focused its rapid growth strategy on stimulating and personalizing the work environment. Providing all the conveniences Gannett/USA Today does, it also has employees select art purchased for their own office spaces. Located just across Interstate 495 (the Capital Beltway) from the Gannett/USA Today Headquarters, the Capital One Financial site holds one office building, a parking building, and acres of open space dominated by a through road and ball fields. These two corporate parks can be seen in Figure 6.28.

Perhaps partially due to Capital One's anticipated future growth and potential need for additional buildings, the site design, beyond providing ball fields for recreation,

Legend

▪ Gannett/USA Today Headquarters

▪ Capitol One Headquarters

Figure 6.28 Capitol One and Gannett/USA Today. These two corporate giants took very different approaches in their campus site planning.

fails to provide engaging landscape spaces or foster ecological sustainability. Unlike the Gannett/USA Today building, which focuses views toward carefully crafted landscape-dominated spaces, the windows of the 14-story Capital One Financial building, shown in Figure 6.29, orient toward a parking building and Interstate 495, away from the open space. A wide access road, Capital One Drive, traverses and bisects the site while vehicular access dominates the building entry. The site detention basin, located in the farthest corner of the site, is neither celebrated as a focal point nor integrated into a larger site composition. Corporations that develop campuses typically have the space and means to include valued open space in areas of rapid growth yet, without clarity of vision from the client or designers, opportunities to integrate cultural and landscape sustainability are missed.

*Figure 6.29 Capitol One Headquarters.
(Credit: Eric Taylor/erictaylorphoto.com)*

The Gannett/USA Today Headquarters design outcome—beginning with the site scale, plan enlargements, sections, and a site detail—are shown in Figures 6.30 through 6.33. The project is analyzed with respect to two central dimensions of sustainable site design process and outcomes: landscape form and landscape function.

Site Design Form

Patterns

A pattern of transition—from formal to naturalized landscapes—is typical of sustainable projects where materials and maintenance regimes transition from areas of primarily human function to areas of primarily ecological function. The site organization is structured around this principle, from the circulation and materials, to plantings.

The site design is broken down into three distinct landscape spaces: a formal landscape adjacent to the building, the central court terrace between the building and stormwater basin, and the active/passive recreation area and knoll. The primary landscape space in terms of the focal point and conceptual connection between the building and extended landscape is the central court terrace. Divided into three zones of treatment and function, this terrace is a sloped transition space between the building and the stormwater pond. The first zone, comprised of

plazas and pathways alongside the building, is minimal, formal, paved, and hard-edged. This is the primary area of use between the building entry and dining terraces outside the cafeteria. This formality, while not entirely lost, devolves in the second zone into a series of grade changes, vegetative layers, and stone wall terraces that direct a small runnel of water on its way to the stormwater basin. This second zone, set in lawn and carefully ordered stone work, is softened with vertical tree forms, scrambling vines, and shifting ground planes. The third zone is naturalized; a wall defines the maintained edge of the central court terrace against the naturalized pond edge vegetation beyond, as shown in the images of Figure 6.34.

Reducing building scale from one tower to two medium-rise towers helped integrate the building into the landscape both formally and experientially. The structures' stepped-back terracing and angled rooflines provide access to the outdoors at multiple roof gardens as well as sunlight penetration and views into the lower parts of the building and site. While large by any standard at 12 and 9 stories high, the scale of the structures is balanced in relation to the 25-acre site with 83 percent of the property retained as open woodland, pond, and lawn area.

The buildings are oriented to focus on the landscape and capture views, as shown in the plan sketches of Figure 6.35. The site slopes away from the buildings down to the stormwater pond then rises again to a woodland knoll. The

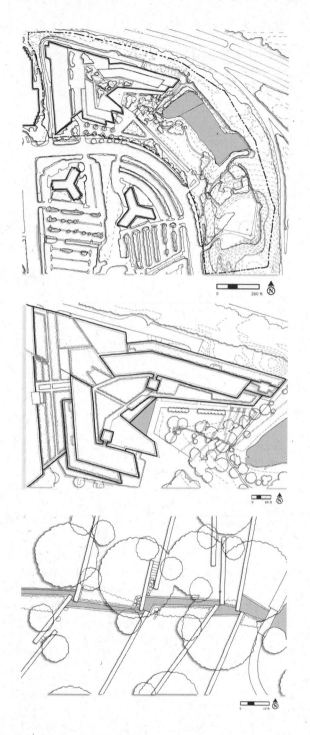

pond and woodland are foreground to distant views toward Washington, D.C., increasing in scale with areas of open lawn in the foreground, dense shrubby vegetation in the middle ground, and canopy trees on the knoll, shown in Figure 6.36.

Materials

In contrast to the polished glass and clean form of the buildings, the material choices for the site, while rectilinear and precisely detailed, are combined in a way to add dimension to the landscape and to reduce the imposing feeling of the structure (see Figure 6.37). In general the formality of materials relates proportionally to the formality of the site zones discussed earlier—more formal near the building and less formal farther into the landscape. A visible material hierarchy addresses each portion of the landscape uniquely. Near the building and site entranceways, pavement dominates and plants are used as accents, as shown in Figure 6.38. The cut-granite pavers feel urban and rectilinear-cut bluestone pavement is broken down with areas of granite cobble. Farther away from the central court with its locally harvested rustic Potomac Basin stone walls, the figure/ground relationship reverses where plants predominate and a single asphalt pathway circles the pond, connecting open space amenities such as the volleyball and baseball areas. The materials of the pavement, stone wall, and water runnels speak to natural process and an organic aesthetic.

Figure 6.30 Gannett/USA Today Site Plan and Enlargements.

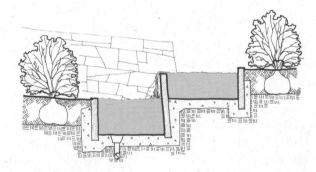

Figure 6.33 Runnel Detail.

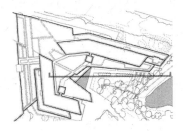

Figure 6.31 Site Section Through the Central Court Terrace to Pond.

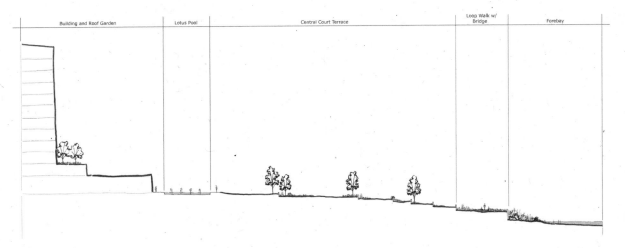

| Building and Roof Garden | Lotus Pool | Central Court Terrace | Loop Walk w/ Bridge | Forebay |

Figure 6.32 Site Section Across Pond.

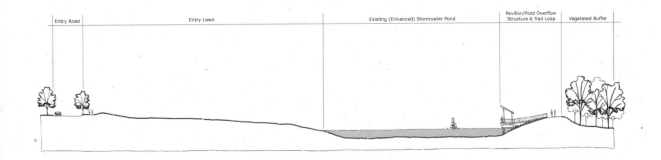

| Entry Road | Entry Lawn | Existing (Enhanced) Stormwater Pond | Pavilion/Pond Overflow Structure & Trail Loop | Vegetated Buffer |

Case Study—Gannett/USA Today Headquarters

Figure 6.34 Formal versus Natural. The central court terrace has a hierarchy gradient from formal near the building to natural near the pond. (Credit: Michael Vergason)

Legend
■ Building Zone - Formal
■ Central Court Terrace Zone - Transition
■ Forebay Edge Zone - Natural

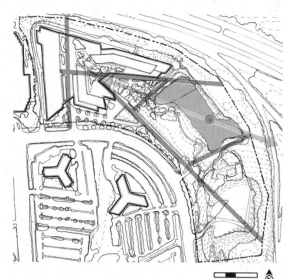

Figure 6.35 Site Organization.

A triangular pool of water, a focal point against the building façade, visually extends the floor level of the interior entry lobby into the landscape. This feature, a *lotus pool* shown in Figure 6.39, creates a reflective horizontal sur-

face, blurring the verticality of the structure with the ground plane. The pool's abstracted forms, lotus plants, and vertical water bubblers create architectural focal points in the otherwise smooth ground plane. Glass and water are used to add interest, extend space, and unify the juncture of building and landscape.

Site Design Function

Natural Systems

The predesign site contained an existing 5-acre stormwater pond that detained water from the surrounding 270-acre watershed—a large portion of Tysons Corner. Regional analysis by the landscape architects assessed the stormwater function, capacity, and health of the existing system and provided cues as to what was missing. Due to its larger function, the general pond shape could not be altered as part of the site improvement plans. However, the landscape architects enhanced the pond by adding a **forebay**, shown in Figure 6.40, to improve stormwater quality. This forebay allows the introduction of a shady buffer planting

Design Efficiency

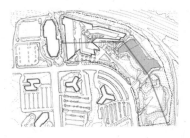

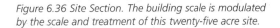

Figure 6.37 Materials. Sensitive use of materials throughout range from urban metallic trellis system on the parking garage façade to the rural accent of Potomac stone walls. A mix of bluestone and cobble pavements melt together to break down the formality of the space just outside the main entry lobby.
(Credit: Michael Vergason Landscape Architects)

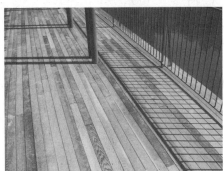

Figure 6.39 Lotus Pond. A lotus pool extends the main hall entrance lobby serving as an extension of the interior ground plane. Its features are architectural focal points within the ground plane.

Figure 6.38 Planting Accents. At the site entry, pavement dominates and plants are used as accents. Vegetation transitions from formal rows to careful plant compositions in the central court terrace. (Credit: Michael Vergason Landscape Architects)

that cools, slows down, and filters incoming stormwater runoff. It allows water to slow and sediment to drop. It also raises and extends the water level, which makes the pond more visible from the building, whose views are oriented toward the pond. A stone pump house functions as a landscape feature as well as pumps water for lawn irrigation and recirculates the central court terrace runnels that aerate the system. This water system is shown in Figures 6.41 and 6.42. Pond-edge bird counts by employees include green and great blue herons—a total of 19 at one time—killdeer, cedar waxwings, spotted sandpiper, hawks, mallards, and wood ducks.

Figure 6.40 Forebay. The forebay in the background, here, slows down and cleanses water coming in from the surrounding development.
(Credit: Michael Vergason Landscape Architects)

Aside from enhancing stormwater quality, the site design, while not explicitly incorporating sustainable construction techniques, such as rainwater recapturing or porous pavement, uses impervious surfaces frugally and employs extensive and dense site plantings. Roof gardens cool terraces, dense native woodland creates buffers, and vines shade parking. The canopy-versus-understory aspects of the site design are shown in Figure 6.43. These techniques were included to improve the human environment but they also reduce the heat island effect and improve site permeability.

The planting approach at Gannett/USA Today Headquarters takes into account architectural and formal qualities adjacent to the building as well as the striated grove-like qualities of a natural system in the wooded knoll and highway buffer areas. Subtle transitions from formal to organic are evident in the vegetation selections and their spacing, as shown in the sketches of Figure 6.44. Widespread linear rows of Ginkgo trees close to the building transition to densely planted native groves and finally to a natural shrubby mix of wetland plants at the pond's edge. According to one avid employee naturalist, wildflowers such as bloodroot, cut-leaved toothwort, May apple, and trout lily are found in the preserved woodland knoll.

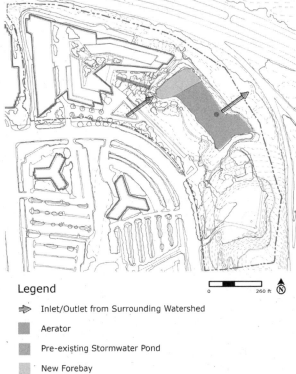

Legend

⇨ Inlet/Outlet from Surrounding Watershed

▧ Aerator

▨ Pre-existing Stormwater Pond

▧ New Forebay

Figure 6.41 Site Hydrologic Sequence. Stormwater from the surrounding development enters the forebay, and flows into the basin where it is aerated. The outfall doubles as a pavilion overlooking the pond.

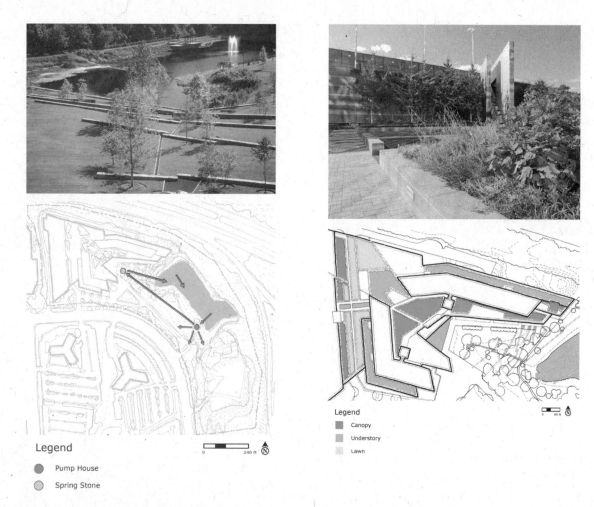

Legend

🔴 Pump House

🔵 Spring Stone

Figure 6.42 Site Water Usage. Water is pumped from the basin to the spring stone in the central court terrace. It is aerated as it flows though the runnels and down falls into the forebay. (Credit: Michael Vergason Landscape Architects)

Legend

■ Canopy

■ Understory

░ Lawn

Figure 6.43 Roof Terrace Vegetation.

Human Systems

The design provides a variety of habitable spaces that integrate the architecture with the landscape. Intensively planted roof gardens at multiple levels and outdoor terraces at ground level provide spill-out areas for gathering, outdoor dining, and working that blend seamlessly with interior spaces. The circulation plan is shown in Figure 6.45. Both the intact and renovated landscapes—from open lawn to shaded woodland to pond edge to plaza—offer multiple uses of the site such as the central court terrace meander, walking paths, ball field, woodland walk, pond pavilion, and seating. In contrast with the surrounding business development where landscapes are dominated by parking lots with no outdoor space except the sidewalk, this landscape provides multiple opportunities to engage with the landscape.

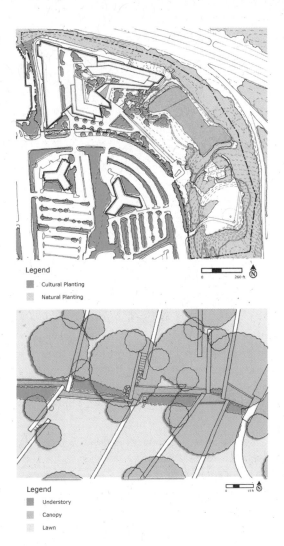

Legend

- Cultural Planting
- Natural Planting

Legend

- Understory
- Canopy
- Lawn

Figure 6.44 Site Planting Plan.

Maintenance

No specific long-term maintenance guidelines were provided by the landscape architect for this project. Currently, however, the maintenance staff is evaluating cost-effective ways to transition to organic land care techniques on the property relative to the stormwater basin and the entire site's health.

Site Design Integration

Engagements

Engagement of the Gannett/USA Today Headquarters site landscape with ecological process occurred through three types of methods outlined in Chapter 7: *restoration*, *creation*, and *regeneration*. Restoration and protection of the largely intact wooded knoll was a primary aim, as well as creation of naturalized ecological landscapes around the pond edge. Regenerative function of the landscape has been created with the improved ecological treatment of onsite and offsite stormwater.

Several factors such as narrative, symbolism, and allusion are utilized in the project design to create a site meaningful beyond just a setting for buildings and site amenities. The design's principal focus, and a source of contemplation and meaning, is the water sequence that activates the central court terrace. Aside from cleansing and recirculating, water is used to reflect, narrate, blur, and enliven space and user experience. Pond water is pumped to a "source stone," then channeled along stone runnels, shown in Figure 6.46, and gets lost among dense vegetation before finding its way into the stormwater pond. While not a primary path, the journey along the runnel, should one investigate, reveals small inviting elements such as stairways and step stone crossings to engage the user. As water cascades down six grade changes, the sequence provides a sense of motion with views that render the central court terrace a place of intrigue and discovery. On a conceptual level, the shifting stone wall feature was initially modeled after natural tree blow-downs that clog and collect debris and create woodland micro-environments (see Figure 6.47). The phenomenon of flotsam and jetsam, or collecting at focal points in the wall junctures, is perceivable in the design and gives the space its own focus and rationale outside of its supporting role to the structure.

Following are specific site design elements that build on the site's ecological enrichment to take advantage of natural phenomenon, site activities, and amenities that combine to engage the user with natural and cultural meaning. These points of cultural engagement are sketched out in the plan shown in Figure 6.48.

Figure 6.45 Circulation Plan.

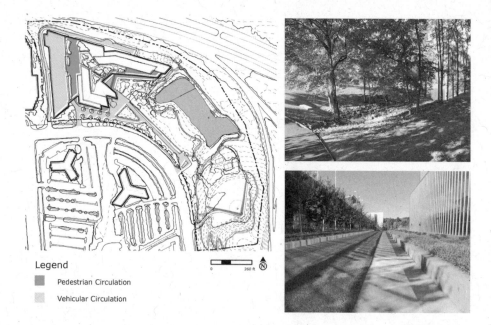

Legend

▮ Pedestrian Circulation

▮ Vehicular Circulation

Views: Pavilion. The existing pond overflow pipe was repurposed as a destination point—a trellised pavilion overlook—along the loop trail and became a focal point of the stormwater pond (see Figure 6.49).

Node: Water Crossings. Where the tilted stone walls intersect, special places for pools and cascades are created. In these areas, small interventions such as hidden steps or small bridges invite the user. This is not just a landscape feature to be viewed from the building windows, but one in which the user is enticed to visit. The photos of Figure 6.50 show these water niches.

Node: Roof Gardens. Two acres of **intensive green roofs** connect interior high-rise spaces with the outdoors. A large open lawn area bordered by tree rows connects the main building to the parking structure above grade. Other, more intimate roof garden areas use retaining walls to provide soil volume for canopy trees, making the interior spaces feel at grade (see Figure 6.51). Despite being intensive roof gardens not designed to manage stormwater per se, they do reduce the heat island effect and capture rainwater, which reduces roof runoff.

Node: Bridge Crossing. The bridge is a small gesture— a place to linger—along the loop path that engages

the pond zone with the central court terrace through the passing over of water that connects the two. Albeit small, a broad mix of ornamental hydric plants calls out the presence of water, as can be seen in Figure 6.52.

Element: Spring Source. Shown in Figure 6.53, a "spring source" stone is located at the top of the central court terrace and begins the flow of collected stormwater down the walled runnel terraces. Located underneath a tree, it is a reference to the simplicity and purity of ground spring sources.

Outcomes

The Program/Site/Context Comparison

Predesign Site/Context Conditions

The sustainable outcome of a project is largely determined by the design team's approach toward three tasks: (1) the development of program goals, (2) choices made in the assessment of the site, and (3) choices made in the assessment of the context. In the chart that follows, the key fea-

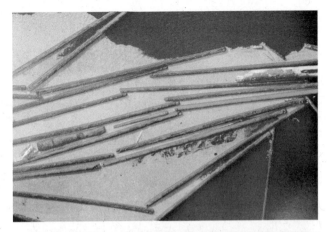

Figure 6.47 Floating Log Design Inspiration.
(Lower Photo Credit: Michael Vergason)

Figure 6.46 Runnel Sequence. Walls, bridge, waterfalls, paths, and stepping stones bring the user in close proximity with the primary feature of the site—the central court terrace.
(Middle Photo Credit: Michael Vergason Landscape Architects)

tures of these three tasks for the Gannett/USA Today Headquarters project are listed in relation to two important sustainable factors: (1) environmental factors and (2) cultural factors.

The relationship shows that the initial program goals of the project were not focused on sustainability, nor did the treatment and planning of the site and region have much ecological or cultural integrity. The site, as it existed prior to the plan inception, is shown in Figure 6.54. The landscape architects introduced sustainable site planning approaches later during the program refinement phase. Sustainable planning techniques were overlain with the basic program goals—and were not an integral part from the project inception.

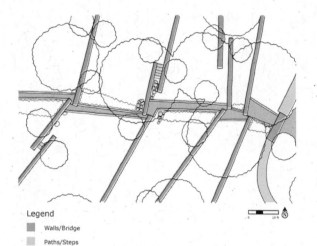

Legend

Walls/Bridge

Paths/Steps

Figure 6.48 Points of Engagement Plan.

Figure 6.49 Engagement—Pavilion.

*Figure 6.50 Engagement—Paths.
(Credit: Michael Vergason
Landscape Architects.*

Figure 6.51 Engagement—Roof Connections.

Figure 6.52 Engagement—Bridge.

Design Efficiency

Figure 6.53 Engagement—Spring Stone.

Postdesign Site/Context Impacts

While clearly walking the line between conventional high-end design and sustainable planning, this project, identified as a *sustainable pioneer,* did impact the context through site improvements. The newly retrofitted regional stormwater basin with forebay and vegetative buffers improves the downstream conditions of Scotts Run. The design draws from the context to enrich the landscape experience through use of local materials and native plants. Therefore, while opportunities for actual connection did not present themselves in this region dominated by sprawl, the Gannett/USA Today Headquarters design improves site biodiversity and downstream hydrology and provides engaging design cues that reference the larger context. The scales most impacted by the design are site and neighborhood as defined by the Scott's Run subwatershed.

The most critical contribution of this project to sustainability is not the details of the project or its connectivity to the surrounding region but the site planning decisions that guided building placement and site resource protection. Three attitudes during the site planning phase resulted in sustainable outcomes. First, early schematics, which had located the structures at the highest site elevation to capture surrounding views, would have destroyed an established native oak woodland knoll—the only ecologically

*Figure 6.54 Pre-Design Site.
(Credit: Michael Vergason)*

*Figure 6.55 Post-Design Site.
(Credit: Michael Vergason)*

intact portion of the site. Instead, when the landscape architects came on board, they recognized that siting new development in construction spoil areas would preserve the woodland knoll as valued **open space**. Second, decisions to keep vehicular circulation to one edge allowed the landscape to dominate as the primary visual feature. Third, the existing stormwater basin was extended toward the building and enhanced to function better and become a feature in the landscape rather than a development limitation. These critical steps during initial schematics laid the groundwork for a rich and functional system of site development, circulation, and hierarchies that drove the remainder of the site design. The outcome is shown in the postdesign photo in Figure 6.55.

The Program, Site, and Context Relationship

	INITIAL PROGRAM GOALS	SITE CHARACTER	CONTEXT CHARACTER
CULTURAL FACTORS	Initial client site goals focused on visibility, highway access, and views. Limited consideration of environmental features	Construction staging area for near-by developments Intact woodland Existing neighborhood stormwater basin	Limited regional planning efforts made to retain existing natural features or to replace or create them
ENVIRONMENTAL FACTORS	To create a corporate campus with state-of-the-art amenities for employees	No cultural site history ·	No precedents in the region that contribute to the cultural richness of the area

Improving Site Efficiency

The following design techniques were used to make use of existing site ecologies and structures, devise multi-purpose details and construction, and ensure a low input maintenance regime, independent of the conditions of the context.

Roof gardens

Incorporating cultural and historic elements

Woodland restoration

Plant community restoration

Stormwater basin enhancement

Improving Regional Efficiency

Despite being a sustainable pioneer this design made moves to improve and to take into account the stormwater and other natural processes that occur outside the site. The design captures some of the resource efficiency goals of the larger region. The following design techniques helped improve the region's sustainability.

Site reuse

Reduced and prescribed maintenance regime

Use of local materials/resources

Plant community restoration

	METROREGION	COMMUNITY	NEIGHBORHOOD°	SITE
GANNETT/ USA TODAY SUSTAINABILITY IMPACTS				

Sustainability Criteria Met?

Five landscape sustainability criteria were presented in Chapter 1 as a means for evaluating landscape sustainability—*Connectivity, Meaning, Purpose, Efficiency,* and *Stewardship.* The design outcome of the Gannett/USA Today Headquarters is evaluated in relation to these criteria as follows:

Connectivity

The Gannett/USA Today Headquarters site design:

- establishes native plant massings that replicate several native habitats, namely woodland, pond edge, and hedgerow.

- uses stone and paving material that references urban uses.

- mimics the natural phenomenon of fallen trees in the forest where material, water, and plants gather. The central court terrace, while a built environment, uses natural processes for its formal inspiration.

- draws users to the landscape because of the variety of experiences it offers.

Meaning

The Gannett/USA Today Headquarters site design:

- fosters curiosity of the hydrologic process with a circular narrative that begins at the spring, flows into a runnel, cascades into pools, and enters the pond and recirculates.

- perpetuates an ecological aesthetic.

- references to natural processes in the central court terrace layout.

Purpose

The Gannett/USA Today Headquarters site design:

- infuses the site with meaning in addition to creating a setting for structures. The site provides both ecological and social functions creating open space and places for people to interact within the landscape features and functions.

- creates a unique landscape in comparison to the indistinguishable parking lot–dominated corporate landscapes surrounding it and beyond.

Efficiency

The Gannett/USA Today Headquarters site design:

- uses a mix of high-maintenance and low-maintenance planting techniques. The low-maintenance vegetation occurs at pond's edge and in woodland and buffer areas. The cultivated vegetation occurs on the roof gardens and along the entry landscape and the Jones Branch Road streetscape.

- recycles pond water for visual and irrigation purposes through the pump house located adjacent to the pond.

- provides opportunities to enhance already established—and create new—low-maintenance vegetation areas.

Stewardship

The Gannett/USA Today Headquarters site design:

- has stimulated the desire in the client to begin investigating organic approaches toward landscape maintenance *vis á vis* the stormwater quality.

- has stimulated the employees to birdwatch and engage with what the landscape provides.

Parallel Projects

The Kresge Foundation Headquarters, Troy, Michigan, USA

When the Kresge Foundation found they had outgrown their existing facilities they took the opportunity to create a workplace that promoted well-being and aligned with their mission to inspire change within the community and be a model of sustainable practices for the nonprofits and communities they support.

Despite the 2.75 acre site's location in an area of suburban sprawl, and its immediate surroundings of acres of parking lot, the site design focused on creating a sustainable pioneer that would preserve its historic features such as a 19th-century farmhouse and barn outbuildings while constructing a new state-of-the-art 17,000-square-foot LEED-rated building. Approximately 72 percent of the site is covered with native plant material meant to evoke the Midwestern prairie. Other aspects are an extensive green roof, geothermal wells, and an aquatic wetland garden. The site is featured in Figure 6.56.

The City of Troy, whose ordinances had once stated that grass must be kept no longer than three inches, was convinced otherwise by this project's goals, and approved the proposed meadow areas. Troy now supports sustainable initiatives to retrofit conventional corporate sites and holds the Kresge project up as a demonstration of alternative development practices.

SmithKline Beecham, West Chester, Pennsylvania, USA

A 300-acre master plan for SmithKline Beecham Animal Health Products corporate campus in West Chester, Pennsylvania, designed by Andropogon Associates, Philadelphia, is a precedent-setting project for the sustainable corporate campus typology. The plan sited buildings, parking, roadways, and developed alternatives to typical stormwater management techniques to improve function and to protect its farmland quality. Rather than designating one maintenance regime throughout, a variety of landscape management zones from formal to natural wetlands were developed. The project also created a greenway link to the township open space plan and became an integrated part of community open space goals. The site can be seen in Figure 6.57.

Figure 6.57 SmithKline Beecham.
(Credit: Andropogon)

Figure 6.56 Kresge Foundation.

7 USER EXPERIENCE

How does sustainable landscape design incorporate "meaning" to connect user and place?

Tanner Springs Park

The diffusion of sustainable landscapes can be accelerated if their functional and informational properties are made tangible and perceivable through direct, physical manipulation. Humans are symbolic animals, and it is through the relationship of form, structure, process, and information content that sustainable landscapes will acquire meaning and depth of experience.
—Robert Thayer

BACKGROUND

The cornerstone of landscape programming is to create opportunities for people to access and inhabit the landscape. The challenge is making gathering spaces, pathways, even parking lots, not just useful but readable, inviting, and meaningful. As a cornerstone of this book's context-informed landscape sustainability framework, *meaning* is a critical aspect of sustainable design because people who are interested and engaged in the landscape have a higher regard for it. Trends toward increasingly personal and virtual environments have diminished landscape design that encourages physical engagement with the natural world and with one another. In addition, environments without *meaning* leave no lasting impression and offer little to the user. As a landscape designer, for example, you know that the ability to identify plants in the landscape makes for a more interesting hike. Likewise, knowledge and meaning in built form, whether explicit or implied, heighten user experience. Sustainable landscapes are particularly fit subjects for assigning meaning and creating rich user experiences. This chapter offers strategies for devising meaningful user experience in the sustainable landscape.

Landscapes have their own history. Previously built sites come with a cultural history to tap into, and every landscape has built-in natural history and character defined by its interdependent site-specific matrix of hydrology, vegetation, and soils. Sustainable landscapes are well suited for user interpretation because of these indigenous qualities. While the site is analyzed for fitness to purpose, in its own right it is a living, changing community of plants and animals (Lynch, Hack 1984). We tend to be more familiar with the meanings inherent in cultural landscapes such as historic gardens and even former industrial sites; however, understanding *ecological landscape* function and history is critical to making appropriate site and bioregional connections. The Whitney Water Purification Facility in Hamden, Connecticut, for instance, replaced its lawn with a meadow indigenous to the Northeast, which now dominates the landscape. A dynamic, evolving, 6-foot-high mix of native grasses and flowers meets the user along narrow pathways. The mixture of species, colors, and textures along with butterflies, birds, and insects provides a connection with natural process, native landscapes, and the site's ecological history. This choice of land cover inspires multiple interpretations and instills the site with a compelling and memorable sense of place.

While buildings are the primary features around which activities of human life are focused, like architecture, landscapes provide shelter, identity, and narrative. Strangely, land use terms such as *residential, commercial,* or *industrial* employ architectural uses to drive the outcome of landscape function. When prompted, however, landscape architects view their projects as multidimensional and land-based, using descriptions such as *a site that tells a watershed story*, *a site repair project*, or *a sustainable and healthy work environment*. Knowledge of place in addition to knowledge of human needs has given landscape architects a unique and needed perspective within the building industry. In a 1967 essay, Ian McHarg laid out a justification for landscape architecture as a profession based on its understanding and consideration of natural systems where he said that ecology offers emancipation to landscape architecture. Incorporating both the natural and cultural aspects of existing sites expands the breadth of landscape function toward more complex program goals. If a site's history is understood, the design outcome can resemble much more than its land use description. It can transform a site into a place that reveals its meaning to users (Krog 1983).

Meaning requires effects that go beyond aesthetics and beauty, to engage users in something active, whether physical or mental. This relies on design that is neither overly prescriptive and one-dimensional nor devoid of any real cues as to focus or message. While good spatial organization contributes to experience of meaning, it is distinct from the elements of meaning. Assigning meaning to the landscape through physical form is not a simple task. It requires crafting of spatial sequences, drama, and materiality. Because user experience is strictly personal and individual, the use of universal materials and techniques allows for multiple readings and speaks to a broad audience, given the audience is listening. A universally accepted meaning can be envisioned in the use of glass to represent water. Or an example of a more intuitive expression is the orange garden wall at the Paradise Valley Residence, which harmonizes with the blue of a framed sky and evokes the red rock landforms of the desert. The following strategies may be employed to expand site meaning to connect user to place in three primary ways—by broadening landscape programs, making natural processes visible, and creating variety in site habitability.

STRATEGIES FOR CREATING USER EXPERIENCE

- *Know your audience.* Think from the point of view of the user. What are the desired uses? What are the required uses? What appeals to some users, most users, or all users? For example, provide benches in easy to reach and difficult to reach locations that appeal to multiple user types.

- *Know the site.* As the site designer, become an expert on the site's ecology and cultural history. Design from the point of view of "sense of place." Knowing the site's former use as an industrial site, for example, can suggest material uses. Likewise, knowing the site is situated along a bird flyway may provide ideas for incorporating habitat.

- *Keep an open mind.* User engagement opportunities may arise late in the design process. The construction documentation and observation phases expose new potentials not revealed earlier. The boulder seating at the Sandstone Visitor Center was conceived of during the construction documentation phase when reference to the site's former use as a quarry became desirable.

- *Provide multiple options to the user.* For example, people tend to gather at water features but can these spaces also be designed to accommodate the lone user?

- *Create human-scaled places for contemplative engagements.* The "spring" that bubbles up from the pavement in the interior of Tanner Springs Park is an intimate circular space. This space contrasts with the wide-open sidewalks, natural spaces, and exposed stairway seating at the edges of the site.

- *Create gathering-scale places for interpretive engagements.* The focus of the Menomonee Valley Industrial Center site is the visible 80-foot-high smokestacks of the former factory, which functions as a gathering and meeting space.

- *Tie leftover spaces together.* Weave together a sequence of natural spaces through the site. Wherever possible, connect to adjacent off-site ecologies. For instance, use an ecotype adjacent to the site to tie disparate pieces such as site boundaries and spaces between buildings together to create a cohesive site and region readable as such by the user.

- *Combine and overlap uses.* Landscapes must be legible. Create intersections between way finding and site features to make landscape patterns readable. If it is a wet site, for example, use the site hydrologic sequence as spatial organization. Or have pathways cross waterways, use benches to call out dramatic scenery, or plant groupings that direct movement.

- *Generate opportunities that appeal to users on two levels—physical and metaphorical.* For example, a pathway that crosses a pond rather than skirts it is an example of a physical engagement. The use of railroad rails for a fence makes a metaphorical connection to the site's former use as a rail yard.

METHODS FOR CREATING USER EXPERIENCE

Engagements

In sustainable design, there is need to address cultural as well as ecological concerns. The intersection of these two conditions, people and natural phenomenon, provides opportunity for physical, intellectual, and spiritual engagements. "Engagement" is a term used here to describe user interaction with ecologies in the natural or cultural environment. The employment of engagements is a sustainable design technique because experiencing the environment is paramount to caring for it and understanding our roles in it (Louv 2006). Two types of land-based engagements, *ecological* and *cultural,* detailed below, forge a connection between people and the landscape and people and their community.

Ecological Engagements

Ecological engagements focus on producing ecological function through restoration, creation, or regeneration of the landscape; they engage the landscape with ecological process. They emphasize *natural processes* in the landscape and in so doing, provide environments that are rich with opportunities for user experience.

Restoration

A restored landscape returns a compromised ecosystem to a stable, balanced, or improved state reasonably close to what would have occurred naturally on the site as an indigenous landscape. Restoration typically applies to soil, hydrologic, or vegetation systems. Restoration is perhaps best applied as an infill approach where natural or human destruction has compromised a small area within a greater intact ecosystem. The Sandstone Visitor Center project was sited on a previously built site within a much larger, intact forested wilderness. Users are engaged with the process of woodland restoration at site boundaries through signage and will witness its change over time as the woodland returns.

Creation/Establishment

Ecosystem creation and establishment occurs in a place where it may or may not have occurred naturally. A fragmented site that seems either too small or too marginalized can be used for ecosystem establishment. The landscape is often viewed and treated as the space between activities with little program of its own. These fragments, however small, can be recreated and connect to other ecological features. For example, small fringes of space adjacent to buildings can become roof runoff swales that provide irrigation to foundation plantings and connect to larger site systems. Improving already existing but not optimum landscapes is another application of creation/establishment. The idea for the meadow and pond biotope at Tanner Springs Park was derived from the historic Tanner Creek and Couch Lake that occupied the site prior to the expansion of downtown Portland. However, this would not be called a restoration because so much time and multiple uses have shaped the site into a completely different condition. The site transitioned between developed and fallow several times over the last century, starting out as a lake, then filled for a rail yard, then abandoned as natural meadow until its new construction as a park. With this design, the site has reached a compromise between the two conditions—part urban and part wilderness.

These created or established ecological landscapes often represent dramatic departures from the site's previous character, attracting user interest and engagement, such as was the case in the Whitney Water Purification Facility's transformation.

Regeneration

Regeneration is the harnessing of natural processes, such as hydrology, vegetative growth, and wind, to provide a landscape that benefits human uses. Often described as *working landscapes,* regenerative design can incorporate agricultural uses that sustainably produce food and other land-based resources, or infrastructure uses such as stormwater management that are conventionally provided with more mechanized, less ecological means. The concept of regenerative landscape design was developed by John Lyle and brought to life at California State Polytechnic University's Center for Regenerative Studies. Here students can learn about, research, and apply processes such as aquaculture, permaculture, composting, wetlands water treatment, solar and wind energy, and more in a live-in campus center. Although these are technological human landscapes, they rely on natural process and are primarily self-maintaining or productive, as opposed to being a resource sink. As technological landscapes they are perhaps most directly engaging of site users. The Menomonee Valley Industrial Center is regenerative in its ecological treatment of stormwater that also allows for recreational and habitat uses of the open space.

Cultural Engagements

Cultural engagements include landscapes that are interpretive, contemplative, or connective. They emphasize user activities in and experience of the ecological and cultural landscape.

Interpretation

An interpretive engagement in the landscape represents, reveals, or draws parallels with natural or cultural phenomena. It includes use of metaphor or demonstration, and is often educative. Understanding our reliance on the landscape for food, clean water, and energy can be achieved passively through natural processes made visible in the landscape itself, or actively through signage and demonstration. Likewise, interpretive engagements provide information either explicitly or subtly about cultural features within our communities. Tanner Springs Park, while a built system, passively (meaning there is no site signage explaining it) demonstrates a natural stormwater process. The circular flow of water that bubbles up from a spring, flows into a vegetated swale and to a pond of standing water, while performing actual stormwater cleansing, represents natural hydrologic flows. Because the majority of usable park space is given over to vegetative and hydrological function rather than human uses, unlike typical urban parks, the park itself represents the push and pull of these two entities.

Contemplation

Contemplative landscapes are places for reflection, quiet observation, and meditation. These provide areas for personal introspection and/or communing with nature. Therapeutic landscapes would fall into this category. While this type of activity can occur naturally on its own, spaces can be designed specifically for contemplation. Areas for contemplation must feel quiet, safe, and must possess inherent interest, beauty, or function. Tanner Springs Park's initial master plan mandate was as a contemplative park and the outcome is a peaceful oasis within a busy urban downtown.

Connection

Landscapes create connections for social gathering in the public realm. Sustainable landscapes are often, but certainly not always, accessible to the public. Public open spaces, however, especially parks, are a key ingredient in sustainability because they foster human interaction and a sense of community identity. Tanner Springs Park lends an organic, intellectual, upscale quality to the high-rise neighborhood it was built to serve. While the majority of the park space is meadow and stormwater pond, the connective engagements are found at the edges of the site. Amphitheater seating is accessible from adjacent streets overlooking a performance space below while a small lawn area, also located at the perimeter, overlooks the meadow.

CASE STUDY—
TANNER SPRINGS PARK

LOCATION: Portland, Oregon, USA
SITE SIZE: 1.2 acres
CLIENT: City of Portland, Parks and Recreation
DESIGNERS: Lead Landscape Architect—
   Atelier Dreiseitl/ Waterscapes, Inc., Ueberlingen, Germany
 Local Landscape Architect—Greenworks, PC, Portland, Oregon
 Civil/Structural Engineer—KPFF, Portland, Oregon
 Wetland Planting Consultant—Sarah Cooke
FORMER SITE USES: Industrial Area/Railway
PROJECT BUDGET: $2.2 million
DATE OF COMPLETION: 2005

Overview

While both cultural and ecological engagements revealed themselves within all of the projects reviewed in this book, the following case study, an urban park in Portland, Oregon, embodies both engagement types. The one-acre site design creates opportunities for seating, viewing, contemplation, learning, relaxing, exploring, and social interaction that reveals the site's former history, the broader regional ecology, and natural processes.

The average conventional park has tree groves in rolling lawn, scattered benches, and a playscape. While these elements are highly desirable, Tanner Springs Park stands as a model for a sustainable park that reaches far beyond this simple prototype. The park challenges the very notion of the traditional urban park by asking the question: *What is nature?* The answer is in the unusual design decision to have a block-long meadow and **stormwater retention basin** as the dominant features. An open pond and a wetland filtration area capture and filter runoff from the surrounding sidewalks on the exterior of the park and clean, store, and recirculate it. In conjunction with the natural features and processes of the site, terraced seating and a boardwalk create a gathering and performance space and allow access to the water. The user experiences were

designed with an understanding of the dynamic between the site's history as first a lake and then as a rail yard. These two events provide several layers of land-based engagements, both cultural and ecological.

Project Inception

Tanner Springs Park, located in the rapidly transforming northeast quadrant of central city Portland, is one of a series of four parks planned for the Pearl District. In 1999, a Pearl District master plan, called the *River District Park System Urban Design Framework,* outlined a dense residential and mixed-use neighborhood with a strong infrastructure of open space and transportation links to its prime location along the Willamette River. According to the master plan, each of the four parks would provide a unique amenity to the district, but each would also retain some common elements to unify them. As of 2008, two of the parks have been realized, Jamison Square and the topic of this case study, Tanner Springs Park, shown in Figure 7.1.

The city of Portland is a national exemplar for sustainable design and planning. From its implementation of an antisprawl urban growth boundary to its Green Streets stormwater treatment program, it has become known for proactive planning and grassroots support of sustainable

Figure 7.1 Bird's eye views of Jamison Square and Tanner Springs Park prior to buildout of the area. Tanner Springs Park is located several blocks from the Willamette River. Jamison is two blocks closer to downtown.
(Credit: Greenworks PC)

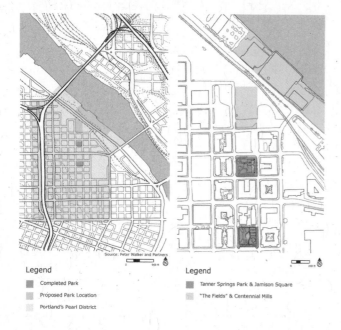

Figure 7.2 Master Plan Components. Two of the four proposed parks have been built. The Master Plan connects neighborhoods in the Pearl District to the Willamette River.

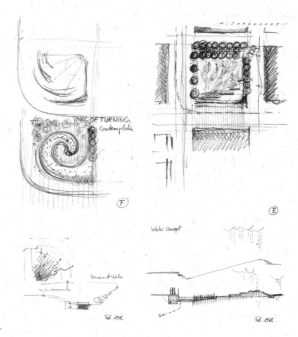

Figure 7.3 Schematic Site Design Sketches. (Credit: Atelier Dreiseitl)

development. The German firm Atelier Dreiseitl, retained as the lead landscape architect, is known for their public design process, water-related design expertise, and overall design excellence. In keeping with Portland's sustainable trajectory, Tanner Springs Park provides compelling form to the ecological sensibility and attention to design excellence that Portland residents and visitors have come to expect.

Design Concept

The specific **programmatic** concept for the Tanner Springs Park site revolves around the creation of a wetland and a **contemplative landscape**. As described by Herbert Dreiseitl, the design sets up the question, "What is nature?" Water features, a trademark of Portland's park system reflective of its riverfront locale and rainy climate, play a part as a common thread in the **master plan,** shown in Figure 7.2, as a link between the Pearl District and the Willamette River, a few blocks north of the site (Portland City Council 1998). Tanner Springs Park features connections to the site and region's historic and ecological character using hydrologic features and native vegetation. The park's name is derived from a local historic creek that used to meander the area on its way to the Willamette River. Its primary visual feature is a **stormwater detention pond** with both urban and natural edges. These features are shown in the early sketches of Figure 7.3 and the design resolution in Figure 7.4. The site design is a dichotomy of rectilinear urban form that contrasts with natural systems, forms, and processes.

Project Philosophies and Approach

The Tanner Springs Park design was a collective vision between four primary entities, the City of Portland, the River District Park System Urban Design Framework master plan, the landscape architecture firm Atelier Dreiseitl, and a local firm GreenWorks, P.C., and input from a series of unique open-forum community discussions. That collaborative vision was a neighborhood park that would provide a place for residential street life activities and the contemplation of nature. Specifically, the goals were to provide for: (1) the creation, contemplation, and celebration of nature in an

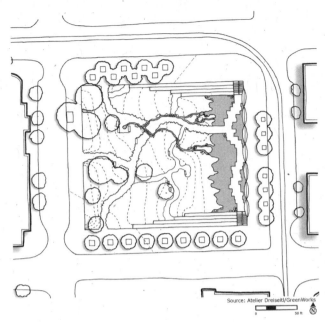

Figure 7.4 Final Site Plan.

Source: Atelier Dreiseitl/GreenWorks

urban environment—different from the way it is celebrated in the countryside, (2) the incorporation of art and artifacts linking to site history, (3) minimal programmed activities to allow for open-endedness, (4) a low-input maintenance regime, and (5) references to the region.

The client and landscape architect's philosophies were critical in forming the site design's sustainable outcomes. On this project, both client and landscape architect shared a vision for sustainable design from the onset. The client for this project, the City of Portland, is well known for its sustainable policies, design, and infrastructure (Centennial Mills Framework Plan). The renewal and master plan of the Pearl District were long in the making with multiple guidelines, design proposals, and reports developed prior to implementation.

The landscape architecture firm, Atelier Dreiseitl, was selected through a Request for Qualifications together with local landscape architects, Greenworks PC. Atelier Dreiseitl, known for spearheading gutsy stormwater design in Germany and on a global scale, has long navigated the pitfalls of achieving sustainable design where high costs, stringent municipal regulations, aged infrastructure, and vocal constituents all factor into changing the status quo of conventional stormwater management. Their design philosophy contends that achieving sustainability is not an "all or nothing" prospect. Rather, each and every development is an opportunity to improve the built environment despite the inevitable pitfalls that often compromise complete sustainability. They believe that designers and municipalities can pursue sustainability in pieces and parts that collectively have an additive regional effect.

Program Type and Development Trend

Program Type: Urban Park

When the first U.S. urban parks proliferated in the late 1800s, the formula for their expected form revolved around the pastoral idea of lawn, shade trees, open water bodies, ornamental gardens, and more recently, active recreational uses provided by play fields and courts. Smaller urban parks have taken on more architectural treatments with formal design and tightly planted canopies to define outdoor rooms in the city, as in New York's Bryant and Paley Parks. These have provided a representation of nature in the city and an opportunity for cultural expression and interaction with the landscape, though not on an ecological basis.

Ironically, many of the natural landscapes that previously existed on the sites of urban parks were obliterated to create the new urban nature. Central Park, for instance, was originally the site of an irregular terrain of swamps and bluffs punctuated by rocky outcroppings, which made much of the land undesirable for private development. During the mid-20th century, great interest and emphasis was placed on the social dimensions of urban parks, as explored through William Whyte's seminal analysis of the "Social Life of Small Urban Spaces," and Lawrence Halprin's design for interactive places such as Levi Plaza.

While these parks and open spaces have been a critical enriching and enduring amenity in urban environments, there is new interest in expanding the possible forms of urban parks to integrate **site memory** and **regenerative landscape function** as steps toward sustainability. As our urban areas and populations undergo change and shifting pressures, there is also interest in how parks in general might be more relevant to contemporary societal needs and desires. Tanner Springs Park, as yet few others in the United States, fits into this new model for urban park design.

Development Trend:
Urban Renewal

Planned redevelopment, or **urban renewal**, of whole city districts can provide new economic opportunities, comprehensive programs of open space, and renewed mixed-use areas. The Pearl District is one such neighborhood in Portland's movement toward urban renewal. Often, this trend employs approaches such as **adaptive reuse** where postindustrial buildings are saved from demolition for residential or commercial uses. This sustainable practice lends immediate character and historic identity to a neighborhood by providing unique, enduring, and adaptable architectural form. Urban renewal can have negative connotations when used as a mechanism for forcing working-class neighborhoods out in favor of higher-cost uses. However, each case varies and many such projects encompass derelict and abandoned city districts. Prime examples of urban renewal that incorporate elements of adaptive reuse are San Francisco's Mission Bay and the South of Market neighborhoods that began their transformations from urban industrial to a mixed-use residential, open space, and commercial district in the 1990s and 2000s. As industrial uses in the Portland's Pearl District became obsolete, the infrastructure and prime location was seen as an opportunity for strengthening Portland's urban core and creating a mixed-use neighborhood where land has lain fallow for many years.

Context

The regional context of Tanner Springs Park is shown in a sequence of scales in Figures 7.5 through 7.9. Regional context analysis infuses the site design process with an understanding of potentials and challenges. It situates the site relative to area history, regional attitudes, and ecological health. Descriptions of landscape form, function, and philosophy of this area of Oregon explore this unique setting and the combination of sustainable factors to which the project design responds.

Regional Form

Natural Patterns

The valley along the Willamette River, which flows northward from its headwaters in the Cascade Mountains to its confluence with the Columbia River at Portland, shown in Figure 7.10, is a fertile agricultural area. For early users of the Oregon Trail, a primary route that brought settlers westward in the 1840s, this region was a natural place to settle. Now home to 70 percent of Oregon's population,

Figure 7.5 Tanner Springs Park—National Context.

this area is the cultural and political heart of Oregon (Portland Bureau of Environmental Services). Though geographically part of the Willamette Valley, Portland is often excluded due to differing cultural and political interests of its urbanized areas in contrast to the rest of the valley's rural and small-town culture.

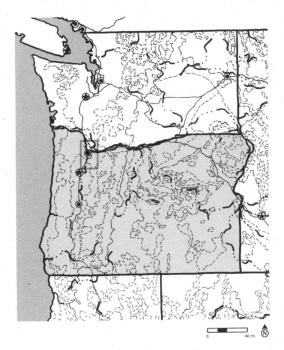

Figure 7.6 Tanner Springs Park—State Context.

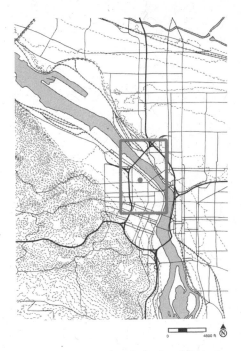

Figure 7.7 Tanner Springs Park—Local Context.

Figure 7.8 Tanner Springs Park—Pearl District Context.

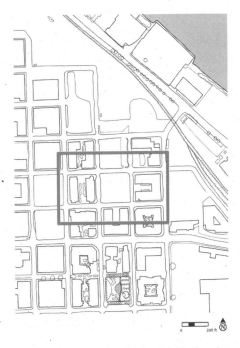

Figure 7.9 Tanner Springs Park—Neighborhood Context.

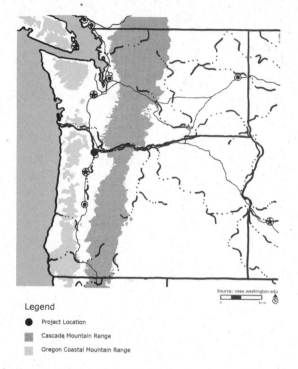

Legend

● Project Location

▰ Cascade Mountain Range

▱ Oregon Coastal Mountain Range

Figure 7.10 Nearby Mountain Ranges.

Legend

▱ Lower Willamette River Watershed (portion)

▰ Tanner Subwatershed

Figure 7.11 Willamette River Watershed and historic Tanner Creek Subwatershed.

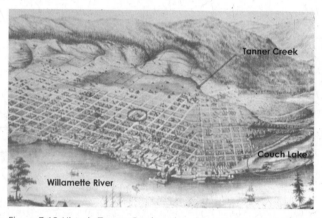

Figure 7.12 Historic Tanner Creek.
(Credit: Library of Congress)

The Willamette River basin is Oregon's largest watershed. Located at the lowest point of the watershed, Portland comprises its most urbanized area in the 17 miles of river that pass through the city. The land uses of the upper reaches of the watershed are largely agricultural or undeveloped. The Tanner Springs Park lies within the Tanner subwatershed (see Figure 7.11). Long since filled, open streams, including Tanner Creek, seen in Figure 7.12, once flowed across this area of downtown Portland's northwest industrial district and into a swampy landscape called Couch Lake. In the mid-1800s Portland was first settled in the area south of the site. By the 1880s, however, development expanded into the north, facilitated by the filling of the area with massive amounts of sawdust, mill wastes, dredge soils, gravel, debris, and trash. These waterways, including Tanner Creek, were diverted into underground pipes, seen in Figure 7.13, originally combined with sanitary sewers. The Tanner Creek diversion pipe runs directly by the site along 10th Street, where it eventually daylights on the western shore of the Willamette River south of the historic Centennial Mills site.

The identity of the region is closely tied to the river and to water in general. In this urbanized area, identity with water is celebrated and fostered with a number of well-known and popular public spaces and landmarks built around water features. Lawrence Halprin's 1966 Lovejoy Fountain and his work with Angela Danadjieva on the 1971 Ira C. Keller Fountain, which explore the processes of nature, are among the many included on a city fountain walking tour (Harvey, Fieldhouse 2005).

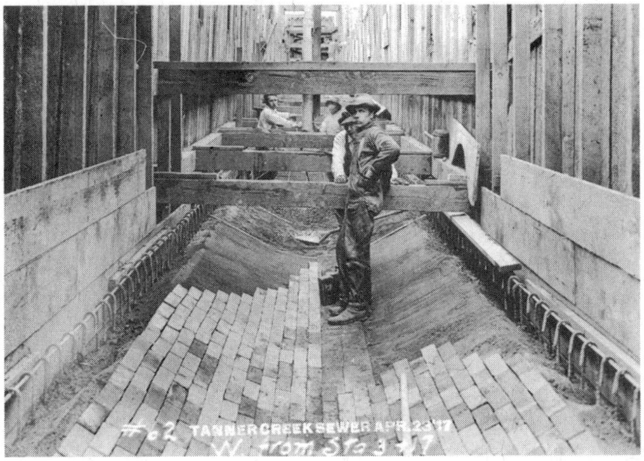

Figure 7.13 Tanner Creek. Tanner Creek was diverted underground where it still flows.
(Credit: Environmental Services, City of Portland, Oregon)

The project area lies in the West Coast Mountains Natural Region, outlined in Figures 7.14 and 7.15. While the mountain ranges on either side of the Willamette Valley are dominated by cedar, hemlock, and Douglas-fir upland forest, historically the Willamette Valley forests were primarily oak savannah—tall grasslands with scattered Oregon white oaks (*Quercus garryana*) as seen in Figure 7.16, and groves of coast Douglas-fir (*Pseudotsuga menziesii subsp. menziesii*). The river floodplains contained extensive wetlands, with stands of ash, willow, alder, and cottonwood, as well as **riparian** forests. Native American inhabitants of the valley managed this landscape by employing fire to

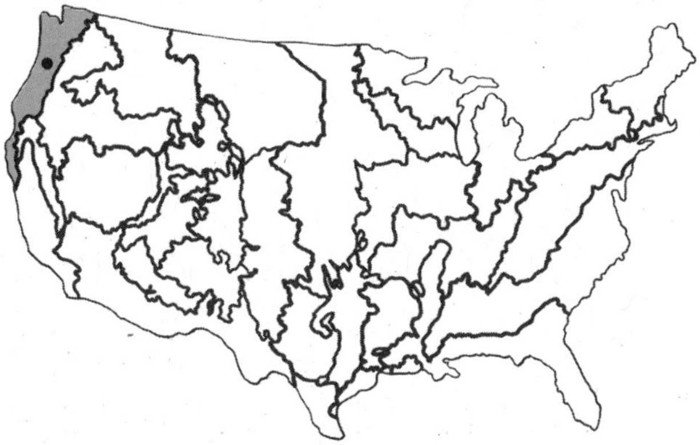

Figure 7.14 U.S. Natural Regions: West Coast Mountains.
(Harker 1999)

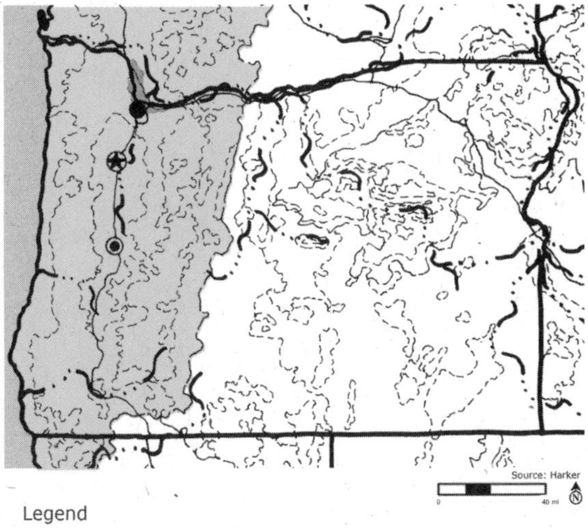

Figure 7.15 Alder-Ash Forest Locations. The lower Williamette Valley and its confluence with the Columbia River was the location of floodplain wetlands inhabited by wet forest types in addition to the drier oak savannas. (Harker 1999)

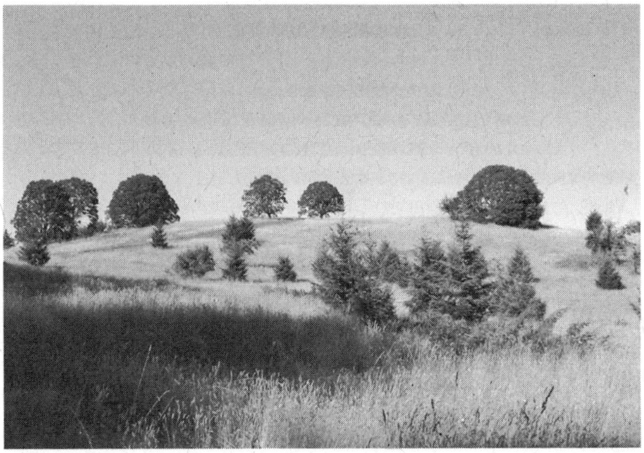

Figure 7.16 Oak Savannah. Native to the area, now very little of the original oak savanna remains.
(Credit: Darin Stringer-Integrated Resource Management)

encourage open grasslands and limit tree growth. Nineteenth-century American settlers used the valley for agriculture, and the remainder converted from grasslands back to canopy forest. Today almost nothing of the early oak savannah remains.

Legend

☐ Portland City Boundary

▨ Portland Urban Growth Boundary

Figure 7.17 Urban Growth Boundary. A controversial boundary around metropolitan Portland of approximately two hundred thousand acres meant to discourage sprawl.

Legend

▨ High Density Developed

▨ Low Density Developed

▨ Undeveloped Grassland/Forest

Figure 7.18 Land Cover. Much of the area surrounding the growth boundary is low-density development or undeveloped.

Development Patterns

Perhaps the most distinctive and influential feature of Portland's sustainable urban form is its **urban growth boundary**, shown as the shaded area of Figure 7.17. While urban growth boundaries are common in Europe, the United States has resisted adopting them due to the prevalence of local control over development. Under Oregon law, each municipality in the state has an urban growth boundary in place that controls development from expanding into pristine or agricultural land (Metro). In the Portland metro region, a consortium of 24 cities in three different counties belong to a regional authority called the Metro Council, which regulates and sets the boundary and provides oversight and regional services such as transit and waste management. This boundary, in place since 1977,

preserves agricultural and natural open space in outlying areas while encouraging densification in urban areas, shown in Figure 7.18. Tanner Springs Park lies in the dense urban center of the growth boundary.

The focus on urban development within the growth boundary has created intense emphasis on the distinctive identity of neighborhoods and districts within the region, seen in Figure 7.19. While today, Tanner Springs Park is located in Portland's well-known art district, in the early 1900s the park site was occupied by rail tracks of the Hoyt Street Rail Yards. Filled with warehouses, industries, and a rail yard, this area was known as the Northwest Industrial Triangle. From 1915 until the end of World War I, the rail yard was a booming passenger line, bringing travelers to the coast to catch steamers to San Francisco. When pas-

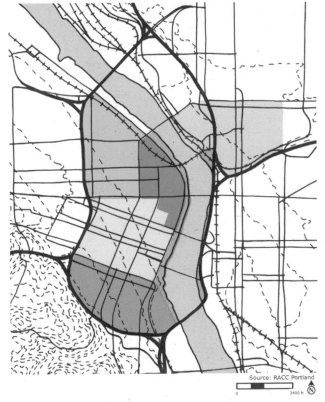

Figure 7.19 Neighborhoods in Downtown Portland. Downtown Portland occupies the west banks of the Willamette River. (Photo Credit: wikipedia.org)

Source: RACC Portland

senger train use ceased, Hoyt Street Yards switched to freight trains and then declined over the next two decades (Hoyt Street Properties). In 1994, developers purchased a 34-acre area in the renamed Pearl District, marking the beginning of planning and redevelopment of the district.

At first, redevelopment took the form of reuse and few changes were visible. Artists moved to the area and lived and worked in lofts, but the primary land uses remained light industry, vacant buildings, and cafes. It is unclear where the Pearl District's name derives from—a local gallery owner may have suggested that old warehouse buildings were like crusty oysters and that the galleries and artists' lofts were like pearls. Soon the area **gentrified** as aging warehouses were renovated into residential units and new buildings filled vacant sites to create a dense mixed-use neighborhood that retains some of its historical character.

Art and culture is an important focus in both the physical and economic development of the City of Portland. The city has a long-standing commitment to public art, bolstered more than 30 years ago when Oregon became one of the first states to commit to consistent public art funding. Today, the city has a public art walking tour of over 80 sites, which includes Tanner Springs Park's Art Wall. The art tour is shown in Figure 7.20. Walking tours highlight Hispanic, Chinese, Japanese, African American, and Native American art that have contributed to the city's current identity. The Cultural District, located in the heart of downtown, south of the Pearl District, is the civic center of the city and home to Pioneer Courthouse Square, known as Portland's "living room." The Park Blocks area, lined by the city's oldest churches and homes, is an historic open space boulevard planted with stately elms and poplars. Museums and other civic institutions are found there as well. The city's arts and culture efforts are highly landscape place-based in their focus on pedestrian connectivity, the public realm, open space, and distinct neighborhood identity.

Because the provision of open space is a critical component of the dense development encouraged by the urban growth boundary, the Portland metro region is well connected with a range of dedicated open space, shown in Figure 7.21. Likewise, the cornerstone of the Pearl District Master Plan is the sequence of open space features that connects the neighborhood to the riverfront.

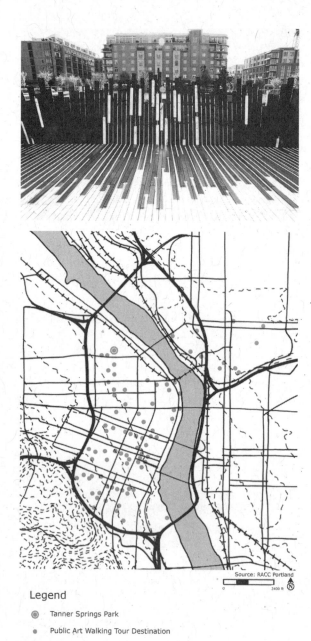

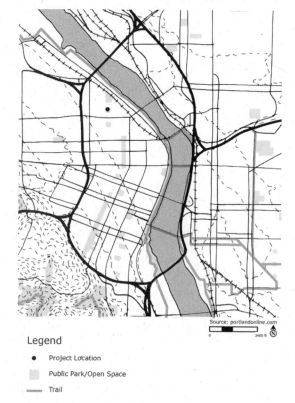

Legend

⊙ Tanner Springs Park

• Public Art Walking Tour Destination

Figure 7.20 Portland's Public Art Tour. (Credit: Braut Kilbes.)

Legend

• Project Location

▨ Public Park/Open Space

─ Trail

Figure 7.21 Regional and Downtown Parks and trails.

Regional Function

Natural Systems

With its critical location at the confluence of two large rivers, protecting and improving water resources has become a primary ecological initiative for the Portland metro region, to which many efforts have been devoted. Its Green Streets program, outlined in Figure 7.22, is nationally recognized as a model for municipal stormwater management. In several locations throughout the city, Green Street projects retrofit existing piped-system streets with curbside planters fed by street runoff, adjacent building rooftops, and porous paving. Ongoing monitoring is undertaken to quantify benefits, improve design and function, and lower maintenance costs.

The name *Tanner Springs* derives from wetlands and a tributary creek that once flowed through the site and neigh-

Figure 7.22 Portland's Green Streets Program.
(Credit: Environmental Services, City of Portland, Oregon.)

borhood and an early tannery built in the 1860s. Now diverted in a culvert that runs under the edge of the site, an early and frequent topic of debate in the development of the parks for the Pearl District was the concept of its day lighting. While it was considered during the design of Tanner Springs Park as a way of returning ecological health and biodiversity to the urban core, it ultimately became too costly and contentious to execute.

Human Systems

Unlike many urban areas, today's Portland is achieving a high level of urban vitality, increased growth, and diversity. New development in the Pearl District has consciously emphasized family-friendliness and, with the addition of new housing, has resulted in an urban baby boom that has roughly doubled the census birthrate in the period between 1991 and 2005 (City of Portland Bureau of Planning).

The urban density planning encouraged by the Portland's urban growth boundary goes hand-in-hand with the employment of a comprehensive program of mass transit. Designed to fit the scale and traffic patterns of the neighborhoods it travels, the Portland Streetcar passes by Tanner Springs Park.

Regional Philosophies

Conservation versus Development

Portland's urban growth boundary is emblematic of the region's long-held value for an integrated approach to conservation and development. This important measure spawned further planning work in the early 1990s when the Environmental Protection Agency formed the Pacific Northwest Ecosystem Research Consortium (PNW-ERC). The principal aim of the group was to offer scientific analyses to help both policymakers and local citizens make better decisions about land and water use in the Willamette Valley region. Studies were developed that looked at a projected population growth from 2.5 million in 2000 to 4 million in 2050. They created three different planning scenarios for how this growth could be accommodated: one that would continue in their then-present planning framework, one that would loosen the existing restrictions on development, and one that would strengthen them. These scenarios show the combined effects of potential policy decisions on urban, rural, residential, agricultural, forestry, and natural lands, as well as water use, across the entire basin through the year 2050. They have helped guide citizens and policymakers to make informed choices about conservation and development direction.

Among other groundbreaking legislation, Oregon passed the Sustainability Act in 2001 with nearly unanimous support from the governor and the legislature. The first of its kind in the nation, the Act establishes a policy of sustainability to guide activities including and beyond those undertaken by state agencies. The legislation created the Sustainability Board, to examine sustainability practices and recommend approaches to both government agencies and the private sector (The Biodiversity Project).

The evolution for urban renewal planning in Portland, begun in the late 1980s, has been characterized by three distinct focuses: (1) the development of a mixed-use planning philosophy, (2) the necessity of reliance on entrepreneurial vision with strategies to identify and shape projects, and (3) the recognition of the ever-growing necessity of true community involvement in renewal programming (Wollner 2003).

Development Design Goals: City of Portland

The following goals guide development throughout the Central City. They apply within the River District as well as to the other seven Central City policy areas.

1. Encourage urban design excellence in the Central City.

2. Integrate urban design and preservation of our heritage into the process of Central City development.

3. Enhance the character of Portland's Central City districts.

4. Promote the development of diversity and areas of special character within the Central City.

5. Establish an urban design relationship between the Central City districts and Central City as a whole.

6. Provide for a pleasant, rich, and diverse pedestrian experience in the Central City.

7. Provide for the humanization of the Central City through promotion of the arts.

8. Assist in creating a 24-hour Central City that is safe, humane, and prosperous.

9. Assure that new development is at a human scale and that it relates to the character and scale of the area and the Central City.

Additional River District Design Goals (1996)

An additional set of goals for the design review process augment the Central City Fundamental Goals. These goals for design review are specific to the River District policy area of the Central City. There are four River District Goals for design review; they are:

1. Extend the river into the community to develop a functional and symbolic relationship with the Willamette River.

2. Create a community of distinct neighborhoods that accommodates a significant part of the region's residential growth.

3. Enhance the District's character and livability by fostering attractive design and activities that give comfort, convenience, safety, and pleasure to all residents and visitors.

4. Strengthen connections within the River District, and to adjacent areas.

(City of Portland)

The planning ethic prevalent in the larger region's efforts to balance conservation and development is also evident at the smaller scales of districts and neighborhoods. The development of the Pearl District emerged through a multifaceted master planning process that began as an urban renewal project in 1998 for the larger River District. More recent planning efforts resulted in a more focused North Pearl District Plan, in the Tanner Springs Park area. The plan establishes a sustainable community concept with goals of family-compatible housing, economic development and "green collar" jobs, multimodal transportation, a natural systems approach to stormwater management, and an emphasis on the street and the public realm.

Cultural Resources

The Portland metro region has an interesting combination of cultural influences that result from its unique position at the edge of a large agricultural region and two vast natural mountain ranges, and the center of an important historical urban hub that began with the arrival of the Lewis and Clark Expedition and settlers streaming in from the Oregon Trail. In combination, these influences create a culture that values outdoor amenities, the public realm, and a sense of history. As has been mentioned, in addition to a strong attitude of sustainability, there is also substantial value and appreciation for design and art. In the Pearl District, with its evolution from an industrial district to an arts hub, these influences all converge to create an eclectic study in contrasts from high-tech to historic, rustic to refined, and open green space to densely developed blocks.

Region as Setting for Integrator Site

As an example of a setting for a sustainable integrator, the region surrounding Tanner Springs Park exhibits several dimensions of sustainability. Through integrated levels of planning, including an urban growth boundary, a multifaceted transit plan, and district master planning, the Portland metropolitan region has systematically created and implemented strategies for smart growth. As they lead the nation in efforts to encourage compact development, their focus on water quality, urban open space, and distinctive design models a livable urban environment.

A paradox of this reputation for careful planning and a commitment to conservation is that it has attracted larger-than-average population growth, which is putting smart growth policy measures to the test (Sprawl City). The prescribed higher density of the urban center depends on the provision of adequate high-quality, functioning open space, such as this project provides.

Site

Design Considerations

Existing Site

Historically the Tanner Springs Park site was a swampy floodplain of the Willamette River and part of the Tanner Creek and Couch Lake system. The initial site development, shown in Figure 7.23, evolved through many transitions that began long ago when these existing wetlands were filled with varied and contaminated debris to accommodate factories and later a rail yard. Then for many years, the abandoned industrial lands lay fallow as meadow. In a sense, outside of its natural and industrial history, at the onset of this project, the site was a clean slate—an abandoned city block near a dense and bustling center city, as can be seen in Figure 7.24. In 2002, the area surrounding the site experienced a rapid transition to high-rise mixed-use development. To the Dreiseitl/GreenWorks landscape architectural team, this evolution—from wetland to industrial to naturalized to residential—found expression in the park design.

Program Development

The scale of sustainable planning and design that most influenced the Tanner Springs Park project design was district planning. The Pearl District master plan put forth a basic site design program that determined the site location and the neighborhood open space sequence. It was determined at the time that this series of four parks would contain common features readable as a contiguous park

Figure 7.23 Development

Figure 7.23 Development Succession. Over the course of ten years, the Pearl District rapidly transitioned from a formerly industrial area that lay fallow for many years to a mixed residential area.

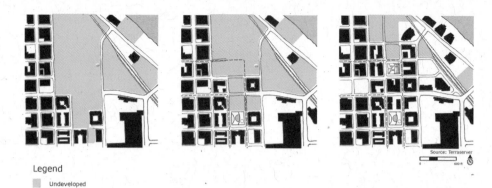

Legend

◾ Undeveloped

sequence ending at the Willamette River while each still forged their own unique character. These common features were an outdoor gallery for community gatherings, a water feature, and a boardwalk along the east side of each park that would form a continuous trajectory toward the river. This basic planning tool guided the process during the schematic phase then allowed the design to take its own course. Several community meetings informed three alternative schematic site plans, developed by Atelier Dreiseitl. These alternative site plans are shown in Figure 7.25. Later, the community voted on the one that best suited the site, its size, function, and local aesthetic. This final plan showed the park's urban edge condition with generous streetscapes with street trees and furnishings, and an interior that transitioned from east to west from formal to progressively more natural areas. Its focal point was a stormwater pond that collects, filters, recirculates, and stores rainwater.

Community collaboration is a feature of the City of Portland's design and programming approach as is often the case on public landscape architecture projects. At Tanner Springs Park, a steering committee was involved from the onset. The community workshops, headed by Atelier Dreiseitl, avoided politically driven themes and instead focused on stimulating creativity and having fun with sketching and stage performances.

The community workshop activities infused the schematic programming phase not with forms or details but with a **gestalt** sensibility for the new park. Workshops were formatted as a combination of party, experimentation, and celebration. Atelier Dreiseitl asked a series of questions to initiate community visioning, such as: *What is*

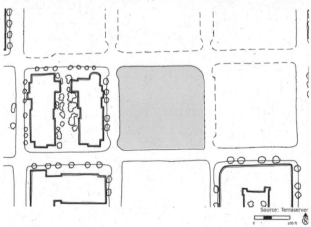

Figure 7.24 Pre-existing Site. The site, just prior to development as a park, was a construction staging area for new high-rise apartment buildings.
(Credit: Greenworks PC)

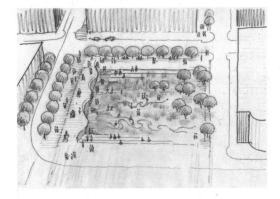

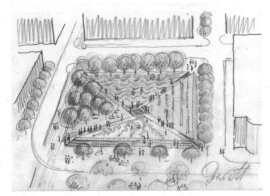

Figure 7.26 Community Workshops. Atelier Dreiseitl's community workshops go beyond charrette-type brainstorming to include engaging coffee and donut hours, interactive performances, and water play. (Credit: Atelier Dreiseitl)

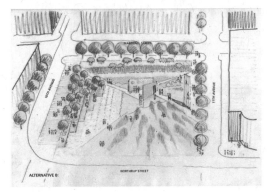

Figure 7.25 Three Schematic Site Plan Alternatives. (Credit: Atelier Dreiseitl)

good/bad/missing?, while impromptu stage performances responded to questions such as: *What would a little spider do in the park?* Kids-only meetings included experiments with water absorption and focused on having fun with engaging stormwater. These workshops included musicians, food, art making, and water games, as can be seen

in the images of Figure 7.26. As Dreiseitl puts it, the community gatherings are not a contest of wills but to gather and define a feeling or mood for the project.

While the district master plan introduced the concept of a wetland park, later programming evolved this idea into much more than just a stormwater pond. Through the site planning, site design, and detail design process, the designers envisioned the park to represent the "peeling back" of the urban fabric to reveal the site's history as part of the historic Couch Lake. While the site's contaminated soils made it necessary to create a closed, circulating stormwater system (rather than allowing stormwater to infiltrate), this lack of ecological function was made up by the scale of the pond gesture that fills up nearly the entire site. The wetland system was designed as a narrative to be followed as water moves and recirculates through the site starting at a spring source, filtered through levels of vegetation, and flowing into the pond. The system provides ecological function through stormwater cleansing, and a biodiverse meadow that provides habitat for birds and insects. Programmatically, the park is unique within Portland as it is for most other cities—a naturalized city block in the midst of an otherwise impervious hardscape urban setting.

	REGIONAL PLANNING	DISTRICT PLANNING	SITE PLANNING	SITE DESIGN	DETAIL DESIGN
TANNER SPRINGS PARK SCALES OF PROGRAM FOCUS					

Again, the mandate of contemplation was dictated by the district master plan and the landscape architect expanded opportunities for contemplation to embrace ecology, site history, and materials. The rich ecological and cultural history of the neighborhood folded into the approach toward vegetation as well as the Art Wall feature, where pieces of stained glass capture light and reflect the ideas of histories past. Also the use of traditional urban materials such as cobble and old railroad rails reference past site uses. These program features bring the essence of the site to the user experience.

A Conventional Urban Park Design

Jamison Square, Portland, Oregon, USA

Jamison Square, located two blocks south of Tanner Springs Park, is named after William Jamison, a prominent river district developer. Designed by Peter Walker and Partners Landscape Architecture (PWP), the park was the first of four built as laid out in the *River District Park System Urban Design Framework, also laid out by PWP.* The focal point of the park is a nearly block-long stone wall that cascades water into a subtly sloped pavement area, shown in Figure 7.27. This intermittent fountain recirculates water as the timed system flows, fills, and stops then drains the basin. This park, popular with families, holds several sculptural pieces including three 30-foot totems. Trees and lawn provide areas for picnicking and shade. The water feature forms a division between a crushed gravel area set aside as gallery and community event space. While the park is animated, well-designed, and a comfortable place to enjoy the water sequence, Jamison Park characterizes one type of park important for outdoor life in the city, yet it has no ecological component. Tanner Springs Park, shown in Figure 7.28, on the other hand, signifies a park designed for people but

Figure 7.27 Jamison Square. Located two blocks from Tanner Springs Park, Jamison Square was the first in the series of parks outlined by Peter Walker Partners in the River District Master Plan called River District Park System Urban Design Framework. Peter Walker Partners designed this park. This park is largely hardscaped and formal. (Credit: Greenworks PC)

where human interactions are in balance with nature's provisions that benefit birds, fish, and plant life and where water's purpose is not only recreational but a resource with multiple meanings.

Figure 7.28 Tanner Springs Park. Tanner Springs Park is the second to be built in the series. In contrast to Jamison Square, this park is largely vegetated and informal.
(Credit: Greenworks PC)

The Tanner Springs Park design outcome is illustrated in the site plan, sections, and detail views shown in Figures 7.29 through 7.32. The project is analyzed with respect to two central dimensions of sustainable site design process and outcomes: landscape form and landscape function.

Site Design Form

Patterns

The site's layout and organization is best understood looking down from the height of the surrounding buildings. Framed by conventionally broad tree-lined sidewalks complete with pedestrian lighting, trash receptacles, and hanging flower baskets, the pattern of the park interior lies in stark contrast to its surroundings. As the patterns shown in Figure 7.33 suggest, pathways, swales, planting, and seating areas meander through the interior of the park and convey a sense of flow, regeneration, and organic form antithetical to the urban grid. Stone dust paths are not smoothly curved but seem to wander, while the deck layout is not linear but syncopated. Despite the irregular grid created by the site pathway layout, as materials change and paths curve, navigating the site is a journey. The primary vertical element is the 7-foot-high Art Wall along the sidewalk. On the park side of the wall, it allows a 6-foot grade drop to the pond, cutting off views across the site. This element is a backdrop for a performance space.

In contrast to the verticality of multistoried structures that restrict distant views, the sight lines of the site are open, as can be seen in Figure 7.34. While visually open because of the relatively few vertical elements, physical access is dictated by narrow pathways through meadow, and makes for a complex site experience. Swaled waterways flow across major access lines while knee-high meadow vegetation sweeps across the site and becomes more naturalized as it nears the pond. At the detail level, the contrast between hard-edged linear walls and soft-edged vegetation occur in many combinations and dominate the ground plane. While the sidewalks are at grade with the street, the park interior is retained 18 inches on the west side and drops 6 feet below the sidewalk, retained by the Art Wall on the east side. This elevation is shown in Figure 7.35. As the grade changes from higher and more manicured to lower and more natural, the transitions in height, material, and formality represent a "peeling back of the city layer" to reveal the historic hydrologic landscape (Dreiseitl 2007).

Materials

The materials employed in the park design are new, salvaged, and repurposed and are utilized in uncommon combinations, as can be seen in Figure 7.36. A variety of materials and techniques, from poured-in-place concrete to hand-laid cobbles to stone dust, create a site that conveys both expert artistry and unplanned informality. Largely minimal and organic, the pathway layout seems incidental with rough-edged transitions.

Portland's commitment to public art was carried through in this design. The Art Wall, which represents the former rail yard, is made of discarded rails set on-end in an undulating pattern that frames park views on one side and retains the sidewalk from the detention basin below on the other. As Figure 7.37 shows, stained glass, inlaid with drawings of dragonflies and extinct insect species taken from period graphics, were reproduced by Herbert Dreiseitl and inserted between the steel rails. Their presence references lost ecologies (Dreiseitl 2007).

A wooden boardwalk, an uncommon choice of sidewalk material, runs along the eastern edge of all parks in the master plan. This element will eventually complete the link from Jamison Square to the Willamette River.

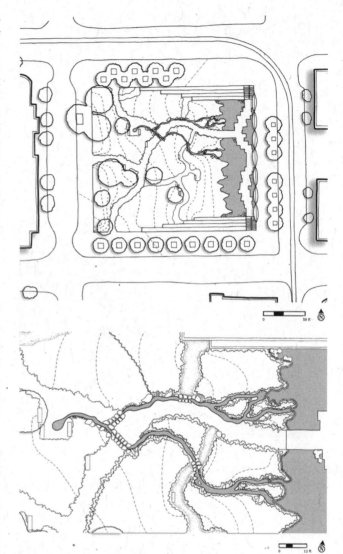

Figure 7.29 The Site Plan.

Site Design Function

Natural Systems

The park manages its stormwater, which means stormwater is not piped off-site into the municipal sewer system. It functions as a large, aesthetic, accessible stormwater detention basin. A shallow, open water pond (12 to 18 inches in depth) at the east end of the park holds and recirculates the rainwater captured from sidewalks and the site. The

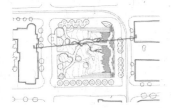

Figure 7.30 Site Section. East/West.

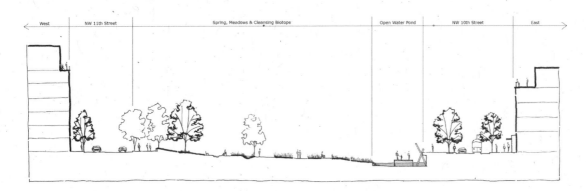

West | NW 11th Street | Spring, Meadows & Cleansing Biotope | Open Water Pond | NW 10th Street | East

Figure 7.31 Site Section. North/South.

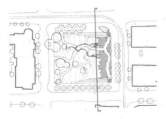

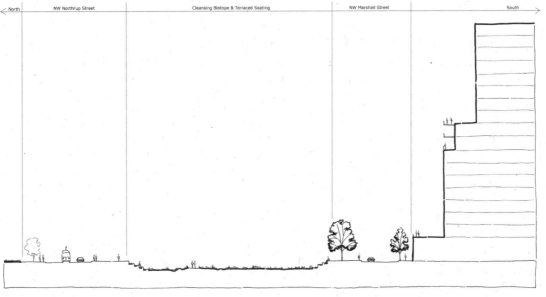

North | NW Northrup Street | Cleansing Biotope & Terraced Seating | NW Marshall Street | South

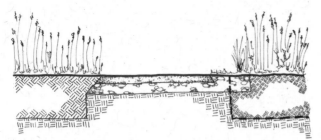

Figure 7.32 Construction Detail. Gravel pavement adjacent to constructed soil of the biotope and meadow.

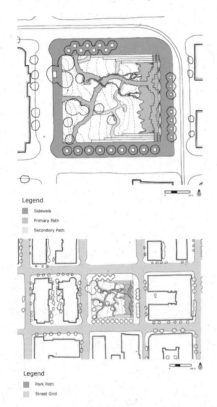

Legend
- Sidewalk
- Primary Path
- Secondary Path

Legend
- Park Path
- Street Grid

Figure 7.33 Patterns of Infrastructure & Path Hierarchy. Pathways, swales, planting, and seating areas meander and convey a sense of flow, regeneration, and organic form in contrast to the urban grid of the park's surroundings. Paths meander through the site with curves that feel organic rather than engineered.

stormwater system functions differently during different seasons. Ninety percent of the rainfall in Portland occurs during the winter months, thus, during the summer, potable water, if needed, augments the stored rainwater for maintaining the pond level.

Figure 7.34 Open Sight Lines.

Figure 7.35 Site Grade Changes. Although the site is open horizontally, the grade changes offer considerable spatial variety. The change of grade is 7.5 feet across the site.

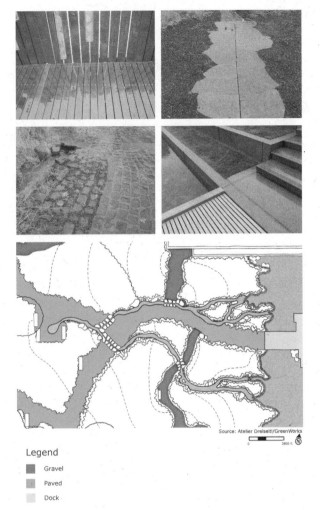

Legend

- ■ Gravel
- ■ Paved
- □ Dock

Source: Atelier Dreiseitl/GreenWorks

Figure 7.36 Materials. A variety of materials from polished to organic transition between paved surfaces and vegetation.

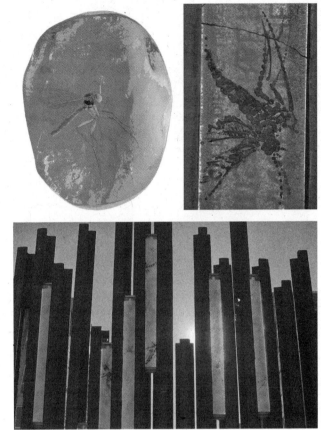

Figure 7.37 Art glass. The undulating Art Wall is made of steel train rail on end imbedded with blue stained glass etched with insects that reference extinct species that once may have existed on site. (Credit: Greenworks PC)

Designed to provide stormwater filtration much like a natural wetland, the designers refer to this system as a "cleansing **biotope**." Because this site is a **brownfield** with contaminated underlying soils, the site is capped with 8 feet of clean fill and the pond is lined. Therefore, the stormwater does not infiltrate the soil and connect to subsurface groundwater (Waterscapes, Inc & Green Works, PC 2003). However, through biofiltration, the system cleanses the recirculated water through a planted, sand-based filtration medium. Biological and physio-chemical processes break down and remove unwanted substances from the water. This water flow pattern is shown in Figure 7.38. By avoiding chemical additives, the cleansing biotope functions as a living water body with its own ecological equilibrium. The recirculated water begins at a bubbling spring source in the center of the park and then flows through paved, and successively more vegetated swales into the pond. This recirculating flow through the vegetation and soil matrixes aids water cleansing. The system manages the rain of a two-year storm event with a 16-inch fluctuating water level in the pond.

The natural versus cultural aspect of the vegetation is shown in Figure 7.39. Vegetation covers more than 80 percent of the park's ground plane. The vegetation transitions between several plant types from multi-use lawn to structurally reinforced grass-gravel paving, to a cleansing wetland meadow (Dreiseitl 2007).

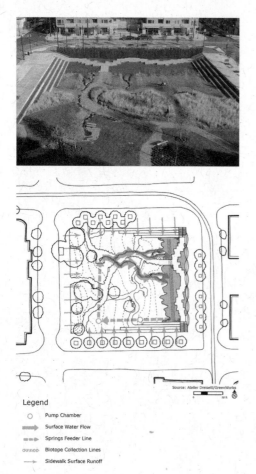

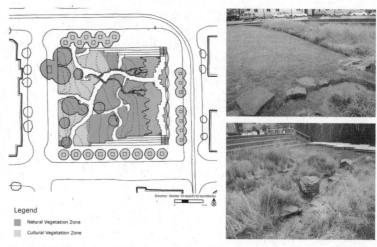

Figure 7.39 Natural vs. Cultural Vegetation. Eighty percent of the site is vegetated. The site transitions from areas of cultural vegetation, such as lawn and ornamental shrubs, to area of natural vegetation of upland and wet meadow.

Legend

○ Pump Chamber

⇒ Surface Water Flow

⇨ Springs Feeder Line

⇨ Biotope Collection Lines

→ Sidewalk Surface Runoff

Figure 7.38 Cleansing Biotope. Stormwater diagram shows the edge of the biotope soil (this is also the extent of the plastic liner), the water collection lines, the pump that brings water to the spring, and the area where ultraviolet light treatment removes bacteria. (Modeled after a diagram provided by Greenworks PC)

Three large, 8-inch caliper Oregon white oak trees (*Quercus garryana*) are planted to represent the native Oregon oak savannahs, which were discussed in the project's regional context section and of which only one percent of the region's original stands remain. The oaks, included in Figure 7.40, are concentrated in a small grove; one is a sidewalk tree. The landscape architect selected trees not for their perfect stature but for their variety and organic form. Trees shade sidewalks and lawn areas; however, the meadow and the cleansing biotope require full sun, and just a few trees used as accents are planted in this area.

Plant selection was of critical importance to the success of the project. Finding wetland plants to grow in the coarse, sandy soil mix was a challenge. The city retained a wetland plant specialist to consult on species selection and techniques to establish the plants in the first two or three years. The meadow has two zones: (1) upland meadow plants such as bent grass and barley, and (2) mesic/wetland meadow plants such as rushes and sedges. The plan for these plantings is shown in Figure 7.41.

Human Systems

In terms of human uses, the park was purposely kept programmatically open-ended. Since the concept promoted the idea of contemplation, much of the site was dedicated to the establishment of a meaningful fragment of nature. While a majority of the site is taken up by the open water feature and vegetative ground plane, multiple opportunities for seating and gathering are built into the grade changes to observe these features. The grassy amphitheater seating at both ends of the pond serves as event seating when the deck is used for performances. Other parts of the site offer seating opportunities within mown portions of meadow, at the spring, and along the sidewalk retaining wall. Lawn areas provide opportunity for passive recre-

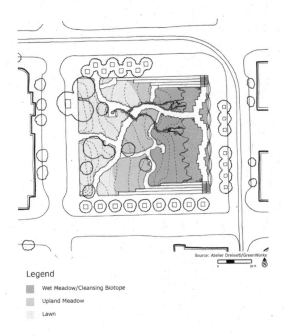

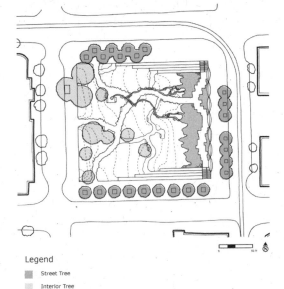

Source: Atelier Dreiseitl/GreenWorks

Legend

- ▪ Wet Meadow/Cleansing Biotope
- ▪ Upland Meadow
- ▪ Lawn

Figure 7.41 Seeding Plan. The grade change demands two types of meadow conditions, upland and wetland.

Legend

- ▪ Street Tree
- ▪ Interior Tree

Figure 7.40 Site Tree Plantings. Relatively few trees are planted·on site in order to make the cleansing biotope habitat, which requires full sun, feasible. Three Oregon white oaks were planted to represent the native oak savannahs that used to cover much of the Willamette Valley.

The latent meanings within site materials, site function, art pieces, craftsmanship, and layout were carefully considered in the Tanner Springs Park design, which is a highly detailed site. The site's hydrological history is readable in the stormwater narrative and its regional connection made with native plantings that attract bird nesting, feeding, and bathing. Symbolism is included in both form and materials. At once functional and provocative, the swales, shown in Figure 7.43, have meaning beyond conveying water that expresses a symbolic connection to the site's historic function.

Unlike many conventional park designs, this park has natural function, is multidimensional, and is alive. The areas created for interaction at Tanner Springs Park vary from active play in a bubbling spring to passive viewing of water in the catchment area where fish spawn and birds nest. This breadth of function and meaning does not occur at nearby Jamison Park where the choreographic sequence of the fountain is intriguing yet provides neither insight nor regional cues for interpretation. Jamison Park is a multi-use park but does not have a "life" of its own that inspires thought or awe for the natural. While the water sequence

ation such as picnicking and birdwatching. Quirky details such as the lawn access ladder, shown in Figure 7.42, were included to provide connectivity and arouse curiosity. The sidewalks, meanwhile, are broad, tree-lined, and are areas to view the site and contribute to the street life of the urban neighborhood where cafes and shops and residential uses rim the site.

Figure 7.42 Details. A small detail invites open-ended uses. This step ladder bridges the grade change between the sidewalk and lawn.

Figure 7.43 A Pathway "Erodes" to a Swale.

Figure 7.44 Multiple Water Interactions. The site offers many ways to access or view water from the bubbling spring to the passive pond.
(Credit: Greenworks PC)

at Tanner Springs Park is a closed system, not connected functionally to area hydrology, and has thus been criticized for its sustainable validity (Thompson 2006), it provides multiple functions, human awareness, and meaning—conditions that engage people with ecological processes, as shown in Figure 7.44. This is critical to comprehending natural landscapes.

Maintenance

As the neighborhood was developed and the open-space network conceived, volunteer groups took interest in park maintenance—and in this park in particular. Adopted by Friends of Tanner Springs, the site is monitored vigilantly in an effort to keep the biotope healthy and functioning. Signage, such as that seen in Figure 7.45, discourages dog walking to protect the water system from excess nutrients and bacteria. While there is no official mechanism for monitoring the vegetation establishment or stormwater quality of the park, a specifically trained landscape contracting company, with volunteers with the Friends of Tanner Springs, maintains the site through hand-weeding and no chemical inputs.

Site Design Integration

Engagements

Ecological engagement of the Tanner Springs Park landscape occurs primarily in the form of *creation* and *regeneration*. The former industrial fill site and its entire metropol-

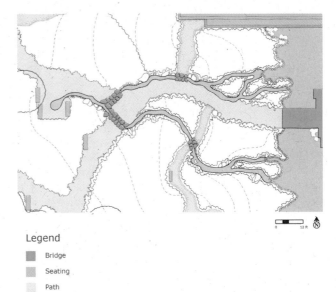

Legend

■ Bridge

▨ Seating

▥ Path

Figure 7.46 Points of Engagement Plan. Areas of specific site design elements that take advantage of natural phenomenon.

itan area had been largely devoid of any natural landscape for over 100 years and its urban nature dictated not a true restoration of the original native landscape, but a created patch of naturalized landscape including wetland and savannah plant zones. Regeneration occurs through the cycling and cleansing of stormwater through site biotopes in a deliberately controlled system of runnels, swales, and open water.

Following are specific site design elements of the Tanner Springs Park design that take advantage of natural phenomenon, site activities, and amenities that engage the user with site and regional environmental and cultural systems. These *cultural engagements* are categorized into elements (objects), views, and nodes (intersection of objects). The engagement plan for the site is shown in Figure 7.46.

Element: Performance and Seating. A variety of seating opportunities, shown in Figure 7.47, are open-ended and integrated within other structures such as walls and grade changes. Backless benches, steps, and retaining walls allow versatile uses. The deck overtop the stormwater pond doubles as a stage and tiered seating, for viewing performances or the ecology at work, and creates an amphitheater setting.

Figure 7.45 Site User Guidelines. Usage guidelines insure that habitats are not disturbed. Management of the cleansing biotope is aided by the city as well as the neighborhood group, Friends of Tanner Springs.

Figure 7.48 Engagement: Art Wall.

Figure 7.47 Engagement: Seating and performance spaces vary considerably: the performance space deck allows interaction with the water, bench seating near swales, seating walls with stepladder access from sidewalk to lawn area, tiered seating adjacent to the deck, and two-sided seating for viewing the meadows or the pond. (Credit: Greenworks PC)

Element: Art Wall. Shown in Figure 7.48, this feature, constructed with vertical rails, divides the sidewalk from the stormwater pond. The wall undulates to suggest the flow of water while drawings of extinct insect species etched into the glass embedded into the wall reference past site ecology. The Art Wall is an element of engagement because it functions on many levels; allowing grade change to accommodate the stormwater pond, referencing the historic rail yard through the use of repurposed rails and incorporating stained glass fragments that capture light.

Element: Water Narrative. The spring, runnel, swale, and pool sequence are engaged separately in unique ways on the site. The spring provides an area of shallow water safe for kids' play and is surrounded by pavement and benches. Meanwhile, the narrow water runnels are designed to be visually and physically accessible as they cross pathways then disappear into meadow. The deck, which spans the pond, allows complete access to the major draw of the park. These small, multiple, and varied areas put the user in con-

Figure 7.49 Engagement: Stone Bridge Across Swale.

Figure 7.50 Engagement: Wood Deck Spanning Open Pond.

Figure 7.51 Engagement: Stairway with Exposed Drain to Pond. (Credit:Greenworks PC)

tact with a variety of qualities of water from bubbling, running water to passive water. This water narrative can be seen in Figures 7.49 through 7.52.

View: Regional River Connection: From the eastern edge of the park, the wooden gallery sidewalk is centered on the bridge over the Willamette River. Although the river itself is not visible, the bridge is a prominent view from the site along this axis and connects the site with the greater regional hydrologic theme outlined in the master plan. The view of the water connection is shown in Figure 7.53.

Figure 7.52 Engagement: Water Combined with Stonework. Used sparingly but effectively maximizes its accessibility and effect. A bubbling spring 'source' expressed in pavement with running water passing through paved runnels. A flagstone 'bridge' transitions between primary cobble and secondary gravel pathways.

Figure 7.53 Engagement: View to Fremont Bridge. The bridge over the Willamette connects the site with the greater hydrologic theme outlined in the Master Plan.

Outcomes

The Program/Site/Context Comparison

Predesign Site/Context Conditions

The sustainable outcome of a project is largely determined by the design team's approach toward three tasks: (1) the development of program goals, (2) choices made in the assessment of the site, and (3) choices made in the assessment of the context. In the following chart, the key features of these three tasks for the Tanner Springs Park project are listed in relation to three important sustainability factors: (1) environmental, (2) economic, and (3) cultural factors.

The comparison shows that the initial program goals of the project focused on sustainability, and that the region's intact natural and cultural systems and regulatory policies supported this goal. It also shows that the program goals drafted by the client were primarily derived from *neighborhood* needs. The design team and client worked together in establishing further-reaching sustainable goals that would connect physically or symbolically to the larger intact regional landscape.

Program, Site, and Context Relationship

Postdesign Site/Context Impacts

While the region is known for its sustainable initiatives, the Tanner Springs Park design may well define a new visual paradigm within the city—one more natural and wild than even Portland has given rise to. The primary contextual impact of the design is its influence at the neighborhood scale. Without the rapid Pearl District redevelopment and the explicit sustainable focus of city government, a park like this would not have been built. The design outcome creates a vital piece of nature in an urban neighborhood in keeping with the sustainable goals of the larger region. View the predesign site in Figure 7.54 against the postdesign outcome in Figure 7.55 to see the impact of this project.

	INITIAL PROGRAM GOALS	SITE CHARACTERISTICS	CONTEXT CHARACTERISTICS
ENVIRONMENTAL FACTORS	Create a wetland	Abandoned industrial site Contaminated soils Former springs and lake	Proactive city policies limit urban growth and manage urban stormwater to reverse problems with the Willamette River
ECONOMIC FACTORS	Create open space for access and viewing from surrounding new high-rise construction Increase area property values and incentivize urban infill	1-acre fallow site	Highly desirable residential real estate in rapidly redeveloping infill area of Portland
CULTURAL FACTORS	Create a place for outdoor contemplation Connect the neighborhood to the Willamette River	Rich industrial history	Precedent of parks with prominent water features by Lawrence Halprin and others as well as art incorporated into daring designs in Portland's urban parks

	METROREGION	COMMUNITY	NEIGHBORHOOD	SITE
TANNER SPRINGS PARK SUSTAINABILITY IMPACTS				

Figure 7.54 Pre-Design Condition. This aerial depicts the relatively recent barren conditions of much of the Pearl District. The project site block is located in the center of the image.

Figure 7.55 Post Design Impact.

Improving Site Efficiency & Sustainability

The specific details and techniques of the Tanner Springs Park site design are critical to site function, spatial quality, and experience of the site user. The following design techniques were used to improve the site, mitigate the impact of development, and create a compelling, functional site design independent of the conditions of the context.

Plant community creation

Biodiverse meadows

Hardscape and vegetated swales

Bioretention pond

Reduced maintenance regime

Improving Regional Efficiency & Sustainability

This design did more than just improve the one-acre site. It resonates within the larger goals of the City of Portland, which include the creation of sustainable stormwater approaches to improve the quality of the Willamette River. Certain techniques used in sustainable site design result in connections with larger processes occurring outside the site. The following site design techniques helped support the Greater City of Portland's sustainability goals.

Community involvement with maintenance

Local material reuse

Public open space

Use of cultural and historic elements

Improvement of site water quality

Sustainability Criteria Met?

The sustainable landscape criteria presented in Chapter 1 are a means for evaluating landscape sustainability—*Connectivity, Meaning, Purpose, Efficiency,* and *Steward-ship*. The design outcome of Tanner Springs Park is evaluated in relation to these dimensions in the following discussion.

Connectivity

The Tanner Springs Park site design:

- establishes a significant area of native plantings that replicates a functioning biome and creates a diverse habitat in an urban site.
- incorporates art and water in keeping with Portland's park tradition.
- provides a community space for people to gather.
- continues the flow of movement outlined in the master plan toward a future park system along the Willamette River, which currently is not accessible.
- creates a micro-watershed that references former ecological features that occupied the site such as Couch Lake and Tanner Springs Creek.
- utilizes hardscape materials to reference former urban use of the site as a rail yard.

Meaning

The Tanner Springs Park site design:

- fosters curiosity about the hydrologic process with a circular narrative that begins at the spring, flows into runnels, enters the pond, and recirculates. The design stimulates questions of how the site works and what it represents.
- introduces natural functions and meaningful materials that initiate contemplation of ideas and places beyond the site boundary.
- perpetuates an ecological aesthetic.

Purpose

The Tanner Springs Park site design:

- provides a park that is "doing something" even when no one is there. The natural processes benefit the environment and create habitat in addition to providing a contemplative open space for people.
- creates a truly local, site-informed, and memorable experience in comparison to the valid yet ubiquitous mown lawn, benches, and rows of trees of most parks.

Efficiency

The Tanner Springs Park site design:

- uses self-perpetuating vegetation that requires monitoring and occasional maintenance but fewer inputs than conventional site designs such as mowing, mulching, irrigation, or annual replanting.
- balances overall inputs. The cultivated portion of the site is kept to a minimum while the natural self-perpetuating areas are maximized.
- uses repurposed local materials, such as cobbles that accent site entrances and are used sparingly elsewhere and rails to create the Art Wall. Other pavement materials are concrete sidewalk pavement, concrete amphitheater steps, stone dust paths, and narrow flagstone bridges over water runnels.
- recycles water within the site hydrological system, collecting rainwater when available.

Stewardship

The Tanner Springs Park site design:

- allows for and requires the stewardship of a community that understands what is required to oversee a naturalized site such as this.
- allows for changes and assumes the site is a "work in progress" as the landscape changes over time.

Parallel Projects

The Stata Center, Cambridge, Massachusetts, USA

The Stata Center, a research facility designed by Frank Gehry at the Massachusetts Institute of Technology in Cambridge, Massachusetts, is set within an urban plaza that captures stormwater in a bioretention system designed by Olin Partnership and Nitsch Engineering, as shown in Figure 7.56. While not a park, the focus of the plaza, like at Tanner Springs Parks, is the bioretention system, which is a constructed wetland that detains and cleanses runoff, maintains wetland plants, and is harvested for reuse in toilets. A solar-powered pump recycles water back into the wetland. Initially, the client on this project was not very interested in sustainability, but realized they could achieve other goals by implementing this idea (Baird 2007). The project was conceived by the landscape architects as a slice of a New England ecosystem. While a highly functional stormwater system that diverts uncleansed stormwater from the Charles River, the design also provides a compelling focal point and spatial and material qualities. Like Tanner Springs Park, it looks a bit out of place in the urban setting where the design compels questions about the systems in place and offers a palette of materials and vegetation that speaks to the greater region.

Figure 7.56 The Stata Center, Cambridge, Massachusetts, USA. (Credit: OLIN)

Living Water Park, Chengdu, China

The Living Water Park, located along the Fu-Nan River in southwestern China, was designed in collaboration with city experts, artist Betsy Damon, and landscape designer Margie Ruddick, among others. While the park may not significantly improve the health of the entire river, water diverted through the park is cleansed, creating a pocket of successively aerated and cleaner water as it passes through. More than just a cleansing system, the park is a place for environmental education, much needed open space, cultural gathering, and habitat creation. The park serves as public open space that communicates and creates experiences involving the qualities, importance, and uses of clean water (see Figure 7.57).

Figure 7.57 Living Water Park, Chengdu, China. (Credit: Betsy Damon)

Glossary

Adaptive reuse

The use of a previously developed area for a different type of use.

Architectonic

Pertaining to architecture or suggesting the qualities of architecture.

Arrested succession

When vegetation systems are held back from maturing due to environmental circumstances such as extreme microclimates, pollution, insect and disease infestations, or management regimes.

Arroyo

Meaning "river" in Spanish, this term refers to a natural dry gully with intermittent wet periods during times of monsoon. Similar to the term "swale" used in less arid areas or "wash" used interchangeably in desert areas.

Bedroom community

A community that originates from and is dominated by residential land use. Residents of a bedroom community commute to a larger city or suburban area for jobs and material needs.

Biomass

Living or recently dead biological material produced by plants.

Biotope

A habitat for a specific assemblage of plants and animals. This term has the same usage as the term "ecosystem."

Biotreatment

The treatment of stormwater by passing it through an open vegetated swale or low-lying area to encourage filtration and infiltration, reducing offsite runoff as well as providing habitat values.

Brownfield

A previously developed site.

Charrette

An intensive collaborative design session in which a group of designers and other interested individuals draft a solution to a design problem. It originates with the 19th century French *Ecole des Beaux-Arts* design training studios, where the *charrette,* or cart, would come down the aisles to collect the designs at the end of a project.

Census-designated place

A community that lacks a dedicated municipal government, but which otherwise physically resembles a legally incorporated city or town. These places are identified by the U.S. Census Bureau for statistical purposes in tracking socioeconomic and other demographic data.

Conservation easement

The purchase of development rights from private landowners not for land ownership, but rather for the protection of natural resources, wildlife corridors, scenic byways, etc.

Contemplative landscape

A landscape that provides opportunity or space for thoughtful observation.

Context

That which surrounds, and gives meaning to, something else.

Copse

A thicket of small trees and bushes.

Corporate campus

A property owned by a corporation designed to represent the company philosophy, meet the needs of the employee population, and often to accommodate growth.

Cultural landscapes

Landscapes in which materials, spaces, and their arrangement are based on human artistic expression and functional qualities. Such landscapes are generally intended to be controlled and molded through intensive maintenance and human care, aimed at an ultimate static mature state.

Ecology

The study of the relationship between organisms and their environment.

Ecotype

A distinct entity of an animal, plant, or other organism that is closely linked in its characteristics to the ecological surroundings it inhabits.

Edge city

A concentration of business, shopping, and entertainment outside a traditional urban area in what had been a residential suburb or semi-rural community. The term was first used in Tom Wolfe's 1968 novel *The Electric Kool-Aid Acid Test* and was popularized in the 1991 book *Edge City: Life on the New Frontier* by Joel Garreau. In the latter book, Tysons

Corner, Virginia, was used as an example of how edge cities are formed—as typically located near airports, having more office space than living space, experiencing rapid change over the last 30 years, being automobile-dominated areas, and so on.

Endemic species
Animal or plant species that are adapted to a particular isolated place and are not typically found elsewhere.

Engagement
A design element that brings the user into contact with an aspect of the site's cultural or ecological qualities.

Environmental remediation
Various methods used to fix the contamination in a brownfield. These generally revolve around two basic options: (1) isolating the contamination by putting an impermeable cap over the contaminated soils so that stormwater does not leach the contaminants into the ground water, or (2) removing the contaminated materials or compounds.

Estuary
A semi-enclosed coastal body of water with one or more rivers or streams flowing into it, and with a free connection to the open sea. Estuaries are often associated with high rates of biological productivity.

Extensive green roofs
Roofs designed for plants and water cleansing primarily for environmental benefits.

Forebay
Or *sediment forebays* help to postpone overall stormwater basin maintenance by trapping incoming sediments. Usually, it is placed at the outfall of the incoming storm drain pipes or channels. A sediment forebay enhances the pollutant removal efficiency of a basin by trapping the incoming sediment load in one area, where it can be easily monitored and removed. (Virginia Department of Conservation and Recreation)

Gentrification
The buying and renovation of houses and stores in deteriorated neighborhoods by upper- or middle-income families or individuals, thus improving property values but often displacing low-income families and small businesses. (American Heritage Dictionary)

Gestalt
The overall sense, or wholeness, of a landscape site.

Green infrastructure
The interconnected network of open spaces and natural areas, such as greenways, wetlands, parks, forest preserves, and native plant vegetation, that naturally manages stormwater, reduces flooding risk, and improves water quality. Green infrastructure usually costs less to install and maintain when compared to traditional forms of infrastructure. Green infrastructure projects often foster community cohesiveness by engaging users in the planning, planting, and maintenance of the sites. (Green Values Stormwater Toolbox)

Green roof
A roof system for a building that uses a continuous coverage of a thin soil profile and shallow rooting plants in place of inert materials to provide a range of environmental benefits including reduction of heat island effects, improved air quality, building insulation, and stormwater management.

Industrial ecology
An interdisciplinary field that focuses on the sustainable combination of environment, economy, and technology. The central idea is the analogy between natural and socio-technical systems. The word "industrial" does not refer only to industrial complexes but more generally to how humans use natural resources in the production of goods and services. "Ecology" refers to the concept that our industrial systems should incorporate principles exhibited within natural ecosystems.

Infrastructure
Systems of roads, schools, utilities, and other community amenities that provide functional networks for entire communities and regions.

Intensive green roofs
Conventional roof gardens with planters often designed as an outdoor room primarily for human benefits.

Landscape narrative
Environmental design that tells a story, explains a process, or defines a sequence.

Landscape matrix
The dominant landscape type (developed, natural woodland, etc.) of a landscape area.

Low maintenance
Little or no active inputs of water or chemicals, and minimized labor for mowing, trimming, leaf removal, and seasonal replanting.

Master plan
A plan where uses are prescribed for each area. (Steiner 2000)

Mesophytic
A moderately moist environment or a plant with moderate water requirements.

Microclimate
Any climatic condition in a relatively small area.

Native plant
Any plant that is indigenous to a specific area, is used within the appropriate climate zone, and has not been found to be invasive outside of its expected range.

National scenic byway

The National Scenic Byways Program is part of the U.S. Department of Transportation, Federal Highway Administration. The program was established to recognize, preserve, and enhance selected roads throughout the United States. (National Scenic Byways Program)

Natural attenuation

An approach toward groundwater improvement not by engineered solutions but by natural processes such as filtering through pools of vegetated bioretention basins.

Natural landscapes

Landscapes in which the design of materials, spaces, and their arrangement generally mimic or exist as natural landscape ecotypes such as meadow, woodland, wetland, etc. They use plants as they relate ecologically to each other and to their environment (soil type and microclimate), in plant communities. Such areas contain primarily native plant materials but do not necessarily replicate the landscape that would be indigenous to the site. These landscapes generally receive little conventional maintenance (regular mowing, pruning, mulching, and watering) after establishment, other than periodic interventions such as the yearly mowing of meadows to prevent succession to forested landscape.

New town

A community that is carefully planned from its inception and is typically constructed in a previously undeveloped area. This contrasts with settlements that evolve in a more ad hoc fashion over time. New towns were especially prominent in the early 20th century, as rapid industrialization and innovation began to transform urban environments, increase mobility, and reduce rural populations.

New urbanism

A land use planning and design philosophy in which traditional town patterns of mixed land uses, pedestrian-focused environments, dense and compact development, a prominent civic outdoor realm, and hierarchical districts are applied to create cohesive, livable communities.

Open space

A relatively undeveloped green or wooded area provided often (but not necessarily) within an urban or suburban area designated as such to connect areas for recreation, commuting, or habitat and to minimize the congested feeling of the built environment. (Adapted from Steiner 2000)

Physiography

The study of the natural features of the earth's surface, especially in its current aspects, including land formation, climate, currents, and distribution of flora and fauna.

Phytoremediation

The treatment of environmental problems using plants. Consists of depolluting contaminated soils, water, or air with plants able to contain, degrade, or eliminate metals, pesticides, solvents, and various other contaminants from the mediums that contain them. Acts in one of three ways: extracting, stabilizing, or transforming the pollutants. It is clean, efficient, inexpensive, and nonenvironmentally disruptive, as opposed to processes that require excavation of soil.

Program

The development of the *functions* of a landscape design including what uses will occur, what features are incorporated, and so on.

Rainwater harvesting

The collection and conveyance of rainwater from roofs and storage in rain barrels or cisterns for another later use. (Connecticut Stormwater Quality Manual 2004)

Regenerative landscape

Integrated design of human landscape systems that results in net production and multiple benefits, as opposed to segregated system design that results in consumption and one-dimensional benefits. For instance, site water systems that utilize stormwater runoff for irrigating plant materials or vegetative systems that are self-sustaining and provide habitat. As opposed to traditional human landscape systems that are consumptive in their use of water, imported soils, and plant material; where stormwater is treated as a separate system from water supply; where management regimes of mowing and intensive pruning waste the very biomass that is created through these inputs.

Regional planning

The layout of regional land uses, infrastructure, and settlement patterns.

Regional vernacular

The built and natural form language that has evolved to characterize a particular geographic region and its cultural development in response to climatic and resource opportunities and constraints, and political and social history.

Riparian

Relating to, living or located on the bank of a natural watercourse (as a river) or sometimes of a lake or a tidewater.

Site design

Specific determination of patterns and form to accommodate site uses that include layout, grading, planting, and detailing.

Site memory

Valued former ecological and/or cultural identity of a site that is integrated into the form and/or function of the new site identity.

Site planning

Overall determination of uses and spatial organization of an entire site, considering structures, circulation, and what areas will be developed or protected.

Smart growth

An urban density and transportation approach that concentrates new development in urban areas rather than unbuilt areas.

Stormwater detention basin

Vegetated ponds that retain a permanent pool of water and are constructed to provide both treatment and attenuation of stormwater flows. (Connecticut Stormwater Quality Manual 2004)

Stormwater retention basin

A permanent pool that collects rainwater, that is normally wet, even during nonrainfall periods. (Virginia Department of Conservation and Recreation)

Stormwater treatment train

A series of stormwater basins that provide sequential treatment and flow of stormwater for a range of small to large storm events. (Menomonee Valley Industrial Center)

Suburb

A developed area lying just outside a core urban area, originating from earlier residential land use but now associated with a mix of uses focused on private commercial, industrial, business, and residential, which are typically segregated from one other.

Suburban infill

Describes the development of land in existing suburban areas that was left vacant or that was developed but then abandoned during the development of the suburb.

Succession

The progressive replacement over time of one plant community by another until a climax (or stable) plant community is established with relatively little change within it.

Successional landscape change

Structural and compositional changes that happen in a landscape over the course of multiple years or decades when the natural growth, maturation, and shifting of plant material is allowed to occur.

Sustainable

Capable of being continued with minimal negative and maximum positive long-term effects on the environment, community, and economy.

Transit-oriented development

Planned new mixed-use development, which is located adjacent to existing or simultaneously planned public transportation hubs and corridors. This is a land use planning strategy to maximize use of public transportation and displace other, more automobile-dependent forms of land use.

Urban growth boundary

A designated boundary line that forms an enclosed area around an existing urban area, within which development is encouraged and outside of which development is discouraged or prohibited.

Urban renewal

The revitalization of often postindustrial areas to provide for a range of housing, employment, and social activities.

Visioning

Employing creative programming approaches with the design team or stakeholders to reach common goals that give direction to a project.

Watershed

The entire physical area drained by a distinct stream or riverine system, physically separated from other watersheds by ridge-top boundaries. (www.basineducation.uwex.edu)

Xeriscape

A planned or designed landscape in which low-water-requiring or drought-tolerant plantings are used; "xeric" environments are those that receive little rainfall, such as deserts. Coined by a group in Colorado, the term embodies seven principles: (1) planning and design, (2) soil improvements, (3) efficient irrigation, (4) zoning of plants, (5) mulching, (6) turf alternatives, and (7) an appropriate maintenance plan. (Colorado Water Wise Council)

References

Preface

Dramstad, Wenche; James D. Olson; Richard T.T. Forman. *Landscape Ecology Principles in Landscape Architecture and Land-Use Planning.* Washington, DC: Island Press, 1996.

Franklin, Carol. "Fostering Living Landscapes." In *Ecological Design and Planning,* ed. George Thompson. Hoboken, NJ: John Wiley & Sons, 1997.

LaGro, James, Jr. *Site Analysis: Linking Program and Concept in Land Planning and Design.* Hoboken, NJ: John Wiley & Sons, 2001.

Lynch, Kevin and Gary Hack. *Site Planning.* Cambridge, MA: The MIT Press, 1998.

Lynch, Kevin. *The Image of the City.* Cambridge, MA: The MIT Press, 1960.

Marsh, William M. *Landscape Planning: Environmental Applications.* Redwood City, CA: Addison Wesley, 1983.

McHarg, Ian. *Design with Nature,* new ed. Hoboken, NJ: John Wiley & Sons, 1995.

Steiner, Frederick. *The Living Landscape, An Ecological Approach to Landscape Planning.* New York, NY: McGraw-Hill, 2000.

Chapter 1

Abrams, M. H. *A Glossary of Literary Terms,* 8th ed. Belmont, CA: Thomson Wadsworth, 2005.

Alexander, Christopher. *A Pattern Language.* Oxford: Oxford University Press, 1977.

Brown; Harkness; Johnston. *Landscape Journal: Eco-Revelatory Design, Special Issue.* Madison, WI: University of Wisconsin Press, 1998.

Carson, Rachel. *Silent Spring.* New York, NY: Fawcett Crest Books, 1964.

Cronon, William. *Changes in the Land: Indians, Colonists and the Ecology of New England.* New York, NY: Hill and Wang, 1983.

Dramstad, Wenche; James D. Olson; Richard T.T. Forman. *Landscape Ecology Principles in Landscape Architecture and Land-Use Planning.* Washington, DC: Island Press, 1996.

Edwards, Andres R. *The Sustainability Revolution. Portrait of a Paradigm Shift.* Philadelphia, PA: New Society Publishers, 2005.

Gore, Al. *Earth in the Balance.* New York, NY: Plume, 1993.

Hawken, Paul. *The Ecology of Commerce.* London: Collins Business, 1994.

Hester, Randolph. *Community Design Primer.* Mendocino, CA: Ridge Times Press, 1990.

Hough, Michael. *Out of Place.* New Haven, CT: Yale University Press, 1992.

Jackson, John Brinkerhoff. *Discovering the Vernacular Landscape.* New Haven, CT: Yale University Press, 1986.

Kaplan, S.; R. Kaplan; and R. Ryan. *With People in Mind. Design and Management of Everyday Nature.* Washington, DC: Island Press, 1998.

Kaye, Jane Holtz. "Little Green Islands." *Urban Land,* 2002, Vol. 61, Issue 2, p. 128.

Kunstler, James. *The Geography of Nowhere.* New York, NY: Free Press, 1994.

LaGro, James, Jr. *Site Analysis: Linking Program and Concept in Land Planning and Design.* Hoboken, NJ: John Wiley & Sons, 2001.

Leopold, Aldo. *A Sand County Almanac.* Oxford: Oxford University Press, 1966.

Lyle, John Tillman. *Regenerative Design for Sustainable Development.* Hoboken, NJ: John Wiley & Sons, 1992.

Lynch, Kevin and Gary Hack. *Site Planning.* Cambridge, MA: The MIT Press, 1998.

Macy, Christine. 2008. "Three Recent University Buildings Led by Mackay-Lyons Sweetapple Architects Illustrate the Participatory Design Process on University Campuses in Canada." *Canadian Architect.* www.cdnarchitect.com.

Mandelbrot, B.B. *The Fractal Geometry of Nature.* New York, NY: W. H. Freeman and Company, 1982.

Marsh, William M. *Landscape Planning: Environmental Applications.* Redwood City, CA: Addison Wesley, 1983.

McHarg, Ian. *Design with Nature,* new ed. Hoboken, NJ: John Wiley & Sons, 1995.

Nash, Roderick Frazier. *American Environmentalism,* 3rd ed. New York, NY: McGraw-Hill, 1990.

Ndubisi, Forster. "Landscape Ecological Planning." *Ecological Design and Planning.* Hoboken, NJ: John Wiley & Sons, 1997.

Rybczynski, Witold. *A Clearing in the Distance.* New York, NY: Simon and Schuster, 1995.

Scarfo, Robert. 1987. "Stewardship: The Profession's Grand Illusion." *Landscape Architecture,* 77:3, pp. 46–51.

Spirn, Anne Whiston. *The Granite Garden.* New York, NY: Basic Books, 1985.

Steiner, Frederick. *Human Ecology. Following Nature's Lead.* Washington, DC: Island Press, 2002.

Swaffield, Simon, ed. *Theory in Landscape Architecture.* Philadelphia, PA: University of Pennsylvania Press, 2002.

Thayer, Robert. .*Gray World, Green Heart.* Hoboken, NJ: John Wiley & Sons, 1994.

The Sustainable Sites Initiative. www.sustainablesites.org.

Thompson, J. William; and Kim Sorvig. *Sustainable Landscape Construction.* Washington, DC: Island Press, 2000.

U.S. Green Building Council. Leadership in Energy & Environmental Design Rating Systems. www.usgbc.org.

Watts, May Theilgaard. *Reading the Landscape of America: An Adventure in Ecology.* New York, NY: The MacMillan Company, 1957.

Woodward, Joan. *Waterstained Landscapes.* Baltimore, MD: The Johns Hopkins University Press, 2000.

World Commission on Environment and Development. 1983. *The Brundtland Commission Report.*

Chapter 2

Aldo Leopold Nature Center. www.naturenet.com.

Aten, Nancy. 2008. Email Correspondence. Menomonee Valley Partners Inc., Milwaukee WI. July 1.

Barnhill, David. *The Six Bioregions of Wisconsin.* Madison, WI: University of Wisconsin, 2005.

City of Milwaukee, Department of City Development. 2004. Press Release: City completes largest environmental clean-up in history, November. www.mkedcd.org/planning/plans/valley.

Communities and Local Government. 2000. *Urban White Paper,* November. www.communities.gov.uk.

Council of Great Lakes Governors. www.cglg.org.

Dorolek, Greg. 2007. Power point presentation: *The Menomonee Valley Park and Shops Redevelopment. From concept to detail: stormwater management as catalyst for economic, social, and recreational growth.*

Dorolek, Greg. 2008. Interview. Wenk Associates, Inc., July 3.

Educational Communications Board of Wisconsin. www.ecb.org.

Franklin, Carol. "Fostering Living Landscapes." In *Ecological Design and Planning,* ed. George Thompson. Hoboken, NJ: John Wiley & Sons, 1997.

Gregory, Michael M. 2004. *A Cultural Resources Management Plan Specific to Menomonee River Valley Redevelopment Project Lands in the City of Milwaukee, Milwaukee County, Wisconsin.* Great Lakes Archeological Research Center. www.renewthevalley.org.

Harker, D. *Landscape Restoration Handbook,* 2nd ed. Henderson, KY: Audubon International, 1999.

Kalundborg Center for Industrial Symbiosis. *Industrial Symbiosis: Exchange of Resources.* www.symbiosis.dk.

Kirkwood, Niall, (Ed.) *Manufactured Sites, Rethinking the Post-Industrial Landscape;* London: Spon Press, 2001.

Leopold, Aldo. *A Sand County Almanac.* Oxford: Oxford University Press, 1949.

Levine, Marc V. 2007. Working Paper: The Crisis of Black Male Joblessness in Milwaukee. University of Wisconsin-Milwaukee Center for Economic Development, March. www.uwm.edu.

Menomonee Valley Partners, Inc. www.renewthevalley.org.

Michael Van Valkenburgh Associates. mvvainc.com.

Milwaukee Journal Sentinel. www.jsonline.com.

Milwaukee River Basin Partnership. www.basineducation.uwex.edu.

Milwaukee Road Historical Association. www.mrha.com.

National Park Service. www.nature.nps.gov/geology.

Paulsen, Eric. June 2003. Piggsville still a secluded community in the Valley. www.onmilwaukee.com.

Sixteenth Street Community Health Center. 2004. Report: *Menomonee River Valley National Design Competition.* www.renewthevalley.org.

Travel Wisconsin. www.travelwisconsin.com.

U.S. Environmental Protection Agency. www.epa.gov.

Webber, David J. January 1996. "Senator Nelson Gaylord, Founder of Earth Day." MU Political Science. www.web.missouri.edu.

Wenk Associates, Inc. www.wenkla.com.

Wenk Associates, HTNB, Applied Ecological Services. March 2006. Report: *The Menomonee Valley Community Park: Transforming the Menomonee River Valley.*

William McDonough + Partners. Port of Cape Charles Sustainable Technologies Industrial Park. www.mcdonoughpartners.com.

Wisconsin Department of Natural Resources. www.dnr.wi.gov.

Wisconsin Historical Society. www.wisconsinhistory.org.

Chapter 3

Bailey's Eco-Regions. www.fs.fed.us.

Bioengineering Group. 2005. Whitney Water Purification Facility and Park: Educational Facility and Park Feature Watershed Best Practices, September 19.

Center for Coastal and Watershed Systems, Yale School of Forestry and Environmental Studies. www.yale.edu.

Connecticut Department of Environmental Protection (CDEP). 2001. Quinnipiac River Watershed Integrated Pest Crop Management Project, January.

Connecticut Department of Environmental Protection (CDEP). 1990. Bedrock Geological Map of Connecticut. www.tmsc.org/geology/bedrock.

Cote, Mel. Lake Whitney Artificial Marsh Treats Urban Runoff. Section 319 Success Stories, Vol. II, Connecticut. U.S. Environmental Protection Agency. www.epa.gov.

Cranz, Galen; and Michael Boland. 2004. "Defining the Sustainable Park: A Fifth Model for Urban Parks." *Landscape Journal.* 23(2):102–120.

Department of Environmental Protection Natural Resources Center: Traprock Ridges. www.wesleyan.edu.

Edgerton Park. www.edgertonpark.org.

Favretti, Rudy. *Highlights of Connecticut Agriculture.* The College of Agriculture and Natural Resources of the University of Connecticut, Storrs, CT, 1976.

Grabowski, Peter J., David E. Pinsky, Edward O. Norris, Peter E. Gaewski, Brian P. Robillard. 2003. Demolition of Regional Water Authority's 100-Year-Old Lake Whitney Slow Sand Filtration Plant. Presented at Joint Regional Conference and Exhibition, Worcester, Massachusetts, April 2; published in New England Water Works Association Journal, March 2004. www.tighebond.com.

Harker, D. *Landscape Restoration Handbook,* 2nd ed. Henderson, KY: Audubon International, 1999.

Holl, Steven. *Steven Holl: Architecture Spoken*. New York, NY: Rizzoli, 2007.

Hudak, John P.; and Mona E. Ellum. Effectiveness of Stormwater Treatment Systems Within A Highly Urbanized Watershed. www.whitneydigs.com.

Jorgensen, Neil. *A Guide to New England's Landscape*. Barre, MA: Barre Publishers, 1981.

Lichtenfeld, L. 1999. A Natural History Study of River Otters, *Lutra Canadensis*, in the Mill River. Yale School of Forestry and Environmental Studies. www.yale.edu.

Michael Van Valkenburgh Associates. www.mvvainc.com.

Smith, Anna. 2006. Park In Edgehill Thrives, September 29. www.yaledailynews.com.

Smithsonian Institute. Marcel Breuer: A Centennial Celebration. www.aaa.si.edu.

Strang, Gary. 1996. Infrastructure as Landscape. *Theory in Landscape Architecture,* Simon Swaffield, (Ed.), 2002. University of Pennsylvania Press.

Sullivan, Mary Ann. Eero Sarinnen's Ezra Stiles and Samuel Morse Colleges at Yale University. www.bluffton.edu.

U.S. Environmental Protection Agency (EPA). Nonpoint Source Pollution. www.epa.gov.

U. S. Fish and Wildlife Service. Atlantic Flyway. www.fws.gov.

Urbanski, Matthew. 2008. Case Study Biography form—Whitney Water Treatment Plant.

Yale Center for British Art. ycba.yale.edu.

Yale School of Medicine. Frank Gehry's Yale Psychiatric Institute. www.info.med.yale.edu.

Wastewater Treatment, King County Washington website. www.kingcounty.gov.

Chapter 4

American Heritage Rivers. U.S. Environmental Protection Agency. www.epa.gov/rivers.

Andropogon Associates. www.andropogon.com.

Coal Heritage Trail. National Scenic Byways Program. www.byways.org/explore/byways/10346.

Covington, Sid. 2005. Sandstone National River/ Gauley River National Recreation Area, Bluestone National Scenic River. Geologic Resources Management Issues Scoping Summary. Report from the National Park Service.

Dockwiller, Tavis. 2007. Viridian Landscape Studio. Telephone Interview.

Fiske, Diane M. April 2001. Architecture Week.

Franklin, Carol. 1997. *Ecological Site Design Guidelines*, developed by Andropogon Associates, Philadelphia, PA.

Guiding Principles of Sustainable Design. National Park Service. www.nps.gov.

Harker, D. *Landscape Restoration Handbook,* 2nd ed. Henderson, KY: Audubon International, 1999.

Louv, Richard. *Last Child in the Woods*. Chapel Hill, NC: Algonquin Books, 2006.

Lynch, Kevin and Gary Hack. *Site Planning*. Cambridge, MA: The MIT Press, 1998.

Milici, Robert C. 2006. *Production Trends of Major U.S. Coal Producing-Regions*. Proceeding of the Pittsburgh Coal Conference.

Miller, Katy. 2007. Librarian, National Park Service. Telephone Interview.

National Coal Heritage Area. www.coalheritage.org.

Potteiger, Matthew; and Jamie Purinton. *Landscape Narratives*. Hoboken, NJ: John Wiley & Sons, 1998.

Sandstone National River. National Park Service. www.nps.gov.

Steiner, Frederick. *The Living Landscape*. Boston, MA: McGraw-Hill College, 2000.

U.S. Fish and Wildlife Service. John Heinz National Wildlife Refuge. www.fws.gov/refuges/profiles/index.cfm?id=52570.

U.S. Geological Survey. Energy Resources Program: Health and Environment—Acid Mine Drainage. www.energy.er.usgs.gov/health_environment/acid_mine_drainage/.

United States Green Building Council. Credit Checklist. www.usgbc.org.

www.rootsweb.ancestry.com/~wvsummer/sandstone.html

Chapter 5

Agriculture in the Classroom—USDA. A Look at Arizona's Agriculture. www.agclassroom.org.

American Society of Landscape Architects. 2007 and 2008 Professional Awards. www.asla.org.

Arizona Department of Agriculture. www.azda.gov.

Arizona Department of Water Resources. www.azwater.gov.

Arizona Humanities Council. Moving Waters. www.azhumanities.org.

Barragan Foundation. barragan-foundation.org.

Bermudez, Julio. 2006. *On the Architectural Design Parti*. http://students.arch.utah.edu/courses/arch6971/parti.pdf.

Bormann, F. Herbert; Diana Balmori; Gordon T. Geballe. *Redesigning the American Lawn*. New Haven, CT: Yale University Press, 2001.

Bureau of the Census. www.census.gov.

Calthorpe, Peter. Winter 1991. The Post-Suburban Metropolis. *Whole Earth Review,* pp. 44–51.

City of Carmel-By-The-Sea California. Land-Use and Community Character Element of the General Plan. www.ci.carmel.ca.us.

Center for Sonoran Desert Studies. www.desertmuseum.org.

Center for Wildlife Law at the University of New Mexico and the Defenders of Wildlife. 1996. *Saving Biodiversity: A status report on state laws, policies and programs.*

Central Arizona Project. 1997. www.cap-az.com.

City of Phoenix. www.phoenix.gov.

Colorado Water Wise Council. www.coloradowaterwise.org.

Davis, Lisa Selin. 2008. "Hope for a Desert Delinquent. What Phoenix, the poster child for environmental ills, is doing right." *Grist Environmental News and Commentary*. May 13. www.grist.org.

Department of Agriculture, Natural Resource Conservation Service. www.websoilsurvey.nrcs.usda.gov.

Dines, Nicholas. Quoted in "Is It Sustainable, Is It Art?" by J. William Thompson, *Landscape Architecture*. May 1992, p. 56.

Harker, D. *Landscape Restoration Handbook*, 2nd ed. Henderson, KY: Audubon International, 1999.

Jenkins, Matt. 2005. Arizona Returns to the Desert. *High Country News,* March 21, www.hcn.org.

Jenkins, Matt. 2006. The Perpetual Growth Machine. *High Country News*, June 12, www.hcn.org.

Jensen, Jens. *Siftings, Johns Hopkins paperback ed.* Baltimore, MD: Johns Hopkins University Press, 1990.

Kaplan, S.; R. Kaplan; and R. Ryan. *With People in Mind. Design and Management of Everyday Nature.* Washington, DC: Island Press, 1998.

Keane, John L. 1998. A Once and Future River. *A Journal of the Natural and Built Environment.* www.terrain.org.

Laseau, Paul. *Graphic Thinking for Architects and Designers, 3rd ed.* Hoboken, NJ: John Wiley and Sons, 2000.

Lluria, Mario R. 2006. Application of Water Resources Management Mitigation Practices in the Southwestern Desert Region of the United States. Salt River Project, Phoenix, Arizona, USA. International Symposium on Transboundary Waters Management. www.uclm.es.

Lutz, Adam M. 2006. Why Infill Is the "In" Thing to Do. *Real Estate Business Online*, September 18. www.rebusinessonline.com.

Martin, Chris A.; Kathleen A. Peterson; Linda B. Stabler. 2003. Residential Landscaping in Phoenix, Arizona, U.S.: Practices and preferences relative to covenants, codes, and restrictions. *Journal of Arboriculture*, January.

McHarg, Ian. *Design with Nature,* new ed. Hoboken, NJ: John Wiley & Sons, 1995.

Moffett, Marian; Michael W. Fazio; Lawrence Wodehouse. *A World History of Architecture.* New York, NY: McGraw-Hill, 2003.

Morrison Institute for Public Policy, Arizona State University. Hits and Misses: Fast Growth in Metropolitan Phoenix. www.asu.edu/copp/morrison.

Mumford, Lewis. *Art & Technics.* New York, NY: Columbia University Press, 1952.

Musgrove, Spencer. 2005. Basin and Range Aquifers for Arizona. *Introduction to Hydrogeology*, Spring.

Nassauer, J. I. "Messy Ecosystems, Orderly Frames." *Landscape Journal*. 14:2, pp. 161–170.

National Park Service. Casa Grande Ruins National Monument. www.nps.gov/cagr/.

Olson, Erik. 2003. *What's On Tap? Grading Drinking Water in U.S. Cities.* National Resources Defense Council, June.

Paskus, Laura. 2007. "The Big Suck." *Santa Fe Reporter*. April 4. www.sfreporter.com.

Power, Matthew. 2008. "Peak Water: Aquifers and Rivers Are Running Dry. How Three Regions Are Coping." *Wired*. April 21. www.wired.com.

Raver, Anne. 2001. "Human Nature; In the Desert's Warm Embrace." *The New York Times*, April 5.

Salt River Pima-Maricopa Indian Community. www.saltriver.pima-maricopa.nsn.us.

Thompson, J. William. "Is It Sustainable, Is It Art?" *Landscape Architecture*. May 1992, pp. 56–60.

Town of Paradise Valley, Arizona. Paradise Valley General Plan, Open Space and Environmental Planning Section. www.ci.paradise-valley.az.us.

Treib, Marc. *Garrett Eckbo: Landscapes for Living.* Berkeley, CA: University of California Press, 1997.

University of Arizona, Pima County Extension Master Gardeners. Xeriscape Garden Plant List. www.ag.arizona.edu/pima/gardening.

University of California Museum of Paleontology. The World's Biomes on-line exhibit. www.ucmp.berkeley.edu.

U.S. Census Bureau. www.census.gov/.

U.S. Geological Survey. http://az.water.usgs.gov/.

Chapter 6

Alexander, Christopher. *A Pattern Language*. Oxford: Oxford University Press, 1977.

Andropogon Associates. www.andropogon.com.

Arend, Mark. 2001. Site Selection Magazine. www.siteselection.com. July.

Chesapeake Bay Program. www.chesapeakebay.net.

Connecticut Department of Environmental Protection. *2004. CT Stormwater Quality Manual.* www.ct.gov/DEP/cwp/view.asp?a=2721&q=325704.

Cooper, Andrea B. 2007. Interview. Conservation Design Forum, Elmhurst, Illinois.

Deere & Company. History of Deere & Company's World Head-quarters www.deere.com/en_US/attractions/worldhq/history.html.

Fairfax County, Virginia. Fairfax County Comprehensive Plan. www.fairfaxcounty.gov/dpz/comprehensiveplan.

Fairfax County Stormwater Planning Division. 2005 Middle Potomac and Difficult Run Watershed Management Plans, PowerPoint presentation to Tysons Corner Coordinating Committee by Woolpert, Inc. and KCI. www.fairfaxcounty.gov/dpz/tysonscorner/nofind/dpweswshed.pdf. December 19.

Fairfax Trails and Streams. www.fairfaxtrails.org.

Franklin, Carol. 1997. *Ecological Site Design Guidelines*, developed by Andropogon Associates, Philadelphia, PA.

Frej, Anne. 2002. Corporate Location and Smart Growth, ULI Land Use Policy Forum Report. April 8–9.

Gannett Company. www.gannett.com.

Gardener, Amy. 2007. "Tyson's Corner: Tunnel Loses Backers as Landowners Unite for Growth"; *Washington Post*. December 2.

Garreau, Joel. *Edge City: Life on the New Frontier.* Garden City, NY: Anchor Books, 1992.

Harker, Donald; Gary Libby; Kay Harker; Sherri Evans; and Marc Evans. Landscape Restoration Handbook, 2nd ed. Henderson, KY: Lewis Publishers, 1999.

Houser, Nancy. 2007. Interview. Director of corporate administration, Gannett Co., Inc.

Kunstler, James. *The Geography of Nowhere*. New York, NY: Touchstone, 1993.

Lebovich, William. 2002. Architecture Week. Corporate Crystals. August 14. www.architectureweek.com.

Louv, Richard. *Last Child in the Woods*. Chapel Hill, NC: Algonquin Books, 2006.

McHarg, Ian. 1993. Ecology and Design Symposium.

Pepsico. www.pepsico.com.

Perrins, Gerald and Diane Nilsen. 2006. "Industry dynamics in the Washington, D.C., area: has a second job core emerged?" *Monthly Labor Review*. December 2006. www.bls.gov/opub/mlr/2006/12/art1full.pdf.

Reston Historic Trust. www.restonmuseum.org.

Schultz, Christian Norberg. 1980. Genius Loci. Rizzoli.

Steiner, Frederick. *The Living Landscape, An Ecological Approach to Landscape Planning*. New York, NY: McGraw-Hill, 2000.

The Kresge Foundation Headquarters. 2006. A Case Study in Building Green. The Kresge Foundation.

Vergason, Michael, Doug Hays, 2007. Interview, Michael Vergason Landscape Architects Ltd. Alexandria Virginia. October.

Virginia Department of Conservation and Recreation. The Natural Communities of Virginia Classification of Ecological Community Groups SECOND APPROXIMATION (Version 2.2) www.dcr.virginia.gov/natural_heritage/ncintro.shtml.

Virginia Sustainable Building Network. Commercial Sustainable Design.

Whoriskey, Peter. 2005. "Soaring View of Tysons Centers on a Downtown." *Washington Post*. www.washingtonpost.com/wp-dyn/articles/A7443-2005Apr21.html. April 22.

Wohlsen, Marcus. 2005. "Office Space: Louise Mozingo Gets the Dirt on America's Corporate Landscapes." *Illuminations: Berkeley's Online Magazine of Research in the Arts and Humanities*. www.illuminations.berkeley.edu/archives/2005/article.php?volume=1&story=1. February

Worden, Eva; Diana Guidry; Annabel Alonso Ng; and Alex Schore. September 2004. *Green Roofs in Urban Landscapes*, Publication #ENH984, Florida Cooperative Extension Service, Institute of Food and Agricultural Sciences, University of Florida. www.edis.ifas.ufl.edu.

Chapter 7

Abbaté, Mike. 2007. Interview. GreenWorks, P.C., Portland Oregon.

Baird, Tim. 2007. *Stata Center Outwash Basin*. www.artfulrainwaterdesign.net.

Bureau of Planning Portland, Oregon. 1998. *Guidelines Outlined by the City of Portland*.

Bureau of Planning Portland, Oregon. 1998. *River District Design Guidelines*.

Central Park. www.centralpark.com/pages/history.html.

City of Portland. www.portlandonline.com.

City of Portland Bureau of Planning. *North Pearl District Masterplan*. www.portlandonline.com.

Connecticut Stormwater Quality Manual, 2004.

Damon, Betsy. Mavor, Anne H. *The Living Water Garden—Chengdu, Sichuan, China*. Sausalito, CA: Whole Earth, 2000.

Dreiseitl, Herbert. 2007. Interview. Atelier Dreiseitl, Germany.

Franklin, Carol. "Fostering Living Landscapes." In *Ecological Design and Planning*, ed. George Thompson. Hoboken, NJ: John Wiley & Sons, 1997.

Harker, Donald; Gary Libby; Kay Harker; Sherri Evans; and Marc Evans. *Landscape Restoration Handbook*, 2nd ed. Henderson, KY: Lewis Publishers, 1999.

Harvey, Sheila; Ken Fieldhouse. *The Cultured Landscape*. London: Routledge, 2005.

Hoyt Street Properties. Hoyt Street Properties Master Plan. www.hoytyards.com.

Krog, Steven. "Creative Risk Taking," in *Theory in Landscape Architecture*, by Simon Swaffield. Philadelphia, PA: University of Pennsylvania Press, 1983.

Louv, Richard. *Last Child in the Woods*. Chapel Hill, NC: Algonquin Books, 2006.

Lynch, Kevin, and Gary Hack. *Site Planning*, 3rd ed. Cambridge, MA: The MIT Press, 1984.

Lyle, John Tillman. *Regenerative Design for Sustainable Development*. Hoboken, NJ: John Wiley & Sons, 1992.

Massachusetts Institute of Technology. *The Ray and Maria Stata Center–Rain Water Harvesting and Flushing Water System*. www.web.mit.edu.

McHarg, Ian L. and Frederick Steiner, Edit. *To Heal the Earth: Selected Writings of Ian L. McHarg*, Washington, DC: Island Press, 1998.

Metro. www.oregonmetro.gov.

Mitchell, Martha S. *Land Use Planning: The Ultimate BMP*. Erosion Control. www.forester.net/ec_0004_land.html.

Oregon Oak Communities Working Group. www.oregonoaks.org/issues.shtml.

Oregon State University Willamette Basin Explorer. The Willamette Story. www.willametteexplorer.info.

Parks and Recreation/Tanner Springs Park. 2008. Bureau of Planning/North Pearl District Plan & River District Guidelines-amended, Arts and Culture.

Pearl District. www.explorethepearl.com/history.htm.

Portland Bureau of Environmental Services.

Portland City Council. 1998. Tanner Creek Park and Water Features Steering Committee Report.

Portland Development Commission. 2006. *Centennial Mills Framework Plan*.

Portland Historical Society.

Portland Metro Council. www.oregonmetro.gov.

Portland OnLine City of Portland. www.portlandonline.com.

Sprawl City. *Outcome of Portland Experiment Still Uncertain*. www.sprawlcity.org/portland.html.

Steiner, Frederick. *The Living Landscape*. New York, NY: McGraw-Hill, 2000.

Thayer, Robert. *LifePlace: Bioregional Thought and Practice*. Berkeley, CA: University of California Press, 2002.

The Biodiversity Project. www.biodiversitypartners.org/state/or/index.shtml.

Thompson, William. *Land Matters*, April 10, 2006. http://land.asla.org/2006/0410/landmatters.html

Waterscapes, Inc & Green Works, PC. 2003. *Stormwater Memo*. North Park Square.

Wollner, Craig; John Provo; Julie Schablisky. 2003. *Brief History of Urban Renewal in Portland, Oregon*.

Index

WILEY BOOKS ON
Sustainable Design

For these and other Wiley books on sustainable design, visit www.wiley.com/go/sustainabledesign

Environmental Benefits Statement

This book is printed with soy-based inks on presses with VOC levels that are lower than the standard for the printing industry. The paper, Rolland Enviro 100, is manufactured by Cascades Fine Papers Group and is made from 100 percent post-consumer, de-inked fiber, without chlorine. According to the manufacturer, the use of every ton of Rolland Enviro100 Book paper, switched from virgin paper, helps the environment in the following ways:

Mature trees saved	Waterborne waste not created	Waterflow saved	Atmospheric emissions eliminated	Solid wastes reduced	Natural gas saved by using biogas
17	6.9 lbs.	10,196 gals.	2,098 lbs.	1,081 lbs.	2,478 cubic feet